The AMA Guide to Management Development

Daniel R. Tobin

Margaret S. Pettingell

American Management Association

New York • Atlanta • Brussels • Chicago • Mexico City
San Francisco • Shanghai • Tokyo • Toronto • Washington, D. C.

This publication is designed to provide accurate and authoritative information in regard to the subject matter covered. It is sold with the understanding that the publisher is not engaged in rendering legal, accounting, or other professional service. If legal advice or other expert assistance is required, the services of a competent professional person should be sought.

Library of Congress Cataloging-in-Publication Data

Tobin, Daniel R., 1946–
    The AMA guide to management development / Daniel R. Tobin, Margaret
    S. Pettingill
        p.   cm.
    Includes index.
    ISBN 978-0-8144-0899-5
1. Management–Study and teaching. 2. Executives–Training of.
3. Leadership–Study and teaching. 4. Mentoring in business. 5. Core
competencies. 6. Career development. I. Pettingell, Margaret S. II. Title.

    HD30.4.T63 2008
    658.4'07124–dc22

                                                                2008001434

Printing number

10 9 8 7 6 5 4 3 2 1

Contents

A PDF file of the AMA Management Development
Compentency Model, as well as other information about
the book, is available at:
www.amacombooks.org/go/AMAGuideMgmtDevelop

Foreword

For the last 85 years, AMA has been successfully developing managers. More than 160,000 people a year will go through our seminar programs worldwide, through open enrollment forums or through customized solutions delivered on site. Companies trust us with their talent, and we take their trust seriously. We concentrate on providing superior programs, webcasts, podcasts, research, and books.

Successful development of managers in your organization involves much more than sending people to a training program. It requires new roles for the organization's leaders, the human resources function, the internal training group, and for all employees and managers in the organization. This book provides expert guidance on actions you can take today to improve your management development processes, no matter the size of your organization, your location, or your industry.

The traditional scope of duties and influence of expanding management responsibilities are constantly changing, but our model will give you a guide for your journey. With this core you can then further sharpen or customize the model to align competency priorities that are important for *your* business. Then you can craft a development model that aligns those priorities with the kind of contributions employees make as their own sphere of influence expands from individual contributor, to manager of others, to managing the business. Your own management development plan for your team will be shaped by the role and responsibility of each team member, his or her contribution, and how it ties to your corporate goal.

Once you know your ultimate goal, you can begin to plan. What skills do your people need to possess in order to get the job done and move your business forward? What capacities do they need to be really strong? In what roles do they need to excel, as part of the mosaic of contributions they make individually and as part of the team effort of doing business?

This is not a recipe book. Crafting a management development strategy and execution plan is not that simple. This is work, and you need a plan. You need to stick to the plan and be ruthless about developing your people to meet the needs of your business AND take them to the next level of professional development. You owe it to your company. You owe it to your employees. You owe it to yourself as a manager. Blissful is that state when all your employees are engaged, aligned, pulling in the same, agreed direction, contributing to the discussion, and anticipating the company's needs.

> "Would you tell me, please, which way I ought to go from here?"
> "That depends a good deal on where you want to get to," said the Cat.
> "I don't much care where. . . . ," said Alice.
> "Then it doesn't matter which way you go," said the Cat.
>
> Lewis Carroll, *Alice in Wonderland*

In the words of the Cheshire Cat, where are you going? What do you want to achieve? What talents do you need on board to accomplish your goals, personal or organizational, and how do those ingredients need to come together to achieve that end? Unlike Alice, we trust that you care . . . otherwise you wouldn't be reading this book. It does matter "which way you go" on this journey, and as you will read, there are many factors to consider. Trust in us, in AMA, to give you a guide, steeped in experience, positive in outcome, that will get you where you want to go.

Pat Leonard
Executive Vice President
American Management Association

Introduction

Over the past eighty-five years, the American Management Association (AMA) has delivered thousands of seminars to millions of participants across the globe. It is rare for us to attend any business gathering without meeting people with fond memories of an AMA program they attended sometime in their career, while many tell us of AMA programs that were important milestones that shaped their career progress.

For example, when Dan Tobin joined AMA several years ago, he spoke with an uncle who retired fifteen years earlier from a sweater manufacturer, where he worked his way up from office manager to company CEO. He said that over the span of forty years he attended half a dozen AMA seminars, and that they ranged from very good to outstanding, and that all were important milestones in his career progression. AMA's CEO, Ed Reilly, recently met a Fortune 500 CEO who told him that early in his career he had attended an AMA seminar on strategic planning, and by using what he learned in that seminar he accelerated his journey from a young marketing manager to eventually becoming the company's CEO.

For years, AMA's corporate customers have repeatedly asked us two questions:

- What is AMA's competency model for individual professionals, first-level managers, and mid-level managers?
- How can our organization best develop its employees so that we have a ready supply of future management and leadership talent to grow our organization?

This book will help answer those questions.

In AMA's history there were attempts to answer the competency question with rudimentary competency models and a concept we called "learning paths." This is not to say that there was no information on the subject generally available. There are many competency models to be found in the worldwide management literature, from consulting and training firms, business school professors, and training pundits, as well as hundreds or thousands of company-specific competency models developed over the past decades. And there are tens of thousands of books offering management advice from hundreds of publishers around the world, including AMACOM, AMA's own book publishing operation.

Starting two years ago, AMA's portfolio management group, which is responsible for defining AMA's program offerings, led an organization-wide effort to define an AMA competency model for individual professionals, first-level managers, mid-level managers, and functional managers. This research examined a number of models that existed in the public domain, including many of the well-researched competencies developed by the Lominger organization, the U.S. Government Office of Personnel Management (OPM), and the UK Management Standards Centre. In this book, we further categorized these competencies into three broad categories, those that deal with:

- Knowing and managing yourself.
- Knowing and managing others.
- Knowing and managing the business.

Please note that even for individual professionals, both those who aspire to climb the management ladder and those who plan to stay in individual roles, there are important competencies required in all three of these categories, for even if an individual professional will never "manage the business," he or she still needs to have some business knowledge and acumen.

The AMA Management Development Competency Model, as presented in this book, is not meant to be the be-all and end-all of competency models, but it provides a realistic framework of competencies on which to base your organization's management development efforts. Because competencies are general in nature, there can be lengthy debate on what to call a given competency, or whether a particular competency is more or less important for individuals at a given level of the organization, or whether your organization's culture puts greater or lesser emphasis on some competencies as compared with others. These discussions and debates are a good sign that your organization is thinking about the importance of developing its management talent to ensure its success.

The second question, "How should our organization develop its managers?," has no one right answer. If there were a single correct answer, there would be one theory, one book, one training program, and one guru on the subject, rather than the thousands that you can find in today's market. This book does not present an outline of a specific training program for managers, but rather offers advice on what your organization needs to do to be effective at developing the managers (through training and many other development methods) who will keep your organization running today and growing tomorrow.

The responsibility for developing managers cannot be left solely to your organization's training group. It is one of our objections to the popularity of "corporate universities" that in too many organizations that have established such entities, managers now feel freed from their responsibilities to develop their employees–"I don't have to worry about that any more because we have the corporate university to handle it." As described in this book, there are vital roles in management development for the organization's executives, the human resources group, the training group, and most importantly, managers and their employees. Without the active participation in and support of management development of all these groups, you will not get maximum value from any development initiative you undertake.

Evaluation of training efforts has become an increasingly hot topic over the years as training organizations try to justify their expenditures on employee training. Most books on training use the last chapter to discuss evaluation methods. We start this book with evaluation. Chapter 1, "Starting with the End in Mind," posits that if you plan your management development efforts well, by tying all such efforts to specific organizational, group, and individual business goals, their value to your organization will be self-evident and you will never be asked to justify the expense *post facto.*

In Chapters 2 through 5, we present the AMA Management Development Competency Model. Chapter 2, "Competence: The Ability to Do Something Well," defines competence, discusses distinctions between "management competencies" and "leadership competencies," and provides background information on the process we used to develop the

AMA Management Development Competency Model. Chapter 3 covers those AMA competencies that deal with knowing and managing yourself, while Chapter 4 describes those included in the category of knowing and managing others, and Chapter 5 defines those related to knowing and managing the business (whatever business your organization may be in).

In seeking people with a given set of competencies, organizations always have the options to either buy those competencies (hire employees who already possess the needed competencies) or build them within the organization's current employee base. Chapter 6, "Selecting for Competence," discusses how to screen external or internal candidates for specific competencies. Chapter 7 deals with employee learning, both self-directed learning and training provided by the organization. Chapter 8 discusses a wide range of options for developing management competencies that fall outside the realm of formal training programs.

Knowing the competencies needed for effective management, and understanding how to develop those competencies, will not get your organization very far unless the right people in the organization step up to take responsibility for management development. In Chapter 9, "The Employee and the Manager: The Key to All Development," we focus on the two people who have the primary responsibility for all employee development. Chapter 10 discusses the vital role that the organization's top leaders must play in building a "leadership pipeline" to ensure that the organization has the management talent it will need in the future to help the organization prosper. In Chapter 11, the focus is on the role of the Human Resources (HR) group in identifying and developing management talent. In many organizations, the training group is part of the HR group, while in other organizations it is separate from HR. For the purpose of this book, we deal separately with the role of the training group in Chapter 12.

In Chapter 13, "The Future of Management Development," we examine some of the current and future trends that are likely to impact the future of your company's management development efforts. We are grateful to Florence Stone, editorial director for the American Management Association, who conducted a number of interviews with leading thinkers in the field on our behalf and to the interviewees, listed below, for sharing their thoughts with us. They include:

- Professor Richard Boyatzis of Case Western University
- Professor Henry Mintzberg of McGill University
- Jay Jamrog, research vice president of the Institute for Corporate Productivity (I4CP)
- Professor David Ulrich of the University of Michigan
- Professor Allan Cohen of Babson College
- Professor Michael Watkins of IMD (Lausanne, Switzerland)
- Executive coaching guru Marshall Goldsmith

This book is not designed to be a blueprint for management development with detailed specifications on every aspect of the process. No two organizations' management development efforts will look alike–nor should they–each should be tailored to the specific needs and culture of the organization. Our hope is that this book will provide some new ideas, and remind you of some longstanding principles, in the broad field of management development that will help you succeed in your organization's efforts. If you get some new ideas, and if this book sparks some debates within your organization on how you should be developing your management talent for the future, we will consider our purpose well served.

Dan Tobin
Peg Pettingell
American Management Association

Starting with the End in Mind

Our plans miscarry because they have no aim. When a man does not know what harbor he is making for, no wind is the right wind.

Seneca (4 BCE–CE 65)

Most books on corporate training strategies and methodologies include a chapter on evaluation methods in the last third of the book. This is not a random placement–most people think of evaluating learning initiatives after the fact. But if you want to make management development, or any form of learning, a real contributor to individual and corporate success, the evaluation process must begin even before you start any developmental activity. You must start with the end in mind.

In this chapter, you will learn how a learning contract enables you to plan your organization's management development initiatives and to build in evaluation measures at the start. We will discuss methods of evaluating learning, including the Kirkpatrick model and return on investment (ROI) analysis, showing how to use the learning contract to plan management development activities that add value and demonstrate how your management development efforts help the organization and its employees meet their collective and individual goals. We will also present several techniques to help you implement learning contracts within your organization.

The Learning Contract

The learning contract starts and ends with the organization's goals. It starts with an understanding of organizational goals and how those goals cascade down to the business unit, group, and individual level (Part I). The learning plan (Part II), where learning methods, schedules, etc., are specified, comes next. Finally, Part III of the learning contract specifies how that learning will be applied to the individual learner's work to make a positive difference in achieving personal and organizational goals and the specific results you expect in terms of individual and organizational goal achievement as specified in Part I of the learning contract.

The learning contract can be used both to plan an organization's overall management development program and to draw up a development plan for a specific individual. We will give examples of both types of use.

The most important feature of the learning contract is that it is negotiated between the manager and the employee *before* any learning or development activity is planned or undertaken. The learning contract thus becomes the planning exercise for all management-related learning and development plans at both the organizational and the individual levels.

Part I: From Organizational Goals to a Learning Agenda

What are your organization's goals? Are they a secret, or are they widely known among employees? Do employees understand how those goals cascade down to their business units, the groups in which they work, and to their personal work? Can they connect their individual work to group and organizational goals? Can they tell you how what they do contributes to group and organizational success? These are not trivial

TABLE 1.1	The Learning Contract	
	Starts with ...	Produces ...
Part I	Organizational goals	A learning agenda
Part II	A learning agenda	A learning plan
Part III	Application of learning	Effects of learning on goal achievement

questions–many employees, whether individual contributors, managers, or company officers, often find it difficult to make these connections. And if they cannot make these connections, they may well be working at cross-purposes to those goals. Seneca had it right–if you don't know in what direction you should be moving, any direction will do. In other words, if you don't know what problem your training program is designed to solve, you can't design a proper training solution (see "What Problem Are You Trying to Solve?").

WHAT PROBLEM ARE YOU TRYING TO SOLVE?

During the 1990s, when Dan Tobin was working as an independent consultant, he received a call from the training director of his state's Department of Corrections. "I was reading an article you wrote on learning organizations. Would you be interested in doing a half-day workshop on learning organizations for the Commissioner of Corrections and his staff and then repeating the same workshop a week later for the state's twenty-two prison superintendents?" she asked.

"I could do that," I replied. "But can we meet and discuss what goals you have set for the program?" We met in her office the next day.

"What is the problem you are trying to solve with this program," I asked.

"Let me make a long story as short as I can," she replied. "The Commissioner has set aside a lot of money this year to create a new 'inmate management system,' and I am co-chairing the task force to plan and implement the new system. In the commissioner's staff meetings, which I attend, everyone supports the idea, but outside those meetings, several members of his staff are nay-saying the idea. And when I take members of the task force out to interview the superintendents, they show very little interest in the project. What problem am I trying to solve? I guess the problem is how to get everyone moving in the same direction and supporting the task force, so we can get our work done."

"And how," I asked, "do you think that my presenting a three-hour workshop on learning organizations will help you solve that problem?" I asked.

"Well, I just finished reading Peter Senge's book[1]," she said, smiling. "I just loved it. And I thought if I could get all of these people thinking like that, it would solve a lot of the task force's problems."

"You are probably right," I said. "But you can't teach the five disciplines in three hours and expect anything to change."

"Why not?" she asked.

"How long did it take you to read the book?" I asked.

"I see," she said. "Then what would you recommend?"

After more discussion, we agreed to interview the commissioner, several of his deputies, and several prison superintendents. Based on these interviews, the diagnosis was that the new system would be a major change for the correctional system, and the system had never handled change well. Because many people felt that this change initiative was probably doomed from the start, based on this history, they didn't want to waste their time working with the task force (a self-fulfilling prophecy). What I finally proposed and implemented was a program on "leadership and change" for the commissioner and his staff and a similar session for the superintendents. Through these sessions, the audiences came to recognize, first, that the new system was vital to their future and, second, that they had to take a leadership role in ensuring that the task force could get its work done. Following those two half-day sessions, we held a full-day joint session to do action planning. Happily, it got the project back on track.

What happened in this scenario is repeated on a daily basis around the world in organizations large and small: Someone reads a book or an article or hears a presentation at a conference and gets so enthused by the idea he or she has heard that he or she immediately proposes to implement this "new approach." Unfortunately, in most cases, this approach doesn't work because the proposer has never answered two basic questions: "What problem are you trying to solve?" and "Will this approach solve that problem?"

The same analogy can be made for many organizations' management development initiatives. If you don't know how your initiatives contribute to the achievement of organizational goals, you will never be able to demonstrate that your management development efforts are contributing to organizational success. It is a basic tenet of evaluation methodology that a program's goals should suggest their own evalua-

THE FIVE HOWS[2]

One method of getting clarity for your goals is called "The Five Hows." For any nonspecific goal, ask "How would you know if you are successful?" Keep asking the same question, focusing on your last answer, until you have a measurable outcome. For example, with respect to a goal of "We will become more environmentally conscious," you would ask: "How will we know when we are more environmentally conscious?" (Round 1). You might answer, "When we exceed our industry's measures for pollution reduction."

Next, you might ask, "How will we know when we exceed our industry's measures for pollution reduction?" (Round 2). You might answer, "When we reduce our hydrocarbon emissions to X parts per million."

Next, ask: "How will we know that we have reduced our hydrocarbon emissions to X parts per million?" (Round 3). You might answer, "We will install new filtering systems in our factory and a new monitoring system to ensure that our hydrocarbon emissions do not exceed X parts per million."

You can now change the original goal from "We will become more environmentally conscious" to "We will install a new filtration system in our factory by year's end and monitor emissions to ensure that hydrocarbon emissions are reduced to X parts per million." When you add a target date to this, you will have a measurable goal.

To move from a "fuzzy" goal to a measurable goal may take up to five rounds of questioning—the Five Hows. And, of course, you need to ensure that each "how" is actually achievable—to say, for example, that you will reduce emissions to X parts per million when the technology to do this does not exist is not an achievable goal.

tion measures. For example, if the goal is to increase sales this year by 10 percent, then you can measure the increase in sales at the end of the year and find out whether you achieved that goal. If a goal specifies that the organization will reduce employee turnover by 20 percent this year, then you can measure turnover at year's end and compare it with the previous year's turnover statistic to determine if you have achieved the goal.

But if a goal is written in "fuzzy" language, it may be impossible to measure. Some examples:

We will improve quality.

We will become more environmentally conscious.

We will make this a better place to work for our employees.

We will beat our competitors.

We will become an "employer of choice."

SALES TRAINING

A product manager came to the training manager. "We've got a great new set of products. They've been getting great reviews in the industry press, and the customers who participated in the beta tests of the products really love them. Our competitors have nothing like them. But our salesforce isn't selling them. I need you to put together a worldwide sales training program and deliver it to our salesforce. I need to get these products moving. Just let me know how much it will cost and I'll get you the necessary budget." (Training managers love people like this.)

"Have you talked with any of our sales reps or sales managers about your problem?" asked the training manager. "Have you asked them what training they feel they need on your products?"

"No, I haven't talked to any of them," replied the product manager. "But it must be a training problem because this is a great set of products, and if they knew about them, they would be selling them—and a lot of them. I've got to get this product line moving. Let me know when you can deliver the program. My team will give you all the help you need."

After the product manager left, the training manager called several sales reps and sales managers. The next morning, she went to see the product manager.

"So, when do you think we can get started with this training?" asked the product manager. "And how much will it cost?"

"Save your money," said the training manager. "This isn't a training problem."

"What do you mean?" asked the puzzled product manager.

"I talked with some sales reps and sales managers. They told me that they have all of the marketing literature on your products, and they agree that it is a terrific set of products."

"Then why aren't they selling them?!?"

"Because they're not on their goal sheets. The sales reps get no credits toward their quotas and get no points toward the annual sales prizes for selling your products. So they focus on selling what helps them achieve their personal goals," reported the training manager.

"So how do I change that?" pleaded the product manager.

"A training program isn't going to help. What you need to do is to talk with corporate sales management. Get them to include your products on the reps' goal sheets. Get them to offer extra points toward the annual sales contest for selling your products."

"So you're turning down my request to do the sales training? I've worked for a number of companies and this is the first time I can recall a training manager turning down an offer of money to build and deliver a program."

"Look, if you want to give my group $50,000, we'll put together a great training program on your products, and some of my people will love the opportunity to travel around the world delivering the training. But it won't change anything. It won't give you the results you are seeking. You'll be better off using that money to create some special sales incentives around your product set—you'll get much better results that way."

Once you have a set of clear, measurable goals for the organization and the individual, you must then ask: "In order to meet those goals, what needs to change?" Changes may be related to management development or they may have no relationship to any learning activity.

Not all of the changes needed to achieve your stated goals will necessarily imply a learning or management development need. Instead, you may need to look at your organizational structure; investments in plant, equipment, or other manufacturing or services technology; product or service improvements; different marketing strategies or tactics;

or, as in the above example, simply getting a product set onto the sales-force's goal sheets.

It is not an uncommon error to propose a training solution to a problem that is not caused by a lack of training, or to propose a training

RADIO SHACK

Retailer Radio Shack proclaims four main values on its website:

- Teamwork
- Pride
- Trust
- Integrity

In explaining its value of "trust," the company website indicates the behaviors to which it is dedicated: "Share the truth, both good and bad." Under *Integrity*, it specifies: "Doing the right thing, even when no one is watching," and, "Honesty and openness in relationships with associates, customers, shareholders and vendors."

In early 2006, it was revealed that Radio Shack CEO, David Edmondson, who had been in that post for twelve years, had falsified information on his resume. The degrees in theology and psychology that he had listed were bogus—he never graduated from college.

How did Edmondson's misrepresentation square with the company's "values" of trust and integrity? And how did Edmondson's boss—Radio Shack's board of directors—view the situation?

When the misrepresentation was first reported by *The Fort Worth Star-Telegram*, the company board issued a statement saying it knew about the matters raised by the report, "and has given due consideration to them," while deciding to let Edmondson stay in his job due to excellent job performance.

It should be noted that Mr. Edmondson resigned his position three days later due to overwhelming criticism from the business press, company employees, and the general public.

agenda that will not remedy the problem it was supposed to solve. Too often, because training is what training organizations do, they quickly offer a training solution to any problem that may arise. To paraphrase Abraham Maslow, if your only tool is a hammer, every problem looks like a nail. One of the key competency areas for managers is problem solving, as will be discussed later in this book. Before recommending a training solution, you need to make certain that the proposed solution will actually solve the problem.

Another challenge in management development is ensuring that the organization's culture and its measurement and reward systems reinforce what you are teaching. Many organizational change efforts have started with large training programs, and large expenditures for training, only to result in nothing changing because while the training participants were taught to behave in new ways, the organization continued to measure and reward them for behaving in the old ways. In the "Sales Training" example, a lot of money could have been spent developing and delivering the requested training program with no results, because the measurement and reward system didn't support selling the new product line. In the "Radio Shack" example, proclaimed company values and executive behavior don't match.

For our purposes, let us focus on those changes that imply a need for learning or other forms of management development to help the organization and its employees meet their goals. These changes form our *learning agenda*, which is the outcome of Part I of the learning contract.

Part II: From a Learning Agenda to a Learning Plan

The learning agenda from Part I of the learning contract specifies what knowledge and skills need to be learned to achieve the changes that will enable the organization to meet its goals. But how will that learning be accomplished? As will be discussed throughout this book, there are many ways to develop managers, ranging from formal, instructor-led training programs to e-learning, to self-study, to a variety of temporary or permanent work assignments, to coaching and mentoring, and more. In Part II of the learning contract, you will develop specific plans for your management development program, for the organization as a whole, or for an individual employee.

The learning plan will include many items, such as:

- The goals of your management development program, and how it relates to and aligns with the organizational and individual goals from Part I of the learning contract.
- The topics that you will include in the management development program.
- The methods you will use to develop managers. Which methods best apply to your learning goals?
- Who will participate in the management development program.
- When management development activities will take place.
- Where management development activities will take place.
- How you will measure whether the desired learning actually occurred.
- The roles of various organizational groups (human resources, the training group, organizational executives, participants' managers and employees) in planning, developing, and conducting the program(s).
- Whether to rely on your organization's own training and development resources or seek external assistance from training firms, professional associations, or universities.

While developing a learning agenda, often in the form of a course catalog and schedule, is a core activity of most internal training groups, where those training groups often fall short is in relating the programs they offer directly to, and aligning them with, the organization's key business strategies and goals. Too often, organizations send their employees to a management development program, internal or external to the organization, without ever helping to tie what they are learning to their individual, team, and organizational goals. This is why AMA recommends that every employee who will attend a training program first sit down with her manager to discuss the content of the program and how it relates to her and the manager's goals.

The final dimension of the learning plan is how you will measure learning achievement or the development of the desired management competencies. This will be discussed later in this chapter.

Alternatives for each of these dimensions of the learning plan will be discussed in other parts of this book. But, in formulating your management development plan, you should keep in mind the basic model of the four stages of learning.

The Four Stages of Learning   The four stages of learning[3] are:

Stage 1: Data

Stage 2: Information

Stage 3: Knowledge

Stage 4: Wisdom

We are all inundated with data (Stage 1). Every word we read on paper, a computer screen, or as a text message on a cell phone, everything we hear and see, everything that is taken in by our senses, is data. In today's world, we are flooded with so much data that it threatens to overwhelm us all.

Peter Drucker said that data, when imbued with relevance and purpose, becomes information (Stage 2). In planning any learning initiative, it is important to help learners sort through the jungle of data that surrounds them to discover what is relevant to their work and has purpose. If we swamp learners with irrelevant data for which they see no purpose, they will ignore it or, worse, spend so much time trying to understand why it is being presented that they will have less time to focus on the information most vital to their work. A primary purpose of the learning contract is to have the manager discuss with the employee how the employee's job will change and what new skills the employee needs today and for the future, thus helping the employee better sort through all of the available data on development opportunities to turn it into useful information to better construct his personal learning agenda.

Most training programs focus on providing information, i.e., data that is relevant and has purpose, but many overwhelm the participant with a plethora of information. Studies of all forms of learning show that participants retain only a small percentage of the information presented through training programs for even a few weeks after completing the training.

What organizations really want is not necessarily for learners to retain large volumes of information, but to apply what they learn to their work to make a positive difference in individual, group, or corporate business results. This leads us to Stage 3 of the learning model: To move *from information to knowledge,* the employee must *apply that information to his work.* That is, I can't say that I really "know" something unless I have used it. Even if we help (or force) employees to learn a lot of information through our learning initiatives, there is little value to them or to the organization from the activity if they never use what they learn.

For example, you can read books and articles on how to ride a bicycle, watch videotapes or take an e-learning program that simulates riding a bicycle in traffic, but you can't say that really *know* how to ride a bicycle until you apply your learning and actually get on a bicycle to master the skills and knowledge you have accumulated from those learning resources.

The final stage (Stage 4) of the learning model is that most precious commodity, wisdom. Wisdom cannot be taught, but can only be developed within the individual. Wisdom comes from a combination of insight and intuition based on knowledge and experience. Harvard Business School professor Shoshanna Zuboff[4] tells the story of a paper mill worker who could "sense" if the mixture of chemicals in a vat on the production floor was correct by the way that static electricity affected his hair as he stood next to the vat. This type of wisdom cannot be taught in a classroom lecture or through an e-learning program. But it can be transmitted by dialogue and demonstration.

When we speak of the looming talent management crisis resulting from the retirement of millions of baby boomers, it is this loss of wisdom, or tacit knowledge, that will be the most difficult to replace.

As will be discussed in later parts of the book, this learning model (see Figure 1.1) can provide a lot of guidance in designing management development programs, such as:

- Ensuring that all content is relevant to the jobs of managers and has purpose for them in achieving their individual and collective goals.
- Giving opportunities for participants in your programs to apply what they learn so that they can turn the information they receive into personal knowledge.
- Developing ways for participants in your management development effort to learn from the accumulated wisdom of organizational

1. Data

2. Information = Data + Purpose + Relevance

3. Knowledge = Information + Application

4. Wisdom = Knowledge + Experience + Intuition

FIGURE 1.1   The Four Stages of Learning

leaders and from their own experiences and to test their intuition as they develop their own wisdom about what will or won't work in a particular situation.

The last two of these items are covered in Part III of the learning contract.

Part III: From Application of Learning to Measuring Effects on Goal Achievement

Traditionally, organizational training groups felt that their responsibilities ended when the employee left the training program, either completing an instructor-led course or finishing an e-learning program. In recent years, there has been more interest and activity targeted at measuring the effects of learning activities once the employee returns to the job. Later in this chapter, we will examine the Kirkpatrick model for measuring the effects of training programs and Jack Philips's addition of return on investment (ROI) analysis to the Kirkpatrick model.

The great difficulty of using many of the evaluation methods that are so widely discussed today is that they are all done *after the fact.* "Now that we have spent all this money on classroom training (or e-learning, or webcasts, or knowledge management systems, etc.), let's go back and see if we can justify our expenditures. Can we can prove that there really is a return on the company's investment in these initiatives?" The learning contract solves this dilemma by specifying, *before* any learning or development activities are planned, the expected benefits *in terms of the organization's and the individual's goals.*

LEADERSHIP TRAINING IN A CONSULTING FIRM

One of the managing partners of one of the world's largest accounting and management consulting firms once told us of a large investment he and the firm had made in leadership education. They had hired one of the leading authorities on leadership from one of the most prestigious business schools and, over the course of the summer, had 3,000 of the firm's top associates attend two days of lectures by him at the business school's facilities. While he didn't mention the budget for this learning event, it probably ran close to a million dollars if you count the fees of the professor, the cost of materials, and the travel and lodging expenses as well as the time spent off the job by the 3,000 associates for the training and travel.

When asked how the associates would use their new knowledge, the partner replied: "These are very smart people. They'll figure out how to use it."

What return on this massive investment did this firm get from this ambitious program? No one knows, because it was never measured. How much more return could it have gotten if all associates were required to complete a learning contract with their managers before attending the program to specify how they would apply their learning to their jobs and to tie their learning directly to the firm's business goals? We would venture that the returns would have been many times greater.

Part III of the learning contract specifies:

- How the employee will apply the learning after completing the development activity.
- What reinforcement the employee will need when returning to the job to ensure correct application of the learning and where the employee will get this reinforcement or coaching, e.g., from his or her manager, from another employee who has expertise in this area, from a member of the training group (internal or external), or from an internal or external coach.

- What other changes need to be in place to complement the employee's new skills and knowledge, e.g., systems, processes, organizational structures, or culture changes.

- The expected changes in business results once the employee has applied the learning to the job (allowing time for mastery of the new knowledge or skill), as measured by achievement of organizational or individual goals.

Comparing the Learning Contract to Other Evaluation Measures

Given that Kirkpatrick's four levels of training evaluation have become the *de facto* standard for evaluating learning initiatives, how does the learning contract relate to the Kirkpatrick model?

- **Level 1: Reaction to Training:** Most training organizations use an end-of-course evaluation instrument, commonly called a "smile sheet," that asks participants for their reactions to the learning program, the materials, the instructor, the learning environment, etc. These are standard measures for most training organizations and will undoubtedly continue to be widely used. The learning contract does not specifically address Level 1 evaluation. This should not stop you from using end-of-course evaluations if you feel that they are a meaningful measure within your organization.

- **Level 2: Measurement of Learning:** Level 2 measurements typically take the form of a pretest and posttest that measure the participant's learning achievement, e.g., if the participant scores 50 percent on the pretest and 90 percent on the posttest, you can point to an increase in knowledge as a benefit of participating in the learning activity. One of the items that the employee must negotiate with the manager in Part II of the learning contract is how to measure learning achievement. Kirkpatrick's Level 2 measurement is an obvious choice for this.

- **Level 3: Behavior Change Resulting from Learning:** Level 3 evaluation deals with how the participant's behavior changes following the learning activity. This is the primary focus of the learning contract. Part III of the learning contract specifies what behavior changes the employee is expected to make following the learning initiative. The benefit of the learning contract approach is that expected changes are specified *before* any learning is undertaken, rather than looking for behavior changes after learning is completed. This measurement of behavioral change is typically accomplished with a follow-up survey of the participant and his or her manager several weeks or months after completing the learning activity. Alternatively, a 360-degree evaluation of the participant before and after the learning activity to measure behavioral changes demonstrates Level 3 evaluation. As will be discussed later, you may encounter resistance from managers to taking the time to do this follow-up evaluation, but this really is the only effective means of conducting a Kirpatrick Level 3 evaluation. The learning contract facilitates this type of evaluation by specifying the expected business results in terms of individual and organizational goals. If you try to do this type of follow-up without the initial discussion required by the learning contract, many managers will have no recollection of why the employee attended the training program (or participated in another form of management development) or the original goals of the learning activity. For all AMA seminars, we ask participants to write an Action Plan during the seminar that specifies what they will do differently when they return to their jobs to apply what they have learned, and then ask participants to review their action plans with their managers upon returning to the workplace.

- **Level 4: Impact of Training on Organizational Effectiveness:** Level 4 evaluation, the measurement of the impact of learning on organizational effectiveness, is greatly facilitated by use of the learning contract. Rather than trying to discover whether a learning activity has had any effect on the achievement of organizational goals, the expected impacts are specified in Part III of the learning contract. More importantly, the learning contract negotiation starts with a discussion of the organization's and the employee's business goals and bases all learning initiatives on those goals, thereby making it much easier to specify the intended impact and, therefore, to measure the actual impact of the learning initiative on the organization.

Jack Philips extends the Kirkpatrick model to a fifth level: Return on Investment (ROI), measuring the actual costs and benefits of a learning activity and calculating an actual return on that investment.[5] The learning contract does not attempt to do ROI analysis, and, we would argue, if the learning contract is fully utilized, i.e., tying all learning initiatives directly to organizational goals from start to finish, organizational leaders will never ask for an ROI analysis because the value of all learning initiatives will be obvious.[6]

R O I

The origins of return-on-investment (ROI) analysis come from the corporate finance world. When a company is faced with a number of investment alternatives, such as whether to build a new plant, upgrade technology, or invest in a new marketing program, financial models are built for each of the alternatives. These models estimate the costs and the projected revenue streams, by year, for the life of each investment. Using financial formulas, the organization can measure the projected rate of return for each alternative. Generally, the investment will be made in the alternative that promises the greatest return on capital, or all may be accepted or rejected if the projected rate of return exceeds its target rate of return or falls below the company's cost of capital. Other methods of evaluating potential investments include net present value (NPV), which uses a fixed cost of capital and calculates whether, using the specified rate of return, the project will show a profit, and break-even analysis, which calculates how long it will take the company to recoup its investment in the project.

In the corporate finance world, ROI is used to evaluate *future* investment alternatives—it is NOT used after the fact to judge whether the investment has shown a return. This is a major fault with using ROI to evaluate management development and other types of training and learning programs. The author's own experience, working with a number of companies over the past two decades, is that if the training group waits until the CEO or CFO asks it to do an ROI study to justify the company's training budget, it is already too late—the company has, in most cases, already decided to slash the training budget or outsource the training function and is only using the ROI study to justify a decision that has already been made.

A key point here is that in the world of corporate finance, ROI calculations correctly include the full range of costs and benefits that will flow from a projected investment—the costs may include capital expenses for new plant and equipment, labor costs for running the proposed operation, materials costs, training costs, maintenance costs, etc. In the training world, many ROI studies isolate the costs of training and separate them from the many other costs involved in an organizational change initiative, but then often attribute all of the benefits of the change effort just to the training program. This is the equivalent of saying that if a company invests in a new manufacturing plant and has to spend money to train its employees on how to run the new plant, the full profits from the plant should be attributed to the training program, because the plant couldn't have been operated without the training.

Is it possible to calculate the ROI on a training investment? It can certainly be done, if undertaken with great care and attention to detail to ensure that you can isolate the direct costs and direct benefits of the training. We believe it makes greater sense to do ROI calculations on the entire change effort, measuring the total costs (including training) and benefits of the change initiative.

We would argue that the learning contract obviates the need to do ROI studies on the individual training components of a change effort because the evaluation measures for the training programs are built in from the beginning and are tied directly to, and supportive of, the organization's business goals. And if the company's executives see that all training and development efforts directly support their business goals, they will most likely never ask for an ROI justification for the training and development budget.

Summary

The learning contract is negotiated by the employee and his or her manager *before* any formal training or development activity takes place. By setting expectations of what will be learned, by tying the learning to specific business goals, and by setting expectations of changes in individual goal achievement *before* the employee engages in any type of learning or development activity, the employee and his or her manager recognize the importance of the activity and where to focus their attention.

To get greatest value from a learning experience requires that participants understand, from the start, what they need to learn, how they will use what they learn (purpose), and what value they and their organizations will get from the acquisition and application of that learning. It is not enough to attend a training program, or to take on a developmental assignment, because "it sounds interesting," or because "my manager sent me," and then try to determine its value after the fact, or just hope that something worthwhile will result from the experience. The use of the learning contract ensures that the employee and the organization will get maximum value from the investment in the employee's development by building in evaluation metrics from the start.

CHAPTER

2

Competence: The Ability to Do Something Well

Competence is defined as "the ability to do something well." This would lead us to believe that if we can define a set of competencies for a job role, and find someone who possesses that exact set of competencies, we should expect that the person will do the job well. That is why some companies go to great expense to define a set of competencies for every job in the company and use each job competency profile to judge people who hold a particular job or aspire to a particular job. It is much like defining a set of specifications for a piece of machinery or a part of a machine: If the specs are followed, the part should fit exactly, and the machine should work as predicted. But people are not machines or parts, and people are not subject to customization to fit a set of job specifications. When an executive recruiter develops a job profile, it contains many exacting specifications to help find the perfect candidate for an open position. But most headhunters will tell you that it is almost impossible to identify a candidate who meets all such specifications exactly, and that they tend to settle for, at best, an 80 percent match.

Even when we can agree on a specific competency, we will find that the nature of that competency will vary with the level of the job. For example, it is commonly agreed that good communications skills are needed for almost every job because people need to work with other people, and good communications skills enable people to work together. But as a person moves from individual contributor to manager to executive, the nature of the needed communications skills will change. A first-level manager needs communications skills to work with individual employees and with the group as a whole. He also needs to learn to communicate with upper-level management. The mid-level manager needs to learn how to communicate with a larger group of employees, most of whom do not work directly for her. A C-level officer needs to learn to communicate with a wide variety of employees through public forums and through other managers, as well as to communicate with a board of directors and with the investment community. Even within a single level, required communications skills may vary widely. Consider the engineer who works as part of a global team, the customer service representative who communicates primarily via the telephone, and the salesperson who must make sales presentations to customer committees. In subsequent chapters, where we explore specific competencies for individual professionals and the three levels of management (first-level manager, mid-level manager, and functional manager) that are the subject of this book, we will examine each competency area for these types of differences.

Management Versus Leadership Competencies

For the past several decades, more and more management theorists and business writers have been telling the world that we need more leaders, that we need leaders (rather than managers) at all levels of the organization, resulting in a strong emphasis on leadership competencies and lesser focus on traditional management competencies.

Marcus Buckingham differentiates the roles of manager and leader as follows:

> The great manager's starting point is the individual. He or she seeks to understand the talents, skills, knowledge, experience, and goals of the individual and then finds ways to help make the person successful. Great leaders' starting point is the "better future" they see in their mind's eye. This future is what he or she ruminates on, defines, and refines. Guided by this clear image of a better future, he or she then rallies people toward it–but through it all, the future remains the focus.[1]

Our point of view is that we need *both* management and leadership competencies at all levels of the organization, but that the mix of the two varies with the level of management. For first-level managers, the mix may be up to 80 percent management competencies and only 20 percent leadership competencies, while at the level of corporate officers, the mix may be just the opposite requiring 70 to 80 percent leadership competencies and only 20 to 30 percent management competencies. The exact ratio of the two types of competencies is not as important as the recognition that managers or leaders at all levels need a mix of both types and that the mix varies by level (see Figure 2.1).

There are literally hundreds of competency models that have been developed by consulting firms, public bodies, industry consortia, and competency researchers, not to mention the thousands of competency models developed within organizations over time. While they are all different, they are also all the same; that is, no one group or researcher or company has discovered a "magic competency map" that distinguishes its managers or leaders from the rest of the pack. The words may be somewhat different, the level of detail may vary (some list dozens of competencies, others have hundreds), and their organization and presentation may appear to be different, but they all describe roughly the same sets of skills, aptitudes, and knowledge. Similarly, some organizations will place greater emphasis on one set of competencies than on others, based on the nature of their business, their industry, the organization's culture and values, and what it views as the organization's core competencies. For example, at one Internet database

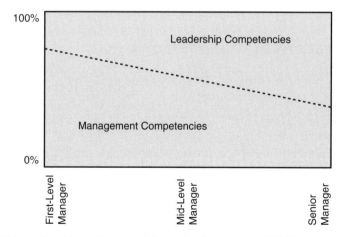

FIGURE 2.1   The Mix of Leadership and Management Skills, by Level

company, all applicants were required to pass a programming aptitude test, regardless of whether they needed programming skills in their work. The founders of the company felt it important that all employees, regardless of position, be able to relate to this core competency that had been defined for the company and that the company would distinguish itself from its competitors by instituting this requirement.

In developing AMA's Management Development Competency Model for individual professionals and the first three levels of management, we examined existing models from several organizations:

- The U.S. Government Office of Personnel Management
- The New York State Department of Civil Service
- Carnegie-Mellon University
- The UK Management Standards Centre
- Lominger

We also focused on key competencies outlined by Drotter, Charan, and Noel[2] in describing career transitions inherent in the management pipeline. Finally, we developed our own list of forty-six key competencies (comparing them to other models to ensure completeness). Because so many of the competencies can be listed for all four personnel categories, we developed a list of illustrative behaviors for each of the competencies, and it is through these behavioral descriptions that we made the distinctions in the requirements at the various levels.

Combinations of Competencies

Each position in a company will need a combination of competencies tailored to the requirements of the job. As mentioned earlier, as jobs grow more complicated, and as the level of the job rises in the organizational hierarchy, it may not be possible to find the exact combination of competencies that are listed in the competency profile. Each organization must therefore develop its own ranking system to determine which competencies are absolutely essential for the job and which are "nice to have." This weighting may be further adjusted during the hiring process, e.g., if the group in which the position exists already has employees who are strong on certain competencies, the hiring manager may place less importance on finding a new employee with those particular competencies and greater importance on competencies that are needed but in short supply within the existing group.

Buying Versus Developing Competence

But just because we list a competency as being important at a given level of management, it does not necessarily mean that the competence can be developed, or that the right way to develop the competence is through training (which is AMA's core business). Sometimes, you hire a person because she has already demonstrated a given set of competencies in her previous job. For example, basic intelligence is not something that any employer can develop–either the employee has it or he doesn't.

Writing in *Harvard Business Review*,[3] Justin Menkes states:

> Thinking critically is the primary responsibility of any manager, in any organization, and a leader's capacity to engage in this process is largely determined by his or her intelligence. Of course, there are many academically brilliant people who might score in the genius range on an IQ test but who could never make it as the CEO of a *Fortune 500* company. That's not surprising, since IQ tests focus on the cognitive skills central to success in school, not success in business.

While some competencies can be improved through training, such as listening skills, time management, and organizational abilities, a well-organized employee who listens well and manages his time well will likely be recognized as having greater management potential than one who doesn't demonstrate these competencies. Other competencies are better learned on the job than in the classroom. For example, developing a broad understanding of the organization's business is better learned by development activities such as assignment to a cross-functional team, job rotation, or an international assignment than by any classroom experience.

You *buy* competencies by hiring employees who already have demonstrated those competencies. Competency models are often used to develop job descriptions and interview guides. Using behavioral interviewing, you can ask specific questions, keyed to specific competencies, about an applicant's knowledge and experience to judge whether the applicant has the required or desired competencies.

Discovering Areas of Competence and Incompetence

Generally, we are aware of our major areas of competence, but often there are areas of competence that we have but don't recognize. Similarly, we may know that we lack competence in some areas, but there are other competencies required for a job that we don't recognize that we lack. Figure 2.2 displays these combinations of competence and incompetence, and those of which we are conscious or unconscious.

For areas of *conscious competence*, we know what we are able to do. We list these competencies on our resumes and talk about them in job interviews. When asked to list our strengths, we focus on these areas of conscious competence.

Areas of *unconscious competence* focus on abilities that others may see in us, but that we do not recognize ourselves. You might say to a colleague: "You did a great job putting together that slide set for the presentation. Could you teach me how to do those special effects you used?" Your colleague may have been doing this type of work for a long time, but never recognized that this was a special area of competence. Or, you might compliment a colleague on how well she handled a customer complaint: "You really put the customer at ease and not

	Competence	Incompetence
Conscious	Conscious Competence: I know what I am able to do	Conscious Incompetence: I know what I am not able to do
Unconscious	Unconscious Competence I am unaware of what I am able to do	Unconscious Incompetence I am unaware of what I am unable to do

FIGURE 2.2   Types of Competence

only saved the situation, but helped us develop a loyal customer for the future." Your colleague might not have recognized that she had this special talent: "Oh, I didn't do anything special–that's just how I have always handled this type of situation." These are areas of unconscious competence, and it behooves managers to help employees discover these types of special abilities that employees may not have recognized on their own.

Areas of *conscious incompetence* are areas for development and are probably recognized by the employee as such. "I've never been very good at getting organized–you can tell by the usual mess in my office."

Areas of *unconscious incompetence* pose a greater problem–the employee lacks a specific competency, but doesn't recognize the need to develop that competency. For example, after an employee has offended other members of the team by using inappropriate language or making a prejudicial remark, the employee may have no idea why he is sensing hostility from other team members because he doesn't recognize that he made a mistake.

Methods to discover areas of competence and incompetence may include:

- Personal assessment
- Manager assessment
- 360-degree assessment
- "Reflected Best Self"

The most common time when an individual may conduct a *personal assessment* of competencies is when she decides to look for a new job, either within or without her current organization. In writing a resume, she will focus on what she considers to be her key competencies and focus on presenting those to a potential employer. Most career guides and books and websites that focus on finding a new position provide tools to conduct this type of personal competency assessment.[4] A personal assessment should focus on all three competency areas that we will use to describe the AMA Management Development Competency Model: knowing and managing yourself, knowing and managing others, and knowing and managing the business. (Remember that even though an individual professional isn't *managing* others or *managing* the business, he or she still requires competencies in the second and third categories related to *knowing* others and *knowing* the business.)

By definition, a personal assessment focuses on areas of *conscious* competence, but will generally fail to include areas of *unconscious* competence. That is why we recommend that you also get an assessment of your competencies from your manager, who may have a different perspective.

COMPARING SELF-ASSESSMENT AND MANAGER'S ASSESSMENT

When I first became a manager, while working at Digital Equipment Corporation many years ago, I attended a week-long program for new managers. Part of the preparation for this program was completing a self-assessment, which included more than 100 competency descriptions. I was instructed to rate each item on two scales: first, on how well I believed I rated on that competency and, second, on how important I felt that competency was to my job as a first-level manager. I was also instructed to give a copy of the same assessment to my manager, so that she could also rate me on the 100+ items on the same two scales. The manager's assessment was sent to the instructor for the program.

At one point in the program, the class was instructed to take out the personal assessments and was then given the managers' assessments to compare with them. There were a number of surprises for me (and others in the class):

- There were competencies on which I rated myself higher than my manager's rating—obviously, we had different opinions on these items and would need to discuss them, for I obviously wasn't demonstrating the knowledge, skills, or behaviors that she was expecting.

- There were some competencies on which I rated myself lower than my manager's rating—again, these were items for discussion and may have been areas of unconscious competence for me.

- There were some competency areas where my manager and I disagreed on the level of importance of the competency to the job. These were areas for discussion as to their relative priorities for my work in this job.

The point here is that without using this instrument, I would not have discovered some areas of unconscious competence and the need to discuss priorities for the job with my manager. I could have assumed that I was doing well, when my manager was dissatisfied with my work. Having the perspective of my manager on the competencies needed for the job and how well I demonstrated those competencies allowed me to learn more about myself and about my manager's priorities, and, therefore, to better plan my work and my personal development in this job.

Dan Tobin

The manager's assessment of an individual's competencies generally focuses on his observations of how well the individual is doing his or her job. It will generally start with technical competencies (knowing and managing the business)—those required for the individual's work, whether the person is in customer service, marketing, sales, engineering, accounting, training, etc. The manager may also comment on interpersonal and communications skills (knowing and managing others)—how well the individual works as part of the team, how well she communicates with peers, her manager, customers, suppliers, etc., as well as personal characteristics (knowing and managing oneself), such as time management, organizational skills, and perseverance. (It is important to remember that a manager's views of an employee's competencies are generally focused on the specific job the employee holds. For example, a new employee may have a broad background in marketing, but it the employee is hired to focus on marketing communications, the manager will focus the evaluation of the employee's competencies on the employee's role in marketing communications and likely forget or overlook the opportunity to review the employee's other marketing skills or contributions.) In the text box "Comparing Self-Assessment and Manager's Assessment," we discuss another approach that works best for individual professionals, first-level managers, and others for whom the organization does not want to invest in a full 360-degree assessment.

An even more comprehensive view of an individual's competencies can be gained by conducting a 360-degree assessment. This involves getting not just the perspectives of yourself and your manager, but also those who work for you and your peers (see Figure 2.3). Doing a 360-degree assessment can be a time-consuming and expensive proposition, and it is generally undertaken by the organization's human resources group as part of a larger effort, such as a talent development program, for a specific training program, or as part of the organization's succession planning process. Sometimes, an individual can request the human resources group to do a 360-degree assessment as part of a personal development or assessment plan, but this is not common (although it never hurts to ask).

It should be noted that there are dozens of vendors of 360-degree assessments on the market. Many have long-established instruments that they will not alter. The advantage of using this static type of instrument is that many of these vendors have developed a comprehensive historical database and can provide norms for various jobs and/or industries to use for comparison with the individual's assessment results. Other vendors will create a customized instrument that can be focused on specific competency areas that are of importance to the individual or the organization. But because each instrument is customized, it will not have a reference database for direct comparison of results. A third alternative, taken by many organizations, is to develop its own 360-degree assessment instrument for use solely within the organization.

Whatever form of 360-degree assessment your organization may use, the results will often be enlightening to the individual, but enlightenment is not sufficient as an end result. As was explained in the learning model in Chapter 1, a 360-degree assessment will provide a lot of

FIGURE 2.3   The 360-Degree Assessment

information, but this information does not have value unless it is applied to improve individual and organizational business performance. There should always be follow-up to a 360-degree assessment, resulting in an individual development plan focused on improving competencies that were judged to be below-par. Without this follow-on process, there will be little value to the 360-degree assessment exercise for the individual or the organization. One approach is to assign each person a development advisor (see "The Role of the Development Advisor").

THE ROLE OF THE DEVELOPMENT ADVISOR

At one company in which Dan Tobin served as director of organizational learning and employee development, a 360-degree assessment was undertaken for each of the "top 150" individuals in the company. The instrument used was based on one purchased from a well-known consulting group, but customized for the company.

Each individual being assessed was assigned a "development advisor"— a senior manager in the company outside the individual's line of command. There were several roles specified for these development advisors:

- Along with analyzing the data from the assessments (development advisors were given training on how to do these analyses), they also interviewed each of the assessors. In some cases, we found that the interviews yielded very different results from the written assessment because, despite promises of confidentiality, some assessors were fearful that their managers would see the ratings they gave them.

- The development advisors had the responsibility to present their findings, from the assessment scores and the interviews, to the company's executive committee (the CEO, the chairman, and other C-level officers) and to lead a discussion of each individual's potential.

- The development advisor was then to work with the individual, the individual's manager, and a designated human resources partner to craft a development plan for the individual.

One longstanding criticism of 360-degree assessments (as well as of typical performance reviews) is that they tend to focus on the negative, on "areas for improvement." Even when the tone of the overall evaluation is positive, people tend to remember and dwell on negative aspects rather than on their strengths. Writing in *Harvard Business Review,*[5] a group of scholars from Harvard Business School and the University of Michigan's Ross School of Business suggest an exercise that they call "Reflected Best Self" to help you focus on your strengths, rather than your weaknesses. In this exercise, you write to a group of current and former colleagues, managers, and family members, asking each to "provide information about [your] strengths, accompanied by specific examples of moments when [you] used those strengths in ways that were meaningful to them, to their families or teams, or to their organizations."[6] Once the feedback is received, the article provides a worksheet to help you "recognize patterns" in the responses and then compose a self-portrait. Using the self-portrait, the authors then recommend that you work with your manager to redesign your job so that it plays to your strengths. One great advantage of the Reflected Best Self exercise is that it is something you can do for yourself, by yourself, without having to wait for the company to include you in a 360-degree assessment program. It can also help you uncover areas of unconscious competence that you can use to improve your performance in your current job and to further your career.

Developing Competence

There are many ways in which people develop competence. For the purposes of this book, we will focus on the actions that companies can take to develop competent managers/leaders at the various levels under discussion, namely:

- Individual professional
- The first-level manager
- The mid-level manager
- The functional manager (e.g., accounting manager, IS manager, marketing manager)

We categorize the actions that a company can take to ensure that employees have or develop the competencies they need as:

- Screening candidates for existing and innate competencies
- Self-study
- Formal, instructor-led training
- Coaching
- Developmental assignments

We will discuss each of these methods briefly here. Following our presentation of the AMA Management Development Competency Model in Chapters 3, 4, and 5, we will devote a chapter to each of these topics.

Screening Candidates

Some of the competencies in our model are innate and the best way of ensuring that an employee has the required competency is to screen for it in the hiring process. In the book, *Smarts: Are We Hardwired for Success?*,[7] Chuck Martin and co-authors argue that some skills are hardwired into our brains, and if they do not exist, no amount of training will enable us to master them. For example, some people are wired to be excellent time managers and some are not. For those who are time-challenged, Martin argues that no amount of training will be able to overcome the brain's wiring.

Individuals build some competencies throughout their lives, in school, at home, and at work, and we often hire people because they already have those competencies. For example, if a job requires fluency in a foreign language, we typically will not hire someone who is not already fluent in the language, no matter how great their general ability to learn a new language. This is not to say that we do not hire people for their potential–if we didn't hire on the basis of potential, we would never hire a new graduate because he or she will almost never have the requisite experience and the full range of competencies we are seeking when people first enter the workforce.

Self-Study

There are some competencies that can be mastered by self-study. By self-study, we mean by reading, using other study materials, or taking an e-learning program. For example, for people with a good aptitude for computer technology, self-study programs have proven effective in learning new technical material to master a new system, new software, or prepare for an industry-certification program. Self-study is effective when you are mastering a competency that requires a Level 2 evaluation (see Chapter 1) that demonstrates that you have learned the material.

Self-study is less successful when trying to master a motor skill or an interpersonal or communications skill, all of which benefit from live practice and feedback. For example, you can read many books and articles on how to drive a car, learn all of the motor vehicle laws from the government booklets, and observe others driving, either live or through watching videos, but you cannot say that you are a competent driver unless you get behind the wheel and practice the skills of driving until you feel comfortable in the driver's seat and receive feedback from an experienced driver to confirm your mastery. While computer-driven simulators are sometimes used for training of some expensive motor skills, such as piloting an airplane, these types of simulations can be very expensive to develop and operate and don't provide the actual practice of live application.

Similarly, you can learn a lot through self-study about how to put together an effective presentation and the skills needed to make that presentation, but you cannot say that you are a good presenter until you have practiced those skills with a coach or a live audience. These types of skills require a Level 3 evaluation–you cannot say that you have mastered these competencies until you have actually used them on the job.

Formal, Instructor-Led Training

Formal instructor-led training is most useful when the classroom is used to help you not just learn, but also to practice new skills in a safe environment. In these cases, the instructor can watch you and coach you as you try out new skills in an environment where making an error can be quickly corrected before the car or the system crashes, or where common errors can be corrected before you become embarrassed by making the error on the job. Of course, this type of instruction requires instructors who have the skills and experience to provide this type of instruction and feedback, and an instructional design that emphasizes this type of experiential learning process.

Coaching

A coach is someone who can watch the individual try out new skills and provide commentary and guidance on the individual's performance. Sometimes, the coach teaches new skills. More often, the coach provides feedback and helps the individual fine-tune her performance. In the organizational setting, the coach is often the individual's manager, but can also be a peer, a subordinate, or another employee who has already mastered the required competency.

Developmental Assignments

Developmental assignments offer a wide range of opportunities for the individual to gain new knowledge and skills and master new competencies. For example:

- In many organizations, a new graduate may be assigned to work with a more experienced employee to "learn the ropes." (The Buddy System)
- A manager may say to an employee, "You've done about 75 percent of the tasks required to manage a total project. Now, I think it's time for you to try managing an entire project on your own, and I will coach you on the areas where you haven't yet had experience." (Job Enlargement)
- An employee who has worked in one area of a company's operations may be assigned to work on a cross-functional task force to broaden his view of the company's overall operations. (Cross-Functional Teamwork)
- In one high-tech company, the comptrollers for the engineering and manufacturing organizations switched jobs for six months to learn more about the other function. (Job Rotation)
- In many large international organizations, a high-potential manager may be given an overseas assignment for one or two years to gain experience working in another culture while learning more about the company's international operations.

You can also combine methods to create an even richer learning experience. For example, you may combine some self-study or instructor-led training with a developmental assignment to provide "action learning" where you provide real-world practice of the skills the employee has learned on her own or in the classroom. Adding coaching to this model makes the learning experience even more complete.

What is importtant in planning for an employee's development is to ensure that the employee has the opportunity to use his newly acquired knowledge and skills on the job. This helps the employee master the needed competencies and ensures that the organization's investment in the employee's development has a real payoff in terms of individual and organizational goal achievement.

Turning Competence into Action

Remember that competence is defined as the ability to do something well. But having the ability to do something doesn't necessarily mean that it will be done in a competent manner. Jeffrey Pfeffer and Robert Sutton of Stamford University studied the problem, which they call the "Knowing-Doing Gap."

> Some organizations are consistently able to turn knowledge into action, and do so even as they grow and absorb new people and even other organizations. Other organizations, composed of intelligent, thoughtful, hard-working nice people, fail to translate their knowledge about organizational performance into action.[8]

Pfeffer and Sutton focus on what company management needs to do to ensure that knowledge is turned into action. Too often have we heard a participant evaluate a training program in this manner: "It was a great program. I learned a lot and I really changed. But then I returned to my office and, while I had changed, my manager and the rest of the organization hadn't. So, no, I haven't implemented much of what I learned in the program."

Referring back to the levels of evaluation discussed in Chapter 1, a Level 2 evaluation, which measures knowledge acquisition by performing pre- and posttests around a learning activity, can demonstrate whether an employee has mastered the learning content, i.e., whether the employee has become competent on the subject matter. But Level 2 evaluation does not guarantee that the employee will apply what he has learned to the job–this requires a Level 3 evaluation, something that most organizations do not require. This is why the third section of the learning contract described in Chapter 1 requires that the employee and his manager agree and specify, *before any learning activity is undertaken,* how that learning will be applied to the employee's work and what changes in individual and business performance are expected to ensue.

The AMA Management Development Competency Model

The AMA Management Development Competency Model, presented in the next three chapters, examines the competencies needed at four levels in any organization:

- The individual professional
- The first-level manager
- The mid-level manager
- The functional manager who has responsibility for a specific functional area within the organization

We include individual professionals in our model because many of the competencies we will describe start with the individual professional—if the individual does not demonstrate these competencies, she will not be considered for a management role. It is also important to remember that the competencies we will describe are *cumulative,* that is, at any level of management, the designated individual must have first mastered the competencies for the previous level(s) along with additional competencies designated for his or her current level in the organization. We use illustrative behaviors for each competency to further demonstrate how the competency may manifest itself at each of the management levels.

Table 2.1 provides a summary of the competencies by category:

- Knowing and managing yourself (10 competencies)
- Knowing and managing others (17 competencies)
- Knowing and managing the business (19 competencies)

TABLE 2.1 AMA Competency Model		
Managing Self	*Managing Others*	*Managing the Business*
Emotional Intelligence/ Self-Awareness	Oral Communication	Problem Solving
	Written Communication	Decision Making
Self-Confidence	Valuing Diversity	Managing and Leading Change
Self-Development	Building Teams	
Building Trust and Personal Accountability	Networking	Driving Innovation
	Partnering	Customer Focus
Resilience and Stress Tolerance	Building Relationships	Resource Management
Action Orientation	Emotional Intelligence/Interpersonal Savvy	Operational and Tactical Planning
Time Management		Results Orientation
Flexibility and Agility	Influencing	Quality Orientation
Critical and Analytical Thinking	Managing Conflict	Mastering Complexity
Creative Thinking	Managing People for Performance	Business and Financial Acumen
	Clarifying Roles and Accountabilities	Strategic Planning
		Strategic Thinking
	Delegating	Global Perspective
	Empowering Others	Organizational Savvy
	Motivating Others	Organizational Design
	Coaching	Human Resources Planning
	Developing Top Talent	
		Monitoring the External Environment
		Core Functional/ Technical Skills

Remember that all three categories apply to all four levels (individual professional, first-level manager, mid-level manager, and functional manager). In the next three chapters we will provide definitions and a list of illustrative behaviors of each competency. It is through discussion of the behaviors that we will make the distinction in how each competency applies to each of the four levels of employee.

Defining Competencies for Your Organization's Employees

Given all of the competencies in the AMA Management Development Competency Model, how can your organization use them, along with their definitions and illustrative behaviors, in planning for the development of managers within your own organization? There are four major ways in which you can use a competency model:

1. Writing job descriptions.
2. Assessing how well employees fit within their current job descriptions.
3. Selecting employees to hire or promote.
4. Developing employees in their current roles within the organization and preparing them for future roles.

The job of writing job descriptions is typically assigned to an organization's human resources (HR) group working with the management team. The HR group often provides a template that is completed by the hiring manager for any new or replacement positions at the individual professional level. At this level, most such job descriptions focus on technical education (for entry-level jobs) or technical skills (for experienced applicants), listing such requirements as:

- This position requires a bachelor's degree in computer science and having earned the certification of Microsoft Certified Systems Engineer.
- The marketing specialist will have three years of experience in direct mail marketing.
- The accounting manager will have a bachelor's degree in business administration and must have earned the designation of CPA.
- The project manager must have five years of project management experience in our industry and have earned the Project Management Professional certification from the Project Management Institute.

While these job descriptions focus on technical skills, training, and certification, they usually have some general statements related to some of the competencies in the AMA Management Development Competency Model, such as:

- Excellent written and oral communications skills.
- Must be able to work in a team-based environment.
- Must be able to handle multiple projects and manage time well.

The AMA Management Development Competency Model, as detailed in Chapters 3, 4, and 5, will give those responsible for writing your organization's job descriptions a much more comprehensive set of competency descriptions and behaviors to use as the basis for writing those descriptions. But before starting to list dozens of behaviors on each job description, the organization must decide which of the competencies and behaviors are most important to building its business and engendering its organizational culture.

Defining the organization's culture and values usually requires time-consuming (and often difficult) discussions between the HR organization and the organization's leadership team, but they are worthwhile and must be done every few years. We have seen many organizations whose culture and values reflected those of its founder. When the founder retired or otherwise left the organization, management found that the culture, which often was built around the personality of the founder, needed to change to better respond to current and future business opportunities as defined by the founder's successor. Without this type of discussion, the old culture and values may continue while the organization's leaders wonder why people aren't responding to the changes they are trying to make. With a common understanding of the organization's values and strategies, people can much more easily align their work with the directions set by the organization's leaders. The competency descriptions and illustrative behaviors for each competency can help to facilitate these discussions, e.g., "How should we prioritize the various competencies in looking for new talent?" or "Look at the behaviors associated with this competency—is it important for our functional leaders to behave in this way?" or "We have always hired a number of new MBA graduates this year, screening them for their technical skills—should we now be considering their teamwork and communications skills in making these hiring decisions?"

The result of these discussions between the HR group and the organization's leadership team should inform the general job requirements for all positions within the company and specific job descriptions for key roles. But it also takes more than rewriting job descriptions (which are rarely consulted except at the time of hiring someone). As explained throughout the latter chapters of this book, developing managers is not the sole responsibility of the HR group or the training function within an organization. There are important roles to be played by those groups, but also by the organization's leaders in building a positive learning environment that nurtures the management development process. As will be explained, management development is not just a training function–there are many ways in which any organization can help develop its management talent to get work done today and to build management strength for tomorrow. And while there are roles for all of these groups, the key roles in developing employees belong to the employees themselves and their managers. So it is vital that every employee and every manager in the organization understand the competencies that they will need and the priorities for those competencies as defined by the organization.

When do organizations assess how well current employees fit within their current job descriptions? The answer is rarely. Logically, this type of comparison is made when a person is hired or promoted into a new job, and perhaps again at the end of a probationary period in the new job (typically ninety days after hiring or promotion). While most organizations conduct annual performance reviews, the judgments made in those reviews are typically based on specific goals assigned to the employee at the beginning of the year. Many performance review forms also ask the manager and the employee to enter ratings on a set of key characteristics, e.g., works well as part of the team, exhibits leadership potential, works in an ethical manner, and so forth.

It is rare for a company to give a poor rating to an employee who is meeting his or her business goals, even if the employee's job behaviors cast him as a difficult person to work with. Many know of a technically brilliant employee who people cannot stand to work with because of his arrogance, his brutal dismissal of ideas from others whom he considers less brilliant than himself, and his refusal to attend team meetings. This type of employee provides a real test of the organizational leadership's commitment to the organization's stated values. Is he allowed to continue offending everyone because of his technical knowledge, or is his behavior not tolerated despite his technical brilliance? At some companies we have seen this type of employee stick around for years, while the organization loses many other competent employees who can't stand working with him. In other organizations, we have seen the organization's leadership and HR groups try to help the individual by assigning an internal or external coach "to smooth out his rough edges" and, if that hasn't worked, subsequently fire him because even though he was technically brilliant, he was too much of a disruptive influence. It all comes down to the company's culture, usually defined by its leadership team, and to how much time the company wants to spend building and enforcing that culture. If the leadership team is committed to building and sustaining a certain culture, the AMA Management Development Competency Model provides many valuable competency and behavioral descriptors that can be used to write job descriptions so that they reflect that culture. If the leadership team does not have such a commitment, the exercise of using the AMA model to write detailed job descriptions can be a time-consuming and very frustrating exercise.

After we describe the AMA Management Development Competency Model in the next three chapters, we will further discuss how the model can be used in selecting new employees and identifying internal candidates for promotion. Following chapters will deal with the tasks involved in developing managers through training and many other means, and the roles that the organization's leadership team, current managers, the training function, and the human resources group need to play to ensure that the organization has the management capabilities it needs for today's business and tomorrow's success.

Summary

With competence defined as the ability to do something well, a competency model includes a set of individual competencies that describe the abilities needed in a given position. Competency models can be used to screen potential employees, as a way of determining an employee's development needs (for his or her current job or for future growth opportunities), or as a way to select employees for promotion up the management ladder. In the next three chapters, we will detail the AMA Management Development Competency Model.

CHAPTER

The AMA Management Development Competency Model

Knowing and Managing Yourself

We start with competencies in the category of knowing and managing yourself, because if an individual cannot master most of these competencies, he will likely never be trusted to manage others or to manage the business. In the category of "knowing and managing yourself," the competencies defined in the AMA model for individual professionals are displayed in Table 3.1.

We will first define each competency and then illustrate each with sample behaviors to further clarify each competency and to demonstrate at which level (individual professional, first-level manager, mid-level manager, or functional manager) each competency becomes important to success. The full AMA competency model, with illustrative behaviors

TABLE 3.1   Competencies for Knowing and Managing Yourself

- Emotional Intelligence/Self-Awareness
- Self-Confidence
- Self-Development
- Building Trust and Personal Accountability
- Resilience and Stress Tolerance
- Action Orientation
- Time Management
- Flexibility and Agility
- Critical and Analytical Thinking
- Creative Thinking

and the levels at which each behavior becomes important, can be found in this book's appendix.

Emotional Intelligence/Self-Awareness

AMA defines this competency as analyzing and recognizing one's own strengths and weaknesses, attitudes, and feelings. An employee with this competence maintains a clear, realistic understanding of her goals, capabilities, and limitations. She seeks feedback about her effectiveness and makes changes in response to that feedback. She is attuned to her inner feelings, recognizing how these feelings affect her behavior and job performance. She expresses her feelings and reactions appropriately.

> **Illustrative Behavior 1:** Proactively solicits both positive and constructive feedback on his or her performance.

> **Illustrative Behavior 2:** Adjusts his or her behavior in response to feedback.

At all levels, a person with this competency becomes self-aware by continuously asking for feedback on his performance, whether that be job performance, performance as a team member or leader, or in managerial duties, to better understand his effects on the people with whom he works, and to adjust his behavior to improve working relationships with peers, managers, and peers. This sensitivity is a key element in emotional intelligence.

> **Illustrative Behavior 3:** Recognizes feelings and concerns heard in conversation to address the other person's expressed and underlying needs.

Emotional intelligence also requires that the employee, at all levels, recognizes the explicit and tacit feelings of others–employees, managers, and peers. Emotional intelligence is not just about managing your own feelings, but also about recognizing and reacting to the feelings of others.

Illustrative Behavior 4: Understands his or her personal preferences for making decisions, solving problems, and working with others; recognizes when his or her preferred style may not be the most effective approach given the situation.

Every person, at every level of the organization, has an inherent style of interacting with other people. In various seminars given by the AMA, we use a variety of instruments to help people recognize their personal styles, or ways they interact with other people. By learning your own style and recognizing the styles of others with whom you work, you can better understand the effects of your style on others, and of their styles on you, and work to flex your style to improve working relationships. This is an important competency at all levels of the organization.

Illustrative Behavior 5: Asks questions that create an atmosphere in which the other person feels comfortable discussing the situation and sharing concerns.

Illustrative Behavior 6: Expresses his or her feelings and reactions in a calm, clear manner.

Illustrative Behavior 7: Communicates tactfully even when others are unhappy or confused.

An employee with good emotional intelligence can control his own emotions and related behaviors and can recognize the feelings of others and adjust his behavior to keep both himself and others calm in tense situations by expressing himself in a calm, collected manner and by helping others to express their concerns similarly. This is an important competency at all levels of the organization, perhaps becoming more important as the employee climbs the management ladder.

Illustrative Behavior 8: Coaches others on the importance of self-awareness and how to become more self-aware.

As important as behaviors 1 through 7 are for the individual professional, when you progress up the management ladder, it becomes important to not only practice all of these behaviors, but to coach your employees on the importance of emotional intelligence and self-awareness and to help them develop this competency. Hopefully, it has become evident to you through these descriptions that self-awareness and emotional intelligence are important competencies for all of the organization's employees. Organizations that work to develop this competency in employees at all levels are much more pleasant and productive places to work.

Self-Confidence

AMA defines self-confidence as acting on the basis of one's convictions rather than trying to please others; being confident in oneself; having a healthy sense of one's capabilities without being arrogant.

> **Illustrative Behavior 1:** Clearly and appropriately states his or her opinions and perspectives, even if others disagree.

> **Illustrative Behavior 2:** Exhibits confidence and conviction when presenting his or her ideas and perspectives, both verbally and in writing.

It is not enough to believe in yourself—you must also have the ability to express your opinions, both verbally and in writing. Often, we have seen introverted people who have great ideas, and believe in those ideas, but who, because of shyness or lack of self-confidence, never speak up to make their ideas heard. These behaviors are needed at all levels, but it must start at the level of the individual professional, for a person at that level who lacks self-confidence and the ability to speak up and fight for his ideas is much less likely to be promoted to a management position.

> **Illustrative Behavior 3:** Demonstrates a willingness to take on challenging new projects or assignments.

A self-confident employee will take on challenging new projects or assignments to demonstrate her abilities and to challenge herself. This behavior can result in greater visibility at all levels and can lead to promotion from individual professional to manager and further up the management ladder.

> **Illustrative Behavior 4:** Quickly and candidly informs others when he or she cannot fulfill a request, and the reason for it, and problem-solves an alternative.

Self-confidence also includes the ability to say "No"—to be able to tell others when he cannot fulfill a request or will be late on a promised deliverable. The self-confident employee knows that in order to make others confident in him, he must be up front in admitting when promises cannot be met. But the key to success in turning down a request or delivering the bad news that a deadline cannot be met is to provide that information as early as possible and to help problem-solve a solution that will help his manager, colleague, or customer find a solution to the problem.

> **Illustrative Behavior 5:** Admits when he or she is wrong or someone else has a better solution and is willing to change direction or reorient his or her actions as necessary.

> **Illustrative Behavior 6:** Demonstrates confidence that his or her plans and decisions will be successful.

There is a big difference between self-confidence and the need to win every disagreement. The self-confident employee will admit when someone else has a better idea or a more logical approach to a problem and be willing to go along with that better approach. Too often have we seen an arrogant employee who has such a great need to win that she insists on doing it her own way, even when there is clear evidence that there is a better way. When an employee is willing to change direction in the face of a better solution, others (managers and peers) will develop a greater respect for the employee when the employee does express confidence that her plans and decisions will be successful. These behaviors demonstrate both self-confidence and reasonableness, and should help the employee climb the management ladder.

Illustrative Behavior 7: Is willing to delegate tasks or assignments that team members may be able to perform better than him- or herself.

A successful manager once told me that the key to his success was to always hire people who were smarter than himself. Part of self-confidence is in recognizing when others can do a task or project better than you and, in so recognizing that fact, delegating the assignment to the better-able employee. A self-confident manager is able to express confidence in others without feeling that this act exposes a weakness in himself.

Illustrative Behavior 8: Takes responsibility for making difficult or unpopular decisions.

A self-confident employee takes responsibility for any difficult or unpopular decision that she needs to make, without trying to slough off that responsibility on others. Such decisions may deal with personnel issues, budget allocations, selection or prioritization of work assignments, for example. This behavior becomes increasingly important as an employee climbs the management ladder.

Self-Development

An employee who has this competency seeks feedback on his strengths and weaknesses and initiates activities to increase or enhance his knowledge, skills, and competence in order to perform more effectively or enhance his career. With this competency, the employee spends time learning new information or ideas and applying them effectively, keeps up to date in his knowledge and skills and learns from his successes and failures.

Illustrative Behavior 1: Routinely asks for feedback on his or her performance and uses both positive and negative feedback to enhance performance.

Illustrative Behavior 2: Receives feedback in a constructive manner.

Illustrative Behavior 3: Probes for concrete examples and suggestions to improve his or her own performance.

Illustrative Behavior 4: Consults relevant sources (e.g., appraisals, reports, videos, customer feedback) to get insight into his or her own performance.

An employee interested in his own self-development regularly seeks feedback and information on how to improve his performance in the current job and to prepare for career advancement. When an employee takes his work seriously, continually challenging himself to improve, the employee often becomes known as someone to consider for the next rung on the management ladder. It should be noted that there is an important difference here between an employee who seeks self-development and one who is so lacking in self-confidence that he continuously asks for feedback to ensure that he isn't doing anything wrong.

Illustrative Behavior 5: Is self-critical; can name both strong and weak points about him- or herself.

Illustrative Behavior 6: Learns from both successes and failures.

Illustrative Behavior 7: Initiates project debriefs to clarify learnings–both what worked well and what could be done more effectively in the future.

An employee with this competency has learned to have a balanced view of herself, knowing both strengths and areas needing development. She learns from both successes and failures. Learning from one's successes is a way of discovering your areas of unconscious competence, while learning from failures helps to uncover areas of unconscious incompetence. One way of learning from both successes and failures is to conduct a debrief of every project, successful or unsuccessful, to learn both what went well and should be repeated and what can be improved in the future. This last behavior becomes increasingly important as the employee climbs the management ladder, for when her subordinates see that their manager learns from failures, and helps them learn from their own errors, it gives them permission to be creative and take prudent risks in their work.

> **Illustrative Behavior 8:** Seeks both formal and informal development opportunities.

> **Illustrative Behavior 9:** Demonstrates a desire to perform above and beyond the requirements of his or her position (e.g., enthusiastically takes on tasks outside of daily responsibilities to learn and grow).

Employees with this competency continuously seek development opportunities, both formal and informal, and recognize that their growth comes not just from formal training programs, but also from self-study methods and from on-the-job experience. By volunteering to take on tasks outside their normal responsibilities, they can not only develop their business acumen but can also demonstrate their ambition to climb the management ladder. This is why many organizations rotate jobs, so that people can learn more about the many aspects of the business. Of course, there is a difference between self-development and blind ambition—we have sometimes seen employees who are too eager to take on too much responsibility too quickly and often just as quickly "burn out" by taking on more than they can handle. However, employees who have shown the willingness to take on new responsibilities are often those who are considered "management material."

> **Illustrative Behavior 10:** Coaches others to focus on self-development.

> **Illustrative Behavior 11:** Builds a culture that encourages learning and continuous improvement.

This is a primary responsibility of any manager at any level—to help his employees develop their knowledge and skills to improve their personal performance on the job. While this takes time (and poorer managers often complain that they have no time to coach employees), this competency is most often rewarded by having employees who are well motivated and are very loyal to the manager. When exit interviews of employees who are voluntarily leaving the organization are conducted by an organization's human resources staff, a frequent reason given for departure is that the manager provided no coaching, no opportunities for the employee to develop and grow.

Building a culture that encourages learning and continuous improvement has been shown to be a major contributor to success in organizations of all sizes. This behavior can be started by managers at any level of the organization, but becomes increasingly important for functional managers and more senior managers.

Building Trust and Personal Accountability

The AMA defines this competency as keeping promises and honoring commitments; accepting responsibility for one's actions; being honest and truthful when communicating information; behaving in a way that is consistent with espoused values; and assuming responsibility for dealing with problems, crises, or issues.

> **Illustrative Behavior 1:** Admits when he or she does not know an answer and takes the necessary measures to locate required information.

In today's world, with the ever-increasing glut of information and expanding spans of control, no employee (individual professional or manager at any level) can know everything. But little is gained, at any level, by bluffing an answer to a query—more is gained by admitting that the employee does not know the answer, at the same time volunteering to find the needed information. Bluffing, or insisting that you know the answer when you really don't, can easily destroy trust.

> **Illustrative Behavior 2:** Treats confidential information with respect and integrity.

An employee who does not respect the need for confidentiality will quickly destroy trust, not just of those people who are affected by the revelation, but by all employees, who will quickly learn to avoid sharing confidential information with that person. And a person who cannot be trusted should not be promoted.

> **Illustrative Behavior 3:** Takes the initiative to provide all relevant information, even when communicating about a problem, mistake, or other difficult situation (e.g., is clear and direct).

> **Illustrative Behavior 4:** Accepts responsibility for mistakes and failures and learns from them (e.g., does not "point fingers").

Being clear and direct in communications, especially about real or potential problems, helps to build trust. Too often have we seen both individual professionals and managers at all levels withhold relevant information or point fingers at others to try to shirk responsibility for a problem. When employees withhold information, or blame others for their own errors, they do not take personal responsibility, and the result is the erosion of trust with peers, employees, and higher-level management.

> **Illustrative Behavior 5:** Keeps promises and honors commitments.

An employee with this competency is "as good as his word"–he doesn't forget what he has promised or the commitments he has made. And if the employee cannot honor a commitment, he lets the affected parties know as quickly as possible and offers alternative plans, rather than ignoring the commitment and hoping that others won't remember. This competency is important at all levels, and a person lacking this competency will generally not be considered for promotion up the management ladder.

> **Illustrative Behavior 6:** Demonstrates consistency between his or her words and actions.

We have all heard the old saw: "Do as I say, not as I do." A trustworthy employee demonstrates consistency between words and actions.

There is an old story of a national sales manager who comes into town to meet with the regional sales manager. "These are hard times for the company," said the national manager. "We need for you to drastically cut your sales reps' expense accounts. No more lunches or dinners with customers."

The regional sales manager replied: "You flew in here, probably in business class, and are staying at one of the most expensive hotels in town. We're having breakfast here at your insistence, rather than meeting at the office, and the bill will be near $100 before you are finished, and you will have me pay for it and put it on my expense account. And yet you are telling me that my sales reps can't spend $25 to take a paying customer to lunch. *Your actions are speaking so loudly, I can't hear a word you are saying.*"

Illustrative Behavior 7: Backs up and supports team members in difficult situations.

Trustworthy employees recognize that all work is interdependent and that supporting team members in difficult situations can only help to build trust. Whether a team member needing help is a peer, your boss, or one of your direct reports, pitching in when the going gets tough can only help to build trust. No one wants to work for a manager or with a colleague who "hangs you out to dry" in difficult situations.

Illustrative Behavior 8: Handles work-related problems in a confident and decisive manner.

Ignoring a problem doesn't make it go away and doing so makes the people who have been, or are being affected by the problem, wary of your intentions. Of course, sometimes problems tend to solve themselves, and few people want to work for a manager who feels that only he or she can handle any problem that arises. The trustful employee/manager encourages people to solve their own problems, but, when the employee has demonstrated that he or she cannot handle the problem, then steps in to help solve the problem in a confident and decisive manner.

Illustrative Behavior 9: Is willing to hold tough discussions with others about taking responsibility for their own actions and decisions.

Few managers are totally comfortable in addressing a performance problem with their employees–this is why doing annual performance reviews is frequently viewed by managers as a chore rather than a desirable part of their job. A manager with this competency knows it is necessary to hold others accountable for their actions and decisions, just as she builds her own reputation for trust and accountability.

Illustrative Behavior 10: Sets an example by behaving in a way that is consistent with the organization's values and principles.

As an employee of, or manager within, any organization, you are expected to behave in a way that supports the organization's values and principles, rather than ignoring them or finding a way around them if you disagree with them. If you find that you cannot support your organization's values and principles, you will probably be better off finding a new employer whose values and principles you can support. And few organizations will promote people to higher-level management if they consistently obvert or subvert the organization's values and principles.

Illustrative Behavior 11: Asks open-ended, nonevaluative questions about work-related problems to encourage people to respond and provide a more complete picture of the situation.

Managers who do not have this competency often jump to conclusions in any problem situation, rather than hearing people out and asking questions to fully understand the situation before reaching a conclusion. When you ask people questions to fully understand the situation, you are building trust with those people.

Resilience and Stress Tolerance

An employee demonstrates resilience and stress tolerance by continuing to perform effectively when faced with time pressures, adversity, disappointment, or opposition. An employee with this competency remains focused, composed, and optimistic in difficult situations and bounces back from failures or disappointments.

> **Illustrative Behavior 1:** Projects credibility and poise under difficult or adverse conditions.

> **Illustrative Behavior 2:** Maintains progress (while maintaining quality) when handling multiple tasks and projects, even under stressful situations or when faced with competing deadlines.

We have all been in these types of stressful situations–you are working on a tight deadline and something goes wrong, or your manager comes in with another "urgent" priority for you to handle (while still expecting you to meet the deadline on your current project). A person with this competency handles these types of situations without panicking and without falling apart.

> **Illustrative Behavior 3:** Is patient, tenacious, and resourceful when seeking information to satisfy a request or complete a project.

> **Illustrative Behavior 4:** Sees issues and problems through to completion.

We have all operated under tight deadlines and often become impatient to get results. An employee with this competency has the patience and tenacity to get the job done. When facing a new urgent project, the employee doesn't just drop the completion of his current project, hoping that no one will notice, but sees all of his responsibilities through to completion. Displaying these behaviors makes him a more desirable candidate for promotion up the management ladder.

> **Illustrative Behavior 5:** Handles contacts with internal and external customers with a high degree of professionalism (e.g., maintains a calm disposition even when others are upset, without conveying impatience or annoyance).

> **Illustrative Behavior 6:** Treats all people with respect and equity, even when under pressure.

Resilience and stress tolerance can be demonstrated by how an employee treats others, both internal and external to the organization. Even though the employee may be under stress, she still treats people with respect, maintaining a professional demeanor. We have all known people who, under stress, start treating other people badly, becoming impatient or displaying annoyance. Employees who consistently display these negative behaviors are unlikely to be promoted.

> **Illustrative Behavior 7:** Finds ways to overcome or eliminate barriers that are hindering achievement of his or her goals.

> **Illustrative Behavior 8:** Views failures and mistakes as an opportunity to learn.

> **Illustrative Behavior 9:** Quickly responds to unforeseen changes in the business.

When facing a barrier, some employees give up–"It can't be done. This person or situation is in the way and won't move," or "this last change makes the whole thing impossible to accomplish." Resilient employees find ways around or through barriers (even if the barrier is their own mistake), staying focused on the goal. This type of persistence is often sought in candidates for management positions.

> **Illustrative Behavior 10:** Keeps team members calm and focused in uncertain or complicated situations.

A manager with this competency not only controls his own emotions when facing a difficult situation, but also keeps his team calm and focused when facing uncertain or complicated situations. Team members find it much easier to tolerate stress when their manager doesn't panic.

Action Orientation

AMA defines this competency as maintaining a sense of urgency to complete a task. An action-oriented employee seeks information rather than waiting for it. She makes decisions in a timely manner regardless of pressure or uncertainty, making decisions quickly when called upon to do so and acting decisively to implement solutions and resolve crises. She does not procrastinate. She is tough and assertive when necessary while showing respect and positive regard for others.

> **Illustrative Behavior 1:** Makes timely decisions based on the best available information (e.g., is not overcome by "analysis paralysis").

> **Illustrative Behavior 2:** Has the confidence to make decisions in uncertain circumstances.

> **Illustrative Behavior 3:** Balances information gathering and analysis activities with an urgency to take action and "drive it forward."

Employees with an action orientation know that not all problems can wait until all possible information is gathered. They demand faster, more timely, decisions and are not afraid to make those decisions. The difference here is between what we call an "academic orientation" and action orientation. When a graduate student is studying for a doctorate in any field, he is being trained on that field's research methodology. His qualifying examinations focus on how well he has learned that research methodology. When he writes his dissertation, his work is not judged on the results of his research, but on whether he applied the research methodology correctly. This is what we call the "academic orientation"–presupposing that if you follow the research methodology correctly, you will get a defensible result, and if you don't follow the methodology exactly your result cannot be valid.

With action orientation, a decision maker says: "We have to make a decision within, say, the next two weeks. Let's learn as much as we can over the next fourteen days to make the best, most informed decision possible." It is not that the decision maker in unconcerned about methodology, but only that making the decision is more important.

> **Illustrative Behavior 4:** Tackles problems or conflict head-on; doesn't procrastinate.

Action-oriented employees do not ignore problems, hoping that they will go away, but tackle them head-on. This does not excuse micro-managers who do not allow their employees time to solve problems before charging in to solve all problems for the employee.

> **Illustrative Behavior 5:** Avoids distraction from less critical activities.

> **Illustrative Behavior 6:** Clarifies priorities and objectives to swiftly accomplish tasks.

Action orientation also requires that the employee be clear about her objectives and priorities and focus on the highest priorities that will help her, and the organization, reach their stated objectives. One of the most important tasks for a manager is to ensure that employees understand their objectives and to help them set priorities among competing tasks.

> **Illustrative Behavior 7:** Takes the initiative to identify and solve work-related problems.

There is an old saying: "Everyone complains about the weather, but no one ever does anything about it." Similarly, employees often face a longstanding problem in the workplace that has annoyed people for years, but no one ever does anything to solve it, even though everyone recognizes the problem. An action-oriented employee, when seeing such a problem, will try to solve it, at the same time trying to ensure that he is not overstepping the boundaries of his job.

> **Illustrative Behavior 8:** Coaches others to be decisive.

An action-oriented manager coaches her employees to be equally action-oriented and to make their own decisions whenever possible. This is the opposite of the micro-manager who will never let her employees make a decision without her input or agreement.

Illustrative Behavior 9: Checks to ensure priorities and objectives are clear among team members.

Illustrative Behavior 10: Refocuses team members on the "big picture" when they appear to have lost sight of it.

This behavior follows on from behavior 8 above–coaching employees to be decisive. When a manager ensures that his employees understand how their work relates to the larger objectives of the team and the organization as a whole, and that they know their own priorities, the manager is much more likely to empower employees to make their own decisions. Without this context, employees can take empowerment too far–making decisions that may benefit themselves in getting their own work done when, in fact, some of those decisions may also obviate the larger work of the team or of the organization as a whole. For example, an organization's lawyer may hold up a vital partnership agreement while sparring with the other party's attorney over inconsequential wording changes while the organization loses business opportunities it would have won if the partnership agreement had been completed.

Time Management

An employee with this competency spends her time appropriately among people and projects to ensure that both internal and external client needs are met. She reprioritizes daily tasks as each day progresses to ensure that newly emerging, urgent issues are resolved, while not losing sight of longer-term projects. She balances her workload when involved in multiple projects.

Illustrative Behavior 1: Shifts attention quickly to respond to the unexpected and simultaneously make progress on planned activities.

Illustrative Behavior 2: Understands what is required to get things done and establishes/implements an effective course of action (e.g., establishes appropriate deadlines and meets them).

>**Illustrative Behavior 3:** Plans each day's work to complete time-sensitive issues before deadlines.

These first three behaviors all deal with balancing day-to-day demands with longer-term priorities. An employee with good time management skills is able to handle the inevitable changes in priorities and tasks on a daily basis with aplomb.

Early in Dan Tobin's career, a week before starting a new job with a high-tech company, he was invited to a group dinner that was taking place as part of a worldwide meeting of the group he was joining. After introductions, his new manager handed him a wrapped gift box. Inside, he found a can of tennis balls. "For the next week," the manager explained, "I want you to practice the most important skill for this job—juggling. You'll have to do it on a daily basis."

>**Illustrative Behavior 4:** Takes ownership for delivering results on multiple projects or initiatives.

>**Illustrative Behavior 5:** Gathers the necessary information to effectively prioritize work (e.g., urgency and importance).

>**Illustrative Behavior 6:** Prioritizes and organizes a complex workload while maintaining focus and staying on track.

While behaviors 1 through 3, above, dealt with juggling priorities, these three behaviors deal with understanding the context for those priorities. Good time managers understand that everything that is important is not necessarily urgent, and everything that is urgent isn't necessarily important. Former U.S. President Dwight Eisenhower once said that only two types of papers end up on his desk—those marked "urgent" and those marked "important." He spent so much time on "urgent" matters, he complained, that he never got around to what was really important.

>**Illustrative Behavior 7:** Reallocates his or her time to ensure the completion of his or her own assigned work/responsibilities as well as helping others perform effectively.

This can be a real challenge for a first-level manager who has been accustomed to just managing her own time. As a first-level manager, not only must she continue to complete her own work, but must also help her employees to manage their own time in line with team and organizational priorities.

> **Illustrative Behavior 8:** Establishes and maintains systems and files to help resolve pending issues and problems in a timely manner.

An individual professional may or may not be able to manage his time without formal systems or files to keep all projects and priorities straight, but as an employee climbs the management ladder, the number of projects and issues for which he is responsible grows exponentially and requires that he use systems or files to keep track of everything for which he and his employees are responsible.

> **Illustrative Behavior 9:** Delegates appropriately to ensure that he or she is focused on longer-term strategic projects.

Delegation is an important component of time management for mid-level and functional levels. By properly delegating work to her employees, a manager at this level can focus her own attention on more strategic issues while entrusting her employees to handle day-to-day operational details.

> **Illustrative Behavior 10:** Reprioritizes work efforts based on changing situations and emerging issues (e.g., in response to organizational, systems, and/or market changes).

This is a primary job for managers—setting priorities for her employees and changing those priorities based on changes in organizational objectives, strategies, systems, etc.

> **Illustrative Behavior 11:** Effectively balances his or her focus on both strategy and operations to achieve optimal results.

This is one of the more difficult transitions for a person who has been promoted to a more senior-level management position. As an individual professional or as a manager at lower levels, he focused on getting work done—his own or the work of his group. At more senior levels, managers must learn to shift their thinking from strictly operational issues to a more strategic point of view. This often requires the manager to learn more about other functional areas, e.g., if a marketing communication manager is promoted to group marketing manager, he must learn about, and value, the work of other parts of the marketing organization. Or, if a marketing manager is promoted to a general business management position, he must learn about and value the other aspects of the business—engineering, manufacturing, customer service, and so on. Learning to balance strategic and operational concerns is a key success factor for individuals new to senior-level management.

Flexibility and Agility

AMA defines someone with this competency as adjusting one's behavior to new information or changing circumstances. Such a person remains open to new ways of doing things and experiments with new methods. He also works effectively in an unstructured or dynamic environment.

> **Illustrative Behavior 1:** Adapts his or her behavior in response to new information or changing circumstances.

In today's ever-changing business environment, nothing is constant except change. A flexible, agile employee understands this and easily adapts his behavior, rather than panicking with every change in circumstances.

> **Illustrative Behavior 2:** Is open to new methods, ideas, or approaches.

This behavior is a key to flexibility and agility. The world is in constant flux and people who are not open to new methods, ideas, or approaches will soon be left behind. Consider that the amount of information in the world is doubling every ten years, or look at what the Internet has done to the world of marketing—without an openness to new concepts, neither the individual professional nor the manager, at any level, can succeed.

> **Illustrative Behavior 3:** Works and collaborates effectively in unstructured or dynamic environments.

The days of a stable bureaucratic environment that defined every position and every reporting relationship within an organization are long gone. The demands of the global business environment and the ever-changing modes of communication have stripped away structure and replaced organization charts with dynamic networks. Today's business environment demands flexibility and agility to work effectively, both as an individual professional and as a manager at any level of an organization.

> **Illustrative Behavior 4:** Adjusts the original objective or plan to allow the best possible results.

A flexible, agile employee will adjust goals and objectives continuously to adapt to changing business requirements and environments, and will consider this as a normal part of the job, rather than as an imposition.

> **Illustrative Behavior 5:** Demonstrates a willingness to embrace new systems, processes, technology, and ideas.

This is a particular strength of the younger generations of employees (GenY-ers and Millennials) who have grown up with the newer technologies and are great fans and avid users of technologies such as instant messaging, text messaging, and Wikis. It is also a source of frustration for many baby boomers and GenX-ers who are not as adept at using newer technologies. No matter what generation, employees and managers at all levels need to be flexible enough to utilize new technologies when and where they add value to the organization.

Illustrative Behavior 6: Stays focused and keeps his or her team focused during times of uncertainty or change.

This is a major component of flexibility and agility for managers at all levels–to help employees at all levels keep focused when uncertainty and change inevitably happen. In times of uncertainty and change, employees look to their managers as leaders to help them find their way.

Illustrative Behavior 7: Coaches others to be flexible and adapt behavior to various situations.

Illustrative Behavior 8: Understands that ambiguity is a normal part of doing business and communicates that to people in the work unit/function.

This is another aspect of the coaching role of managers at all levels. Too often, an organization's management team spends a lot of time and energy dealing with uncertainty and change, finally making its decisions, but then expects employees to embrace the changes instantaneously, not recognizing their own struggles with the changes. But just as the management team had to work its way through the transition, managers must coach their employees to help them similarly make those transitions.[1]

Illustrative Behavior 9: Anticipates changes in the internal and external environment (e.g., organizational, market, products, and systems) and adapts accordingly.

This is a primary responsibility of more senior levels of management–anticipating change in the company's markets, in technologies, and among its constituencies and competitors, and both adapting to those changes and helping employees at all levels deal with the needed changes.

Illustrative Behavior 10: Uses new ideas to reengineer work processes or make changes in how resources are allocated within the business.

This is, again, a major responsibility of senior management (with input from those actually doing the work)–to reengineer work processes and reallocate resources to respond to change.[2] The pioneering work in reengineering done by Hammer and Champy is among the most misunderstood of business methodologies–while we believe that they have great merit, many businesses used the term "reengineering" as justification for massive layoffs without actually doing any of the work required to reengineer.

Critical and Analytical Thinking

An employee with this competency regularly questions basic assumptions about work and how it gets done, identifying underlying principles, root causes, and facts by breaking down information and data and their implications, and drawing conclusions based on their analyses. They understand the complexity of certain issues and crystallize the components of those issues to make them more manageable by applying sound reasoning.

> **Illustrative Behavior 1:** Challenges established thinking, processes, or protocols with company success in mind.

This is the very definition of critical thinking–questioning assumptions. In every organization, employees work under a set of assumptions. These assumptions may be based on past rules and decisions or more tacit elements of the company's or a group's culture. Too often, employees at all levels make suboptimal decisions based on incorrect assumptions. Employees with this competency will make tacit assumptions explicit and question those assumptions if they believe that operating under those assumptions will lead to less than optimal business results.

> **Illustrative Behavior 2:** Quickly and systematically analyzes the root cause of work-related problems before taking corrective action.

> **Illustrative Behavior 3:** Recognizes and communicates the implications of data/information.

Illustrative Behavior 4: Is able to clearly frame a problem, identify and collect the necessary data, and make recommendations for solving the problem.

Illustrative Behavior 5: Takes complex issues or problems and breaks them down into manageable components.

There is an old story about an Indian chicken farmer who lived outside of New Delhi. For many years, he successfully raised and sold his chickens to support his family. One morning, when he went to feed the flock, he found several dead chickens. Not knowing what to do, he packed a bag, took a train into the Himalayas, climbed a high mountain and found a guru. "Oh, guru," he wailed, "some of my chickens have died!"

"What do you feed them?" asked the guru.

"I feed them corn," replied the farmer.

"You must change their diet to wheat," declared the guru.

The farmer descended the mountain, took the train home, and changed the feed from corn to wheat. For several weeks, everything went fine. But one morning, he went to feed the flock and found several more dead chickens. So he packed his bag again, took the train, climbed the mountain, and found the guru. "Oh, guru—more of my chickens are dead!"

"How do you give them water?" asked the guru.

"I have wooden bowls that I fill with water," replied the farmer.

"Troughs!" declared the guru. "Go home and build troughs."

Again the farmer returned home, built troughs, and his flock thrived for the next several months. But one morning, the farmer found more dead chickens. Back to the guru! "Guru! More chickens are dead!"

"How do you house the chickens?" asked the guru.

"I built wooden chicken coops for them."

"You need a new ventilation system," declared the guru.

Back home, the farmer spent his savings to build a new ventilation system. For two years, his business was better than ever—until, one morning, he went to feed the flock and ALL the chickens were dead! Back at the guru's cave, the farmer cried, "All my chickens are dead!"

"That's too bad," said the guru. "I had many more solutions."

Clearly, the guru did not have the competency of critical and analytical thinking and jumped to many conclusions without ever understanding the problem.

> **Illustrative Behavior 6:** Understands how data and recommendations may impact other functions and departments.

> **Illustrative Behavior 7:** Relates problems to one another and to strategic objectives to recognize opportunities for dealing with several related problems at the same time.

These behaviors illustrate some of the major challenges when employees take more general business management positions after having worked in a single functional area for most of their careers–understanding how solving a problem in one area may cause even greater problems in other areas. To develop this competency, managers must learn to view the organization as a complex system in order to trace problems to their source and to make decisions that optimize the entire system. Too often, managers new to general business management overrely on the function in which they started their career.

Creative Thinking

This competency involves reexamining traditional strategies and practices, and proactively looking for new ideas and ways to improve products, services, and work processes. An employee with this competency looks at problems and opportunities from a unique perspective, seeing patterns and themes that are not immediately apparent to others and taking time to refine and shape a new idea so it has a higher likelihood of success.

> **Illustrative Behavior 1:** Suggests ways to improve processes and create efficiencies (e.g., is willing to question current approaches in the interest of maximizing efficiency, suggests better ways to do the work).

> **Illustrative Behavior 2:** Demonstrates creative approaches to solving problems and generates innovative approaches.

While the first behavior is similar to "critical thinking," it goes beyond questioning underlying assumptions to encompass brand new approaches to create both effectiveness (doing the right thing) and efficiency (doing things right). A creative thinker considers brand new approaches as well as modification to current approaches.

> **Illustrative Behavior 3:** Demonstrates creative approaches to locating and applying information to meet internal and external customer needs.

> **Illustrative Behavior 4:** Proactively identifies ways to improve current workflow and procedures to better meet internal and external customer needs (e.g., challenges the status quo).

Many people feel that really creative individuals have different ways of thinking, that their brains may be wired differently. In reality, most people have the capacity for creative thinking, but may need a spark to ignite it. Often this spark can come from reading articles, taking field trips, visiting customers, doing benchmarks on other companies (both within and outside or the organization's own industry), and using other methods of locating information relevant to the organization's work and the needs of its customers. Of course, creative thinking has no value unless the new ideas are applied to the employee's and the organization's work to make a positive difference in personal and organizational performance.

> **Illustrative Behavior 5:** Recognizes patterns or themes in data/information that may not have been readily apparent (e.g., looks for relationships among issues/problems rather than assume they are distinct and independent).

Again, this is related to the previous competency of analytical thinking–seeking patterns or themes that may not have been readily apparent in order to find root causes of problems and opportunities for future improvements.

> **Illustrative Behavior 6:** Solicits input from others who have unique or vastly different perspectives when shaping an idea or plan.

This behavior is especially important for managers at all levels. Too often, when an employee is promoted to a management position, at any level, he feels that he must have all the answers himself, without the benefit of consulting other people. To the contrary, the competent manager will solicit ideas from a wide variety of sources to expand his own thinking and to plan the best way forward for the group he manages.

> **Illustrative Behavior 7:** Coaches others to think creatively and encourages brainstorming when solving problems or making decisions.

A competent manager knows that she alone cannot be the only creative thinker in her group or function if she wants to succeed. She therefore encourages employees to practice creative thinking and coaches them on creative thinking techniques, rewarding them for their good ideas, at the same time allowing that not all creative ideas will be successful.

Summary

While there are many competencies to consider and master within the category of "knowing and managing yourself," we should remind you that it is virtually impossible for any one individual to master all of these competencies, not to mention the two other competency categories (knowing and managing others and knowing and managing the business) that will be presented in the next two chapters.

Our best advice for individuals is to identify areas of strength and areas that need strengthening, to work with your manager to identify which of those areas are most important for you, and to work to capitalize on your strengths and compensate for your weaker areas. For managers, we recommend that you examine not only the strengths and weaknesses of individuals, but also to try to assemble a team where individual employees can build on each other's strengths and compensate for each other's weaknesses.

The AMA Management Development Competency Model

Knowing and Managing Others

Every employee has to deal with other people–peers, managers, employees, customers, suppliers, and many others. In this chapter, we will focus on the competencies needed to effectively relate to and deal with others in the workforce.

The AMA competencies in the "knowing and managing others" category cut across the organization and affect everyone from individual professionals to executives. Remembering the cumulative nature of the AMA competencies, discussed earlier, competencies acquired at the individual professional level continue and are built on and refined as one ascends the management ladder.

The competencies addressed in this chapter are listed in Table 4.1. Once again we discuss each competency and the level of the organization where it first becomes obvious or needed and then comment on how the competency may change as the employee climbs the management ladder.

Oral Communication

AMA defines this competency as being able to convey ideas clearly to others. It includes projecting credibility, poise, and confidence, even

TABLE 4.1   Competencies for Knowing and Managing Others
• Oral Communication
• Written Communication
• Valuing Diversity
• Building Teams
• Networking
• Partnering
• Building Relationships
• Emotional Intelligence/Interpersonal Savvy
• Influencing
• Managing Conflict
• Managing People for Performance
• Clarifying Roles and Accountabilities
• Delegating
• Empowering Others
• Motivating Others
• Coaching
• Developing Top Talent

under difficult or adversarial conditions. People with this competency speak enthusiastically and use vivid language, examples, or anecdotes to communicate a message; they make use of unambiguous language, gestures, and nonverbal communication. This competency requires the basic skills of considering the needs of an audience and how it is likely to react, talking to people in a way they can understand, listening attentively to others, and using appropriate grammar and vocabulary.

> **Illustrative Behavior 1:** Uses effective listening skills to identify important information in conversations and to engage people (e.g., pays attention to orally communicated facts and details, discerns and responds to the feelings and underlying messages of others, paraphrases, asks relevant, open-ended questions).

Everyone, at every level in the organization, needs listening skills. It is important to pay attention when people communicate facts, details, and ideas orally. Good listeners pick up on feelings and respond to those feelings and to underlying messages conveyed in a conversation. Good listeners are good questioners; they can paraphrase other's ideas and ask appropriate open-ended questions to gain more information. Whether in a meeting or in one-on-one situations, listening is always important. At higher levels of the organization, it takes on even more importance because most executives are totally dependent on others to bring them information about situations, problems, and future directions. Good listening and questioning skills help those executives sift through the information to make appropriate decisions and determine appropriate action steps.

Illustrative Behavior 2: Clearly articulates ideas, opinions, and information so others understand them.

Everyone needs to be able to express ideas, opinions, and information in a way that others will understand. This includes use of appropriate vocabulary, sentence structure, and logical patterns of putting ideas together in a conversation so others can easily follow and grasp the meaning of what is communicated. Too much slang or inappropriate humor can hinder understanding.

Illustrative Behavior 3: Uses appropriate medium (e.g., voice-mail, face-to-face, one-on-one, team meeting) depending on the information being communicated.

Selecting the media for a message is not just a matter of personal preference. Certainly we all do have preferences for how we like to communicate, and we would like to use them exclusively. But some media are more personal, some are more easily misunderstood, and some are more appropriate for the particular message being conveyed. The business literature is filled with stories of inappropriate use of e-mail, from companies that delivered termination notices to the individual who criticized upper management decisions. It is good to remember that e-mail never disappears; it is easy to pass around and leaves a record to be retrieved. E-Mail is efficient and easy, but the personal and emotional touch is missing. Any message dealing with personnel issues needs to be conveyed face-to-face so people have that personal connection and a chance to ask questions, express feelings, and hear the rationale in a dialog. Media selection is part of the message.

> **Illustrative Behavior 4:** Adapts his or her communication strategy to the audience.

Most of us have heard it is important to adjust to an audience, but doing it is hard. This is a particularly big adjustment for the first-level manager. As individual professionals, most of us craft our messages from our point of view, with the idea of being heard and getting our message across. We focus on presenting it logically, being enthusiastic, and "fighting" for adoption or implementation. Managers, beginning at the first level, must begin to think of what will reach and motivate the recipient of the message–the audience he or she is talking to. There requires a mindset shift. No longer is it sufficient to present a message just logically or enthusiastically. Thought must be put into shaping the message to address the audience's concerns, so the audience understands and is engaged and motivated to take appropriate action. Managers and executives need to take the pulse of their audiences and craft their messages accordingly.

> **Illustrative Behavior 5:** Ensures that people are provided with clear, timely, and accurate information about issues that may affect their work.

Beginning at the first-level manager, the ability to identify information that people need to do their jobs and to deliver it to employees when they need it is a critical competency. Prior to being a manager, people share ideas, but their focus is on their own performance. Managers must develop the "radar" necessary to determine who needs to know what and when they need to know it. Sharing information and discussing issues at the appropriate time not only enables employees to get the job done, it builds the trust necessary for the team to function well.

> **Illustrative Behavior 6:** Exhibits confidence and enthusiasm when presenting information.

For the mid-level manager and the functional manager, the ability to communicate enthusiastically, with credibility and poise, inspires trust and confidence in employees. When conditions are good, this fosters the feeling of teamwork and promotes pride in the organization and its leadership. When conditions are difficult, it inspires confidence in employees that the leadership is aware of the difficulty and is working to remedy it. In either case, confidence and enthusiasm are read as competence by employees.

> **Illustrative Behavior 7:** Effectively facilitates group conversations in order to clarify issues and establish direction.

Much of the work of mid-level managers and functional managers depends on leading group discussions and encouraging teamwork in identifying issues and solving problems. They need to bring out the best thinking in each of their direct reports, get employees working together, and keep the group focused on the issues at hand. Knowing group dynamics and how to draw some people out, while quieting others, are critical skills.

> **Illustrative Behavior 8:** Delivers presentations to both small and large groups in a well-organized, clear, and articulate manner.

Mid-level and functional managers spend a lot of time presenting information to different-sized groups; they need to project both competence and confidence as they do so. To effectively convey their messages, they need to organize the message so recipients can follow it easily, providing only essential information, appealing to the interests and issues of importance to the audience, and projecting a warm and caring presence. These presentation skills enhance the possibility of the listeners' understanding the message.

> **Illustrative Behavior 9:** Understands when "skip level" communication may be appropriate and necessary (e.g., stays in touch with front-line employees without diminishing the authority of his or her direct reports).

Sometimes a functional manager needs information from the front line. An essential competency is knowing when, and how to, maintain contact with front-line employees without hurting the authority of his or her direct reports. This is called "managing by walking around" in some management books, and it enables the functional manager to gather critical information about what is happening in the business. To be effective, the manager must maintain the trust of his or her direct reports so they do not feel micro-managed or threatened by the possibility of being second-guessed on how they are handling their responsibilities.

Written Communication

AMA defines the written communication competency as expressing ideas and opinions clearly in properly structured, well-organized, and grammatically correct reports and documents. This competency requires the use of language and terminology appropriate to the reader and using appropriate grammar and punctuation.

All but one of the illustrative behaviors for this competency apply at every level of the organization. The last behavior, "placing material in a broader, organizational context, pointing out connections and relationships," is most critical at the mid-level and functional manager levels.

> **Illustrative Behavior 1**: Uses language that is clear to the reader.

> **Illustrative Behavior 2**: Writes documents free of grammatical or punctuation errors.

> **Illustrative Behavior 3**: Presents ideas or opinions clearly and succinctly in writing.

Writing well is a critical lifelong skill for everyone in the organization. With the proliferation of electronic communications, documents and ideas circulate freely. Well-written documents are more easily and quickly read, more readily understood, and convey confidence in the ideas presented. Poorly written documents are frustrating to read and often misunderstood. According to Lynne Truss, author of the runaway best selling grammar book, proper grammar and punctuation are courtesies that help readers to understand what was written without stumbling.[1] Those courtesies are appreciated by readers, help convey the author's ideas effectively, and need to be used by all in the organization. Sloppy usage or low standards project indifference toward the message being conveyed.

> **Illustrative Behavior 4:** Uses e-mail as an appropriate medium (understands when a face-to-face or telephone conversation would be more effective).

E-Mail is most effective for sharing a quick, straightforward message with little emotion attached, for transporting large documents, and for creating a paper trail when documentation is needed. It is not appropriate for lengthy discussions, issues where reasoning might be misunderstood, or where emotional reactions are anticipated. Personal messages and issues are best shared in face-to-face situations, not in e-mail.

> **Illustrative Behavior 5:** Writes with a logical structure (e.g., introduction, supporting information, conclusion).

> **Illustrative Behavior 6:** Breaks down a complex concept so that is easily understood by the target audience.

> **Illustrative Behavior 7:** Uses examples that are suitable and relevant for the target audience.

Logical structure makes communications easy to read and digest; it makes a document reader-friendly. Since most readers today are in a hurry, better-structured documents are quicker to scan and easier to understand. When Peg Pettingell was with Accenture, one of her responsibilities was teaching new consultants an inductive reasoning structure advocated for all senior executive level and client communications because it was believed C-level executives want the bottom line first, then supporting evidence. Whether the organization relates best to inductive or deductive reasoning, structuring your document helps ensure it will be read and understood. At the same time, conveying ideas simply and appropriately for the audience holds their interest and compels them to read to the end. Purging your written communications of redundant phrases and excess words allows the core ideas to emerge clearly.

Illustrative Behavior 8: Places material in a broader organizational context, pointing out connections and relationships.

Mid-level and functional managers have a broader understanding of the issues facing an organization. They can draw on that knowledge to convey important concepts to employees. This helps everyone understand the organization's mission and operations better; it helps employees see beyond their small portion of the organization's business and put their job in the context of the whole.

Valuing Diversity

AMA defines this competency as demonstrating respect for individual differences. This includes cultural differences, as well as diverse ways of thinking or approaching issues. People with this competency are able to establish a climate in which all people can be comfortable and productive; they evaluate the work of others in a culturally neutral way. This competency includes selecting and developing people in multiple cultural settings and being able to communicate effectively with and in multiple cultures. This competency is expressed by understanding how culture influences people's behavior and adapting one's style and behavior to meet cultural norms and expectations. People with this competency can take advantage of their unique cultural knowledge, capability, or information to develop or enhance products or services.

In today's global business environment, this competency has taken on more importance during the last few decades and will continue to grow. It is a competency needed by everyone in the organization, but some behaviors are particular to the manager levels.

Illustrative Behavior 1: Relates effectively with people of diverse backgrounds (both cultural backgrounds and those who have different ways of thinking or approaching issues).

Illustrative Behavior 2: Adapts his or her style and behavior to meet cultural norms and expectations.

Each year most of us encounter more and more coworkers, clients, and customers who are from backgrounds different from ours. Being sensitive to cultural differences means you treat everyone with respect and dignity; you try to learn the norms or expectations that are different, and that you were not previously aware of, and adapt to them. This goes beyond just cultural concerns to include tolerance of different thinking and operating styles as well. Effective organizational teams are composed of people with differing styles, people who can complement each other's strengths and make up for the other's weaknesses. Convergent and divergent thinkers bring very different skills to the table, and, in concert, can bring more depth and perspective to a project–more than either style would achieve individually. Recognizing and working with people from other cultures and with different styles, and blending the strengths of each, makes for a richer organization.

Illustrative Behavior 3: Reaches agreement with people who share different opinions.

Illustrative Behavior 4: Includes people of diverse backgrounds in his or her informal network.

Illustrative Behavior 5: Challenges others who make racial, ethnic, or sexually derogatory comments.

Recognizing and accepting differences goes beyond mere tolerance. It means including people in networks and social events, making them feel a true part of the team, and treating them as others are treated. It also means standing up to individuals who poke fun at or criticize different cultures, races, or styles; it means taking a stand to let those individuals know that behavior is not tolerated in this organization. In short, these behaviors are evidenced by actions that individuals consistently exhibit in their work unit.

> **Illustrative Behavior 6:** Coaches others on how cultural norms and expectations influence behavior.

> **Illustrative Behavior 7:** Demonstrates a respect for individual differences by creating an environment in which people can be themselves.

> **Illustrative Behavior 8:** Evaluates team members' performance in a culturally neutral way.

Managers at all levels have even more responsibilities in supporting diversity. Managers teach by example; employees observe their behaviors to see how they handle situations and how they evaluate people's performance. By constantly modeling respect for differences, managers establish an open environment where all can be comfortable and feel respected. For the good of the work unit, managers must continually assess team members' attitudes and behaviors with respect to diversity and work with team members who are not as tolerant of, or comfortable with, differences. This ongoing coaching demonstrates the manager's commitment to a culturally neutral environment and helps employees learn.

> **Illustrative Behavior 9:** Leverages unique cultural knowledge, capability, and/or information to develop or enhance products or services.

> **Illustrative Behavior 10:** Appreciates the contributions of different functions across the organization and involves them appropriately and in planning and decision making.

Mid-level managers and functional managers work across teams, departments, and divisions. They encounter more diversity and more cultural differences simply because they are exposed to more people, both inside and outside the organization. They are in a unique position to recognize the knowledge and capabilities of the people they encounter; they need to harness those abilities for the good of the organization. Managers need to be open to crossing functional lines and to involving people who can contribute special knowledge and talents to business undertakings.

Building Teams

To AMA, this competency means facilitating the constructive resolution of conflict; increasing mutual trust; and encouraging cooperation, coordination, and identification with the work unit. People with this competency are seen encouraging information sharing among individuals who do not know each other and who may represent different cultures. People with this competency include others in processes and decisions regardless of geographical distance or location; they find creative ways to minimize the effects of different time zones on the quality and frequency of interactions.

This competency is important at every level of the organization, with more implementation responsibilities coming into play at the first-level manager, the mid-level manager, and the functional manager levels.

> **Illustrative Behavior 1:** Acts on opportunities to collaborate across the organization, regardless of geography or cultural differences.

> **Illustrative Behavior 2:** Proactively helps team members both within and outside of his or her group.

Everyone in the organization shares the responsibility for working cooperatively within teams, even when team members are scattered in different places. Each individual needs to be assertive in helping the team function smoothly. This means sharing information, supporting team members, keeping in contact, attending meetings, etc. For a team to function smoothly, everyone is responsible for contributing to success.

Illustrative Behavior 3: Shares credit for successes with team members (i.e., gives credit where credit is due).

Illustrative Behavior 4: Solicits and offers feedback on how people could work most effectively together.

When individuals join a team, at any level of the organization, they take on some responsibility for helping that team function effectively. One responsibility is to recognize and support other team members, acknowledging their contributions and not trying to take credit for their ideas, their work, or their successes. Another responsibility is to speak up when he or she has ideas on how the team could function better and to ask others for their opinions and ideas on that as well. That creates an open environment where all share freely for the betterment of the team's work.

Illustrative Behavior 5: Encourages frank and open discussion of a disagreement.

Illustrative Behavior 6: Encourages cooperation and teamwork among people who depend on each other to get the work done.

Illustrative Behavior 7: Coaches people to partner with colleagues across the organization, regardless of cultural differences or geography.

Managers make special contributions to teams. Because they are responsible for seeing that work gets done, managers must continuously support team cooperation and the healthy exchange of ideas. If and when dissension occurs, the effective manager sees that it is acknowledged and fosters an open exchange of all viewpoints, making sure all individuals are respected in the process. Managers continue to coach the team, and individuals on the team, in ways to resolve their differences and work productively together. To extend the concept of teamwork, managers encourage their teams to reach out beyond their work unit to find the resources and information they need to do their job, even when it is in a different locale.

Illustrative Behavior 8: Recognizes conflicting priorities across the organization and initiates joint problem solving to determine the best course of action for the organization.

Illustrative Behavior 9: Encourages and facilitates cross-unit cooperation and coordination.

Mid-level managers and functional managers have a broader organizational perspective. Because of their knowledge of higher level organization initiatives, issues, and concerns, they see more interrelationships and have ideas on how people who might not know one another could be working together for the organization's benefit. They are in a unique position to make the necessary introductions and to foster that exchange, particularly when they see conflicts that threaten organization initiatives. Their responsibility to help solve problems requires them to call on the best people, across the organization, to contribute to solutions.

Networking

This AMA competency is defined as socializing informally. It includes developing contacts with people who are a source of information and support and maintaining those contacts through periodic visits, telephone calls, correspondence, and attendance at meetings and social events.

All the behaviors are important at every level of the organization—an unusual occurrence. That underscores the importance of this competency for everyone. The more people network and keep in touch, the better for them and for the organization.

Illustrative Behavior 1: Relays relevant experiences and passes on knowledge unselfishly.

Illustrative Behavior 2: Maintains contacts with people in other areas of the company or in different organizations who can be useful sources of information or resources.

Illustrative Behavior 3: Does favors (e.g., provides information, assistance, political support, or resources) to maintain good working relationships with people whose cooperation and support are important.

Illustrative Behavior 4: Attends meetings and social events to continually solidify and grow his or her network.

Connecting with other people helps "grease the wheels" for getting a job done. Informal relationships help an individual get the information he or she needs and keep abreast of what is happening in other areas of the organization. Mere contact is not enough; information and experiences need to be shared on a frequent basis to keep relationships current and top-of-mind. One way to ensure the continuing exchange of information is doing favors for others in the organization. The favors can be simple, like sharing information, or more complex, like providing resources or political support. Networking helps everyone build support and become known across the organization, while it also helps people know what is happening in other areas and what political situations are emerging. Because of the importance of networking for staying informed, everyone must continually grow his or her network by participating in social gatherings and meetings, getting to know new employees, and continually keep in contact with their network members.

External networks are also important and can be developed through professional organizations and attendance at various conferences and specialized meetings. Those external networks bring an added dimension due to the fact that people from different organizations will have differing perspectives. They can help you think things through with a fresh eye and, in turn, have other people in their networks to call on for help.

Illustrative Behavior 5: Uses his or her network to solve problems efficiently and effectively.

Illustrative Behavior 6: Actively designs his or her network in anticipation of future needs or plans (e.g., has clear goals in mind when building his or her network).

One of the main reasons for networking is to have help in getting the work done. Knowing whom to go to, who can point you in the right direction, who has confronted similar problems previously, who is a good sounding-board or mentor, or who has a good reputation for solving difficult situations is a tremendous benefit when issues arise. It can help any individual make better decisions in timely fashion. At the same time it is well to keep an eye out for people who are outstanding in their abilities, or perhaps new to the organization and well thought of, and include them in your network. As you progress in the organization, you may have a need to call on their expertise.

Partnering

AMA sees partnering as identifying, building, and managing external partnerships that add value to the company. This competency includes initiating and leveraging opportunities to work with others across the organization to maximize individual and organizational effectiveness and working effectively across organizational boundaries to accomplish a shared objective. This competency requires developing networks and alliances across the organization to build influence and support for ideas. It is important at every level of the organization, with two behaviors most evident and needed at managerial levels.

> **Illustrative Behavior 1:** Builds relationships with colleagues in other functional groups (e.g., proactively shares knowledge and best practices with people in other groups, understands the objectives of other functional groups and their effect on the company's success).

> **Illustrative Behavior 2:** Readily shares information, knowledge, best practices, and ideas with people across organizational units.

Reaching beyond your unit of the organization is a great way to expand your understanding of the total operation and how all units fit into the bigger picture. As you talk with people in other units, you gain an understanding of the complexity of the business enterprise and the part everyone plays in contributing to success. Those relationships are dependent upon freely exchanging information, being sure to share what your unit does, thereby helping others understand your unit's function and role in the business's success, as well.

> **Illustrative Behavior 3:** Asks consultative questions of customers, colleagues, managers, and others to identify business needs and solutions.

> **Illustrative Behavior 4:** Forms alliances with people in different organizational units to work toward mutual objectives.

Effective partnering requires your discovery of needs and solutions for present and future business opportunities. Being interested in what is going on in other departments, and with your customers, coupled with good questioning and listening skills helps you probe for those opportunities. Once a need or solution emerges, you want to be able to work with people in other units to successfully achieve business objectives for the good of the organization. Effective alliances smooth the way for such communications.

> **Illustrative Behavior 5:** Coaches team members to consult with other departments/work units in solving problems and making decisions.

First-level managers, mid-level managers, and functional managers need to coach their direct reports to partner within the organization. Indeed, they also may have to help identify and create opportunities to make this happen. Team members may not see the connections that can be made, so making suggestions, offering advice, and using effective questioning skills will enhance their understanding.

> **Illustrative Behavior 6:** Manages external partnerships according to agreed-upon plans and standards.

> **Illustrative Behavior 7:** Identifies and builds external partnerships that add current or future value to the company.

Mid-level and functional managers are responsible for reaching outside the organization and developing relationships that are, and will continue to be, valuable to them and to the enterprise. Memberships in key organizations and on boards, as well as community involvement activities and personal business contacts, all serve this purpose. Being tuned into the business and professional community, staying abreast of political issues, and determining emerging opportunities are valuable skills for higher level managers.

Building Relationships

AMA defines this competency as being skilled at detecting and interpreting subtle clues, often nonverbal, about others' feelings and concerns. People with this competency display empathy and sensitivity to the needs and concerns of others and support others when they are facing difficult tasks. When you have this competency, you enjoy dealing with people and working with people of diverse styles and backgrounds. All of the behaviors are critical at all levels in the organization; getting along with people is a critical skill for everyone.

> **Illustrative Behavior 1:** Seeks out people and actively shares information instead of waiting for others to connect with him or her.

This competency requires you to be proactive in reaching out to others, not being afraid to share information before you are asked. When you are open and willing to communicate, it establishes a friendly, open atmosphere in the workplace. People respond to that and tend to be more open in return.

> **Illustrative Behavior 2:** Promptly returns all forms of communication to others including e-mail, voicemail, and more traditional forms.

Timely responses to the communications of others makes other people feel that you care about them and deem them and their communications important. No matter what mode of communication you prefer, it is usually best to return a message via the same medium that it was communicated. The message originator is showing a preference, and you acknowledge that when you use the same vehicle.

> **Illustrative Behavior 3:** Displays empathy when a person is dealing with a difficult problem or situation.

When a colleague is facing a difficult issue, it is important to be able to lend an ear and understand how hard it is for the person at that moment. It isn't necessary to offer advice or to try to solve the problem; it is enough to "be there" with understanding and compassion for what the person is going through.

> **Illustrative Behavior 4:** Understands and adapts to the different working styles, personalities, and cultural backgrounds of the people he or she works with.

This is a critical skill for all in the workforce, as no two employees are alike. There must be some tolerance for differences as people work together. Everyone comes from a different background, with his or her own view of the world, and each has had different life experiences. All of this brings richness to the work environment.

> **Illustrative Behavior 5:** Offers to provide advice and support when a person is facing a difficult problem or issue.

> **Illustrative Behavior 6:** Listens actively to detect both verbal and nonverbal cues in conversation.

Offering advice to a person dealing with a difficult situation depends upon listening actively. You want to be sure the person is actually seeking help and not just venting. Active listening skills enable you to read both verbal and nonverbal cues to more accurately determine what the person means and if he or she is receptive to, and seeking, advice.

Emotional Intelligence/Interpersonal Savvy

AMA defines this competency as being attuned to how others feel in the moment, sensing the shared values of the group, and using that insight to do and say what's appropriate. This includes understanding others' feelings, motives, and reactions and adapting one's behaviors accordingly, as well as appreciating the effect of one's behavior on others. People with this competency are at ease when approaching others during social occasions, able to make and maintain a favorable impression, and able to mingle effortlessly.

> **Illustrative Behavior 1:** Demonstrates awareness for others' feelings and adapts own behavior accordingly.

> **Illustrative Behavior 2:** Encourages others to speak or share their perspective on a situation.

> **Illustrative Behavior 3:** Is attentive to others' needs.

> **Illustrative Behavior 4**: Is at ease in social situations; makes others at ease.

These behaviors demonstrate sensitivity to the thoughts and feelings of others. When this sensitivity is present, an individual or manager senses the underlying emotions and messages in a communication and delivers the correct response in conversations, providing the verbal and nonverbal support the other person needs. Appropriate responses are possible because of this "radar" that provides insight into what is needed at the moment. This intuition smooths the way in social situations and puts everyone in the group at ease with one another.

> **Illustrative Behavior 5:** Intuitively detects and avoids potentially problematic situations before they take place.

> **Illustrative Behavior 6:** Shows empathy for others' problems and concerns.

> **Illustrative Behavior 7:** Knows when to talk and when to listen.

These behaviors help an individual manage almost any situation. Being sensitive and tuned in to what is happening, and how others are feeling about it, enables an individual or manager to react appropriately and smooth over almost any situation. Some call this "a sixth sense." It is definitely an intuitive response that seems to be coupled with the sense of knowing when to talk and when to listen during any exchange. People also sense this competency in others and gravitate to them when they have a problem or concern because they are certain of being heard and understood.

> **Illustrative Behavior 8:** Understands how others may perceive his or her words and actions and that his or her intent may not always yield the desired impact.

People who demonstrate this behavior seem to understand how what they do or say affects others. They know they might be misunderstood in any exchange, but are comfortable enough with themselves that they realize the interpretation of their words and actions is beyond their control.

> **Illustrative Behavior 9:** Helps team members develop the ability to take into account others' concerns and perspectives.

The last behavior in this grouping is particular to the management level. It is demonstrated when managers help their direct reports and team members develop sensitivity to others and the intuition to analyze what is happening in communication situations. It involves managers in coaching others when they are insensitive and providing educational opportunities for them to develop their interpersonal relationship "radar."

Influencing

AMA defines this competency as using techniques that appeal to reason, values, or emotion to generate enthusiasm for the work, commitment to a task objective, or compliance with a request. This includes using appropriate tactics to change a person's attitude, beliefs, or behaviors.

This critical competency applies to every person in the organization, and all but one behavior is paramount to all positions.

> **Illustrative Behavior 1:** Talks in a persuasive manner about the importance of achieving tasks or objectives.

> **Illustrative Behavior 2:** Describes a clear and appealing vision of what can be accomplished with a person's cooperation and support.

These behaviors manifest an individual's commitment to, and clarity about, what needs to be accomplished. When a person is able to communicate his or her vision clearly, concisely, and in a compelling manner, he or she is very persuasive. These behaviors are particularly valuable when trying to influence people over whom you have no control or authority.

> **Illustrative Behavior 3:** Develops enthusiasm for a task or project by appealing to a person's needs or values (i.e., accomplishing a challenging task, beating competitors, doing something never done before).

> **Illustrative Behavior 4:** Adapts style or approach to meet the other person's style.

> **Illustrative Behavior 5:** Explains the benefits of the task objectives to others.

These behaviors demonstrate a compelling delivery style that appeals to the audience at hand, whether colleagues or upper management. Enthusiasm is contagious; how can you expect someone else to be enthusiastic about a project if you don't demonstrate your own enthusiasm? Knowing exactly what will appeal to another person requires knowing your own style and reading the clues other people give you to signal how they might prefer to be approached. Emphasizing the benefits of particular interest to other people goes a long way in persuading them to do what you want. Many of AMA's courses rely on assessment instruments to help participants determine their style of communication for just this purpose: Everyone needs to be able to identify the preferred style of other people and flex his or her own style to influence others. Flexibility can be difficult, but it results in the other person's feeling good about how he or she was approached and being more likely to comply with the request, particularly if the benefits are presented well.

> **Illustrative Behavior 6:** Demonstrates willingness to incorporate input from others.

> **Illustrative Behavior 7:** Listens to others' points before making his or her own points.

These behaviors emphasize the need to be open to others, to evaluate their ideas fairly and not be so enamored by your own ideas that you can't see the value of ideas presented by others. This requires good listening skills, skills referred to several times before under other competencies. It depends on sensitivity to the feelings of others, as well. No one likes his or her ideas dismissed without being considered. It is hard to work with someone who only appreciates his or her own ideas.

> **Illustrative Behavior 8:** Does not rely primarily on his or her position power to influence others.

This behavior obviously is one that applies at upper managerial levels, the mid-level, and functional manager levels, because those managers are the people with more power in the organization. Telling people to do something "because I said so" breeds resentment and mistrust. Managers at those levels will get more accomplished if they continue to use their enthusiasm and style-flexing abilities to present their ideas.

Managing Conflict

This AMA competency is defined as recognizing the potential value of conflict for driving change and innovation. This means knowing when to confront and when to avoid a conflict and understanding the issues around which conflicts revolve. It includes identifying the goals and objectives of the parties involved and finding common ground. It means looking for those win/win solutions and seeking agreement on a solution while eliciting commitment to making it work effectively.

This is a competency of great importance at all levels of the organization because conflict can be a creative force or a disruptive one, depending on how it is managed. Everyone shares the responsibility to manage it.

> **Illustrative Behavior 1:** Tries to understand another person's perspective during a discussion or disagreement (e.g., does not rush to refute each point the person makes, listens attentively, paraphrases the other person's point of view).

This behavior is evidenced, once again, by good listening skills: being attentive, paraphrasing the other person's point of view, and not rushing to refute every point the other person makes. Questioning skills also help to draw out the other person's thoughts so a more thorough understanding of his or her position is possible.

> **Illustrative Behavior 2:** Wins concessions without damaging relationships (e.g., creates "win/win" situations, makes appropriate compromises).

> **Illustrative Behavior 3:** Modifies his or her proposals or plans to deal with concerns and incorporate suggestions to reach a compromise that benefits the business.

When conflict arises, a focus on maintaining the relationship of the individuals involved is critical to successful resolution. All people need to show a willingness to take suggestions from others and to concede some of their own positions. The focus should be on what benefits the business as a whole, and the relationship between the individuals, not on what benefits any one individual.

> **Illustrative Behavior 4:** Challenges people in a way that is constructive and nonthreatening.

> **Illustrative Behavior 5:** Confronts and facilitates conflict in a way that helps people engage in conversation to yield a better solution.

> **Illustrative Behavior 6:** Understands when conflict should be confronted and when it should be avoided.

> **Illustrative Behavior 7:** Identifies the likely source of a conflict before taking action.

Maintaining a calm demeanor, using effective listening skills, probing to determine what the conflict is really about, and knowing when to make the call to confront or avoid conflict are all invaluable and important skills that require thought and practice over time. Certainly people with emotional intelligence have an advantage because they are sensitive to others and used to dealing successfully with people in a variety of situations. They generally have good listening skills and can question appropriately. Those skills are particularly valuable in conflict situations.

> **Illustrative Behavior 8:** Coaches others on how to resolve conflict in a constructive behavior.

Obviously a managerial skill, this behavior is needed from the first-level manager and beyond. The ability to coach others depends on the experience and skills gained and exercised at the individual professional level, accompanied by experience gained as you are responsible for the behavior of others in a team atmosphere.

Managing People for Performance

AMA defines this competency as setting clear performance targets and gaining a personal commitment to accomplishing those targets. This includes checking on the progress and quality of the work and providing specific feedback on a regular basis so others understand what they have done well and how they can improve in the future. It means addressing performance problems by gathering information and setting goals for improvement in a fair and consistent manner. This competency is particular to people in the managerial levels of the organization, as you would expect.

>   **Illustrative Behavior 1:** Sets goals that are clear, specific, and measurable (i.e., quantifiable or verifiable).

>   **Illustrative Behavior 2:** Conducts periodic performance meetings with direct reports to review progress against goals and ensure that goals are relevant and realistic.

>   **Illustrative Behavior 3:** Provides balanced, specific feedback on a regular basis.

All performance management systems list goals, periodic meetings, and feedback as critical steps in managing people. Obviously this begins with the first-level manager and continues up the organization. This is an invaluable process for the monitoring and development of employees, and all elements are critical skills for managers. The focus here is to target behavioral goals and help direct reports improve skills, correct problems, or address issues as they arise and before they become major problems. The secret here is vigilance, regularly scheduled meetings, and frequent exchanges of information and problem solving together. Follow-up sessions and continuous coaching are integral components for success.

>   **Illustrative Behavior 4:** Addresses performance problems in a timely and fair manner by clearly defining where expectations are not being met.

>   **Illustrative Behavior 5:** Develops a sense of commitment in others to meet challenging, yet realistic, performance targets.

Performance management is not a once-a-year responsibility. If the manager manages performance well, there will be absolutely no surprises at the time of the annual written performance review.

Managers must be on top of performance issues, because if they are not addressed immediately, the issues tend to grow quickly. This requires an honest and straightforward appraisal of problems coupled with a discussion of realistic changes in performance. There is an art to crafting those realistic performance targets and measurement methods; they must be created together, with both parties agreeing that they are achievable and yet challenging enough to indicate change and growth. By approaching it as a joint venture, the manager develops the employees' commitment because they helped set the goals.

> **Illustrative Behavior 6:** Holds first-level managers accountable for managing others (not only for technical work).

Mid-level managers have a special responsibility as they manage new managers. New managers are often most comfortable with the technical aspects of the work and will feel comfortable managing them, since, after all, they were probably promoted because they were very good technical professionals. The challenge for the mid-level manager is making sure new managers also recognize and follow through on their responsibilities for managing others, with all the personnel issues, performance issues, and emotions that entails.

> **Illustrative Behavior 7:** Holds people accountable for achieving their performance goals.

> **Illustrative Behavior 8:** Offers tangible, realistic suggestions for how people can enhance or improve their performance.

As part of their job, managers at every level must embrace the responsibility of working with their direct reports to help them achieve the organization's and the individual's goals. This includes helping the employee set realistic goals and providing the support and coaching the individual needs. It often falls to the manager to help identify where an individual can improve and to help come up with suggestions the employee can consider as avenues to improvement.

> **Illustrative Behavior 9:** Ensures that goals are aligned with organizational strategy and objectives; clarifies and communicates cross-functional/departmental interdependencies.

Mid-level and functional managers are in positions that require working with other leaders and departments to accomplish the organization's goals. Because of this, they must communicate more across the organization and work to ensure their area of responsibility is aligned with the efforts of other departments and divisions and with the larger organizational strategy.

Clarifying Roles and Accountabilities

AMA defines this competency as being able to communicate with others to make clear what is expected of them. It includes conveying expectations about timelines and the quality of the employee's work and helping people understand how their roles relate to the broader objectives and success of the organization.

> **Illustrative Behavior 1:** Clearly explains expectations about the quality and timeliness of a task or project.

> **Illustrative Behavior 2:** Specifies a date or time when a task or project should be completed.

Everyone in the organization shares the responsibility for explaining tasks and projects clearly and completely and for specifying timelines and deadlines. Without clear communications, the organization's work will not get done, and people will be in a constant state of confusion. Problems and issues arise when directions are misunderstood or misinterpreted. If tasks are well explained, there is less likelihood you will hear "You never said it was due tomorrow," or "I didn't know you wanted it done that way." Clear communication saves time and effort in the long run and helps avoid irritations and conflict among employees.

> **Illustrative Behavior 3:** Explains how one's role relates to the broader objectives of the company.

> **Illustrative Behavior 4:** Explains what objectives or aspects of the work have the highest priority based on the current business environment, organizational initiatives, strategy, and other parameters.

All managers need to put work assignments and roles into the context of the total organization's strategy. That message helps build employee commitment to the organization and its work. It also helps emphasize the importance of each role in the total business operation. When the explanation includes the rationale for priorities, the employee better understands why he or she is being asked to do something and the importance of following the directives. It also gives the employee confidence that upper management has valid reasons for its requests or for directing that the work be done in a particular way.

> **Illustrative Behavior 5:** Sets task goals that are clear and specific (e.g., quantitative targets to be attained in the next quarter or year, activities to be completed by a given date).

> **Illustrative Behavior 6:** Tailors instructions to a person's skills, experience, level of confidence, and other needs.

When managers define work, they are responsible for being specific about what is to be done and the timeframe in which it is to be completed. To be understood, they need to assess the individual's skills and experience and position the message appropriately for that individual. They are also well advised to ask the person to repeat back the assignment in order to clarify the employee's understanding of the task.

> **Illustrative Behavior 7:** Takes the initiative to meet with a person who is not meeting expectations to clearly define what is expected and why it is important for the business or work unit.

When employees are not working up to expectations, they may be unaware of that fact. Managers are responsible for being proactive and bringing it to their attention. Emphasizing the interdependency of the entire unit's work helps the employee see how his or her performance affects others, something he or she may not have considered. Knowing that he or she is hindering the performance of others may motivate a change in behavior.

Illustrative Behavior 8: Coaches others to convey expectations about the quality and timelines of projects and tasks.

Mid-level and functional managers share this responsibility because of their unique positions in the organization. Their charge is to "marshal the troops" and accomplish the organization's work as defined by senior management. They set the timelines and quality standards to obtain certain business advantages. They need to make other managers aware of the urgency to produce the quality needed in the time allocated and coach the managers appropriately to make that happen.

Delegating

Delegating is a management responsibility at all levels. AMA defines delegating as not only assigning responsibilities to direct reports, but also giving them the authority to carry the assignments out. Effective delegating includes maintaining the proper level of involvement without abdicating or micro-managing. Managers who delegate well assign tasks that are a good fit with the person's capabilities, and when tasks are assigned for development, they provide guidance to ensure success. Effective managers always debrief assignments to reinforce learning.

Illustrative Behavior 1: Gives clear instructions (content, deadlines, decision-making authority) on delegated tasks and projects.

Illustrative Behavior 2: Clearly communicates the desired results of the delegated assignment.

When delegating, managers need to map out the assignment, specifying the content, deadlines, decision-making authority, and results expected. The more explicit the manager is, the better. Managers do well to leave the specifics of "how" the assignment will be carried out to the employee. That encourages creativity and reinforces the confidence the manager has in the employee to perform the task.

Illustrative Behavior 3: Delegates assignments designed to meet direct reports' individual development or career goals as well as assignments that enable better time management.

Managers have the responsibility for selecting assignments that will help an individual grow and develop new skills or capabilities. They do not just delegate things they don't like to do or are bored with. Effective managers think of an employee's current skills and what will move that person's performance to the next level, or what will broaden his or her potential career opportunities. Tasks then need to be selected for the opportunity to develop that potential.

Illustrative Behavior 4: Provides ongoing coaching and support without micro-managing delegated assignments.

Managers at all levels must find the balance between giving too much and too little help with delegated projects. Once a task is delegated, the employee needs to feel ownership and responsibility. If a manager continuously offers advice, makes suggestions on how to do things, and generally interferes in the project, the employee will abdicate that responsibility. A good guideline is to be available and interested in how things are going, but offer advice only when asked or when you genuinely sense that the employee is uncertain how to proceed.

Illustrative Behavior 5: Debriefs delegated tasks and projects to identify key learning and provide both positive and constructive feedback.

Finding the lessons learned from all tasks and projects is an important part of any assignment. Managers need to discuss the learning with employees while it is fresh in their minds. By doing this, the employee is reinforced in the positive decisions he or she made and/or gets to examine how things might have been handled differently.

Illustrative Behavior 6: Coaches managers on the importance of effective delegation for developing and retaining talent.

Mid-level and functional managers hold a special responsibility for coaching other managers about the importance of delegating. They need to continually feed the leadership pipeline with people who are learning to take on more responsibility and growing their skills. They need to help other managers see that employees learn new skills so employees are motivated to stay and contribute to the organization. When not fulfilled, employees take their talent elsewhere, and the organization suffers. This is increasingly important today, with the potential shortage of available people to fill jobs looming on the horizon.

> **Illustrative Behavior 7:** Systematically reviews own responsibilities and identifies opportunities to delegate projects or initiatives to ensure he or she is focused on strategic issues.

Functional managers need to continuously purge their tasks and assignments, selecting developmental and growth assignments to delegate to their direct reports. It helps them continue to develop their staff and, at the same time, free themselves for more time to do the strategic planning and outreach that will benefit their division and the organization.

Empowering Others

Empowering others, as AMA defines it, means giving people the authority, information, resources (e.g., time, money, equipment), and guidance to make decisions and implement them. Because of the nature of this competency, it falls primarily to managers. However, individual professionals may exhibit the first illustrative behavior and, as they approach promotion to manager, may exhibit the behavior more.

> **Illustrative Behavior 1:** Provides people with the information they need to do their jobs well.

Everyone in the organization needs to share information freely so that all can perform to the best of their abilities. When information is withheld or is incomplete, it hinders the effective accomplishment of a task. Knowing that a person needs information, an effective employee sees that the person gets what is needed and doesn't necessarily look for the individual to find it on his or her own.

Illustrative Behavior 2: Allows direct reports to make important decisions and implement them without prior authority.

Illustrative Behavior 3: Presents an assignment in general terms and allows others to determine action steps for implementation.

Illustrative Behavior 4: Encourages others to come up with solutions or ideas on their own; acts as a sounding board when needed.

Managers at all levels need to allow their direct reports some leeway in determining how they do their jobs. Letting go of the need to control what happens enables an employee to be more creative in approaching a task. Continuing to maintain control and to direct people hinders an employee's initiative. Effective managers stand ready to listen, but help people think through solutions on their own.

Illustrative Behavior 5: Demonstrates confidence in people's capabilities; gives people the benefit of a doubt.

Employees quickly sense when a manager has confidence in them. They pick up on subtle cues and feel good about their jobs and their abilities when they sense that confidence. They strive to work to the best of their abilities to demonstrate that the confidence is well placed.

Illustrative Behavior 6: Ensures people have the resources they need to accomplish a task or objective.

Managers are responsible for seeing that people have what they need to do their jobs. Without resources, the work cannot be accomplished. A vigilant manager anticipates what will be needed and provides it in a timely fashion. Employees then have what they need and can accomplish their work.

Illustrative Behavior 7: Asks people in the work unit/function for feedback on the extent to which they feel empowered to make decisions.

Mid-level and functional managers need to be confident enough to solicit feedback from direct reports on how they feel things are working. If people don't feel empowered, little will happen beyond the basic job and tasks assigned. When people feel empowered, they exhibit a creative energy that enables them to share ideas for improving processes and products. Upper-level managers need to establish an environment that ensures that energy exists in the organization so progress is possible.

Motivating Others

AMA defines this competency as the ability to set high standards regarding the quality and quantity of the work to be done. It includes displaying a commitment to the organization and enthusiasm for its products and services. It is demonstrated by conveying confidence in others' capabilities and appealing to others' unique needs, motives, and goals to motivate them to achieve. It culminates in celebrating others' successes and praising them for a job well done. AMA looks to the management levels of an organization for demonstration of this competency.

Illustrative Behavior 1: Sets high standards for performance.

Employees know when a manager has high standards. They sense it through the everyday exchanges of what quality of work is acceptable and what needs to be redone because it is not up to snuff. They see it demonstrated in how a manager critiques their work, in what is accepted, and in what is rejected. Employees take pride in meeting high standards and in having a manager who demands the best from them.

Illustrative Behavior 2: Models excellence and enthusiasm for the work.

Illustrative Behavior 3: Speaks positively and enthusiastically about the organization's products/services and future direction.

Illustrative Behavior 4: Inspires others to a greater effort by setting an example in his or her own behavior of courage, dedication, or self-sacrifice.

Employees look to managers to model the behaviors that are acceptable in the organization. When a manager displays enthusiasm for the products and services, dedication to the organization's mission, and when the manager speaks well of the future plans proposed by upper management, employees are motivated to adopt similar thoughts and feelings and to work hard for the organization. What a manager does speaks louder than mere words.

Illustrative Behavior 5: Identifies and appeals to individual needs and motives.

Illustrative Behavior 6: Establishes challenging, yet realistic, performance goals that tap into people's interests and motives.

Employees feel good when a manager takes the time to identify what appeals to them and taps into their needs and interests when assigning tasks. Employees like to be challenged to learn what will benefit them and to tackle tasks that help them grow. They appreciate realistic performance goals that help them meet their personal goals. Managers are challenged to look at each individual and identify what best motivates him or her to work effectively.

Illustrative Behavior 7: Rewards and recognizes others for a job well done.

All managers need to remember how motivating praise and celebration are. Everyone likes to be praised for a job well done; teams like to celebrate when their job is finished. Managers need to acknowledge both people and teams when they have done a good job. The size of the praise or the celebration is not the issue—people just want to hear that they did well. That goes a long way in motivating them to work as hard the next time they receive an assignment.

> **Illustrative Behavior 8:** Uses others as a sounding board for generating ideas and plans; acknowledges their expertise or perspective when asking for their opinions.

Employees are flattered when a manager acknowledges their talents by asking their opinions. A wise manager knows this and takes every opportunity to include direct reports at the idea stage of problem solving and decision making. Employees will work harder on a project when they feel they were brought into the process early on.

> **Illustrative Behavior 9:** Coaches others on ways to motivate.

Mid-level and functional managers are responsible for coaching their direct reports on motivating their employees. As with all coaching, this requires upper-level managers to observe what is happening in the division or unit and to counsel their direct reports when they see opportunities for them to motivate their employees.

Coaching

This critical management competency is defined by AMA as providing others with the opportunity to develop new skills. It includes clarifying expectations, offering instruction and advice on the skills, and providing support and feedback to enhance performance. This competency is required at all managerial levels and is extremely important for a first-level manager to learn early and practice continuously.

> **Illustrative Behavior 1:** Explains why he or she thinks a person's performance is good.

It isn't enough for employees to know that they are performing well; they need to know how that is determined, what they are specifically doing that makes the performance good, and the criteria by which their performance is being judged. A manager needs to be able to put that into words and concepts readily understood and easily conveyed to employees. Thus coaching is used to reinforce good performance, not just to improve poor performance.

> **Illustrative Behavior 2:** Offers to provide advice or assistance when a person needs help with a difficult task or problem.

> **Illustrative Behavior 3:** Provides extra instruction or coaching to others to help improve job skills or learn new ones.

When employees confront a new or difficult task, they often need help getting started. Managers who are effective coaches provide that assistance, not by taking over, but by stepping the employee through the thinking and planning process. Employees need a manager who will be patient and answer their questions, giving any additional instruction that might be needed when they face a difficult task or problem.

> **Illustrative Behavior 4:** Encourages people to create a personal development plan.

Managers are responsible for developing their people. They know that development cannot occur unless a person buys into the idea and helps formulate the plan. Employees do not always see what they need to improve, and a wise manager can help them realize the opportunities. Effective managers work with their direct reports to help them identify skills to develop and make suggestions for ways to design plans for acquiring them.

> **Illustrative Behavior 5:** Provides feedback both on the spot and through periodic meetings to monitor progress against goals.

> **Illustrative Behavior 6:** Helps people understand the impact of their behavior on their peers, the work unit, the customer, and others involved.

Employees do not always understand how they are perceived by others, nor can they be impartial judges of their own behavior. Managers can help with timely and constructive feedback. Such feedback helps employees realize the impact of their actions and words and can help them in their development efforts. Managers can also use feedback sessions to help steer employees to more effectively reach their goals.

> **Illustrative Behavior 7:** Makes him- or herself available as a resource to direct reports (e.g., provides information, helps to remove barriers to their effectiveness, acts as a sounding board to generate ideas).

Managers need to be there for their direct reports. Employees may not have all the information needed, or they may encounter barriers they are helpless to remove. Sometimes they merely need someone to act as a sounding board to generate or react to their ideas. Managers need to be there to provide what is needed in a timely manner.

> **Illustrative Behavior 8:** Is patient and helpful when giving complicated explanations or instructions.

Employees taking directions or being confronted with new tasks are often hesitant or uncertain. They frequently need directions repeated or rephrased; they may need additional encouragement and bolstering as they confront new challenges and opportunities. Managers need to be patient in explaining things and in supporting employees as they take on new responsibilities.

> **Illustrative Behavior 9:** Offers helpful advice on how people can advance their careers.

Managers are in a unique position to assess people's talents and developmental needs. They must also be thinking of building the leadership pipeline for the organization. Managers are obligated to share their assessments and offer advice on how people can further develop and advance their careers. They can be very instrumental in finding opportunities for people to advance, even if it means transferring to another department, division, or leaving the organization. Helping employees develop their careers motivates those employees and makes them very loyal to their managers.

Developing Top Talent

AMA defines this competency as being able to consistently attract, select, develop, and retain high performers. With this competency a manager raises the performance bar for his or her work unit or team so that it consists of top performers and provides people with the opportunity to develop new skills, carry out challenging assignments, and accept new responsibilities. This competency requires a manager to hold people accountable for their performance.

> **Illustrative Behavior 1:** Does not tolerate mediocre or poor performance; swiftly addresses performance problems.

Setting high standards does little good unless there are consequences for not meeting those standards. Effective managers set those high standards and are then quick to identify and deal with nonadherence. That sends consistent signals to their staff that the standards are real and that mediocre or shoddy work will not be tolerated. Solid performers lose motivation when managers allow some employees to coast along with poor job performance.

> **Illustrative Behavior 2:** Ensures continuous and open lines of communication and feedback.

> **Illustrative Behavior 3:** Gives coaching and support to improve team and individual results.

Ongoing, open communication is a key to maintaining top performance. Being open to the comments, suggestions, problems, and ideas of staff members helps a manager support top performers and know when they need help, resources, or support in performing their work. An effective manager is constantly in touch, coaching the team and individuals and providing what they need when they need it.

Illustrative Behavior 4: Makes maximum use of the different talents of team members.

Managers are responsible for identifying and utilizing the special strengths of each team member. This helps the team function efficiently and allows each individual to be appreciated for his or her unique talents. This means a manager recognizes talents that are evident and also recognizes the potential an individual has for developing new talents.

Illustrative Behavior 5: Raises the bar for performance within his or her work unit by setting challenging objectives and measuring performance against them.

The effective manager is never content with just "what is"; he or she is constantly working to improve performance and reaching for "what could be." This requires stretching the team to reach objectives that might seem beyond reach, but are truly possible with the talent available. Once set, it requires assessing the team's performance against those higher performance measures.

Illustrative Behavior 6: Provides people with the opportunity to develop new skills and accept new responsibilities.

Even though a manager has top-performing talent on staff, he or she must continually develop that talent. Top performers need constant challenges to be happy; they can easily become bored with the same old activities. A manager must constantly search for, and come up with, challenging assignments that will appeal to those talented people and then help them succeed in those new ventures.

Summary

Effective organizations are staffed by people who know how to work together. A critical part of that is learning about other people in the organization, treating them with respect, and adapting to their styles and needs to get the job done. The competencies identified in AMA's category of "knowing and managing others" help everyone in the organization work together more efficiently and effectively.

The AMA Management Development Competency Model

Knowing and Managing the Business

The third set of competencies in the AMA model revolves around knowing and managing the business. While these competencies may vary depending on the business you are in and certainly are defined differently at various levels on the management ladder, including the individual professional, there are a number of universal categories that apply to all businesses and all levels of employees, for while individual professionals may have very limited roles in managing the business, they must have general knowledge of the business of the company and specific business knowledge and skills particular to their individual jobs.

The AMA competency model includes nineteen competencies in this category (see Table 5.1). The complete AMA competency model, with illustrative behaviors for each competency, can be found in the Appendix.

In this chapter, we will define each of these competencies and explain each further with a number of illustrative behaviors.

Problem Solving

AMA defines this competency as identifying work-related problems, analyzing problems in a systematic but timely manner, drawing correct and realistic conclusions based on data and information, and accurately assessing root causes before moving to solutions. Problem solving is a

TABLE 5.1   Competencies for Knowing and Managing the Business
• Problem Solving
• Decision Making
• Managing and Leading Change
• Driving Innovation
• Customer Focus
• Resource Management
• Operational and Tactical Planning
• Results Orientation
• Quality Orientation
• Mastering Complexity
• Business and Financial Acumen
• Strategic Planning
• Strategic Thinking
• Global Perspective
• Organizational Savvy
• Organizational Design
• Human Resources Planning
• Monitoring the External Environment
• Core Functional/Technical Skills

competency needed at all levels of the organization–however, as one rises up the management ladder, the problems tend to become more complex.

> **Illustrative Behavior 1:** Anticipates potential problems and takes actions to prevent them.

Problems arise in every job. The key here is to anticipate potential problems and try to prevent them. Employees at all levels must learn from experience–their own experience and, through sharing knowledge with others, from the experiences of others–to avoid reinventing solutions to problems that have already been solved by others.

> **Illustrative Behavior 2:** Quickly and systematically analyzes the causes of work-related problems before taking corrective action.

Illustrative Behavior 3: Works to see all angles and perspectives on a problem or issue before drawing conclusions or moving forward with plans or decisions.

Because no employee can be expected to be omniscient, to be able to foresee every potential problem, employees must learn how to systematically analyze work-related problems to help them pinpoint the correct solution. As in the story of the Indian chicken farmer related in Chapter 3, continually jumping to the wrong conclusions can lead to disaster. These types of problem-solving skills can be taught in a class or through coaching from a manager or a more-experienced colleague.

Illustrative Behavior 4: Identifies the appropriate tools, resources, and expertise across the organization to develop the best solution to resolve a problem or issue.

Many employees will always try to solve the problems they encounter themselves, without asking for help from their colleagues or their managers. This is a natural tendency–we want to prove that we are able to do our jobs, and there is natural tendency to not want to be the bearer of bad news to one's manager.

It is up to managers, at all levels, to identify when a problem can best be solved by seeking other tools, resources, or expertise outside the local team. Because the manager's purview is wider than that of any individual employee, the manager often has more experience and a better perspective on when the employee is spending too much time on a problem (and thus spending too little time on other parts of his job), and can call in other resources, ranging from asking another employee to help solve the problem to installing a new procedure or tool to prevent such problems in the future, or calling on resources external to the group, or perhaps outside the organization, to help analyze and solve the problem.

Decision Making

The competency of decision making includes generating and evaluating alternatives before making a decision or taking action, considering the risks associated with each option and selecting the option that has the best balance of risk and reward, encouraging input from others when it is appropriate, standing by decisions without reconsidering unless information or circumstances make it necessary to do so, and evaluating the effectiveness of decisions after they have been made.

> **Illustrative Behavior 1:** Anticipates the consequences of decisions.

Decision making is a forward-looking activity. It involves making a choice among options, because if there were no options to consider, there would be no decision to be made. There is always a minimum of two choices: to do something or to do nothing. In considering what to do, an employee must anticipate the results of a decision–what will happen if I decide to do this? What alternatives do I have, and what are the likely consequences of each choice? What would happen if I decided to do nothing?

> **Illustrative Behavior 2:** Involves people appropriately in decisions that may impact them.

Being part of a team or an organization implies that you must work with other people. It is important to include others appropriately in considering decisions that may affect them. Of course, there are times, especially for a manager, when it is not appropriate to include others in the decision-making process. For example, in having to deal with a performance issue, it is the manager's job to manage the problem employee's issue, and it is usually inappropriate to involve others in this type of decision.

> **Illustrative Behavior 3:** Makes decisions, sets priorities, and chooses goals based on risks and rewards.

Most decisions involve risks. In considering alternatives, the employee must examine her priorities and the potential risks and rewards of each before deciding on a course of action.

Illustrative Behavior 4: Quickly responds with a back-up plan if a decision goes amiss.

Because no employee is omniscient, it is likely that some decisions will not yield the anticipated result. (In the game of baseball, even the best batters in the history of the game only got hits two out of five times.) A competent decision maker recognizes this fact and responds to errant decisions by quickly devising a back-up plan. The back-up may be one of the alternatives originally considered but not chosen, or the errant decision may have yielded additional information that leads to a completely different decision. What is important here, for continued development, is to learn from such errors so that they are not repeated.

Illustrative Behavior 5: Proactively identifies and prioritizes the key issues involved to facilitate the decision-making process for his or her team or group.

A key behavior for mid-level and functional managers is teaching the people within their organization how to make optimal decisions. The manager should help employees identify key issues and priorities in order to improve their decision-making skills. When the manager does this successfully, he can better focus on the more strategic issues at his level, rather than micro-managing day-to-day decisions that are better left to his employees.

Illustrative Behavior 6: Sticks to a decision even when faced with resistance or opposition (e.g., stays confident in the decision, does not give in or falter).

Many times, more senior managers must make unpopular decisions based on information and priorities that are unknown to her employees. It is important that, when making such decisions, the manager stay confident in the decision, not faltering or giving in when faced with opposition from employees who do not have complete information. This may not make the manager the most popular person, but it is a necessary part of the manager's job.

Managing and Leading Change

This competency involves putting opportunities and threats to the organization in context and clarifying how the organization needs to be different and why; communicating a vivid, appealing picture of what the organization needs to look like in the future; clearly communicating the need for change and gaining people's commitment; putting a realistic plan in place to achieve the desired outcome and ensure it is resourced adequately; preparing people to adjust to the change; keeping people informed about the progress of change; and celebrating successes.

> **Illustrative Behavior 1:** Defines clear targets and milestones for change efforts and gains people's commitment to them.
>
> **Illustrative Behavior 2:** Proactively identifies and addresses causes of resistance to change.
>
> **Illustrative Behavior 3:** Clearly communicates the rationale for and benefits of proposed changes.
>
> **Illustrative Behavior 4:** Provides clear, timely, and accurate information about a change.
>
> **Illustrative Behavior 5:** Answers questions related to the impact of the proposed change directly and with candor.
>
> **Illustrative Behavior 6:** Solicits people's feedback about how a change effort is progressing and how people are doing.

Managers at all levels need to help their employees deal with change. This starts by defining clear targets for any change effort, explaining why change is necessary, laying out milestones for the effort, and gaining employees' commitment to the change. Change is difficult for everyone–in general, people resist change. The old way may not be as good as the new way, but we know it and are comfortable with it. Managers need to identify employees who are resistant to the change effort and work with those employees to help overcome their resistance and assist them in implementing the change. This starts with a clear explanation of the reasons why the change is necessary and taking the time to answer employees' questions about the change, then following up, listening to feedback, and ensuring that milestones are met.

Illustrative Behavior 7: Adapts own behavior to support organizational change; acts as a role model for others.

"Do as I say, not as I do" doesn't work. Employees who are struggling to deal with a change effort will abandon the effort if they see that their managers, at all levels, are ignoring the change themselves: "If they don't need to change, why should we?"

Illustrative Behavior 8: Determines a plan to introduce and manage a change in line with the company's strategy and available resources.

Illustrative Behavior 9: Evaluates systems and processes to ensure that they are aligned with and supportive of change efforts.

While first-level managers may have to implement any change program, it is the responsibility of higher levels of management to do the necessary planning before introducing the change: Is the proposed change in line with the company's strategy? What resources are available to help implement the change? How do the company's business systems and processes need to be altered to support the change effort? Who needs to do what to make this change happen?

Illustrative Behavior 10: Gains the commitment of first-line and mid-level managers early in the change process.

Illustrative Behavior 11: Ensures that the necessary resources are available in the function or work unit to implement change; revises plans if needed to reflect available resources.

This is the job of higher-level management–not just to mandate change, but to explain to lower-level managers the need for the change, the benefits that will come from the change, and the resources they will have to implement the change. This is a primary leadership role. Less effective managers just tell their people about the changes they need to make without explaining the reason why change is necessary and without consideration of resources available and call this "empowerment." But this tactic is more aptly called abandonment, rather than empowerment.

Driving Innovation

Driving innovation requires managers to foster a climate that encourages creativity and innovation. Managers who are effective at driving innovation allow others to challenge and disagree. They take prudent risks to accomplish goals and assume responsibility in the face of uncertainty or challenge. They champion new, untested ideas and build support for those ideas among stakeholders. They celebrate successes and worthy attempts at innovation and learn from failures. Effective innovation managers build and maintain open channels of communication for the sharing of ideas and knowledge throughout their organizations.

Driving innovation is a management competency that enables employees to develop their own creativity.

> **Illustrative Behavior 1:** Recognizes and rewards others when they suggest innovations and improvements.

The best way for a manager to encourage employees to be creative, to constantly seek new and better ways of doing their work, is to recognize and reward this type of behavior. Recognition can take many forms—it does not necessarily need to be monetary (although everyone appreciates a few extra dollars).

> **Illustrative Behavior 2:** Allows others to question and positively challenge ideas and issues.

To drive innovation, a manager, at any level, must be open to new ideas and must allow employees to question and challenge the status quo. At the same time, the manager must ensure that the challenges are positive in nature—too many good ideas are sunk by naysayers who resist any type of change. We all know the many types of idea-killers that are used to challenge any new idea: "That will never work here!" "Who asked you?" "We tried that years ago and it didn't work." Being open to new ideas is a learned behavior and takes practice for people who are accustomed to resisting change. But it is a behavior that must be mastered in order to achieve this competency.

> **Illustrative Behavior 3:** Takes calculated, prudent risks to achieve important objectives.

> **Illustrative Behavior 4:** Takes prompt action to implement a promising idea.

> **Illustrative Behavior 5:** Fosters an environment where people feel "safe" taking risks (i.e., acknowledges that mistakes and failures occur and focuses on learning from them rather than placing blame).

A competent manager realizes that innovation can be risky—not every new idea will work or yield the anticipated benefits—but takes prudent risks to achieve important objectives.

To foster a climate of innovation, managers must act quickly to implement a promising idea. In many companies, management has implemented a suggestion system to get new ideas from employees. But if the ideas placed in a suggestion box never see the light of day, employees will soon become frustrated and stop making suggestions. Employees must feel safe in challenging the status quo—if an employee were to try something new, have it fail, and then be punished for it, it will not take much time before employee creativity is stifled because employees don't want to put themselves in jeopardy.

> **Illustrative Behavior 6:** Provides forums for team members to share ideas and knowledge and brainstorm new approaches.

> **Illustrative Behavior 7:** Creates and reinforces a culture of being proactive and taking initiative to improve existing processes and procedures.

A manager who is competent at driving innovation doesn't just wait for employees to suggest new ideas, but stimulates those ideas by creating a culture of creativity and innovation. This can be done in many ways, from the age-old suggestion box (which only works if the suggestions are read and responded to) to creating innovation forums for brainstorming new approaches to taking employees on field trips to stimulate creative thinking. While a first-level manager can initiate many of these ideas and methods, it is up to more senior management to create a culture of innovation throughout the organization.

>**Illustrative Behavior 8:** Sponsors innovative approaches to new business/markets that improve current results/performance.

Major innovation efforts such as these must be sponsored at the level of functional managers and above, because the risks are greater and the resources needed to implement these new approaches are generally not within the purview of first-level or mid-level managers.

Customer Focus

Employees who have customer focus demonstrate a concern for the needs and expectations of customers and make them a high priority. They maintain contact with their customers, both internal and external to the organization, and use their understanding of customer needs as the basis for decision making and organizational action.

>**Illustrative Behavior 1:** Responds to a customer's inquiry or problem in a timely and effective manner.

No matter what jobs employees hold within an organization, their ultimate goal is to satisfy the customer, for without customers, the organization would not exist. So, regardless of whether a customer inquiry is directly related to the job of the employee, he should take responsibility to help that customer–to try to solve the problem or to find someone else in the organization who can do so.

Illustrative Behavior 2: Conveys realistic expectations to internal and external customers.

Illustrative Behavior 3: Effectively manages customer expectations (e.g., reshapes incorrect/inappropriate assumptions, establishes realistic timeframes, pushes back as necessary).

Nothing irks a customer, internal or external to the organization, more than being given promises that a problem will be solved and then having those expectations violated. Employees at all levels must learn to set expectations realistically and then to live up to those expectations. And, if the employee has set an expectation and finds that she cannot meet it, it is incumbent on her to notify the customer as soon as possible, rather than to wait until the last minute to reset the expectation.

At the same time, the employee must make certain that customer expectations are realistic and sometimes must push back on the customer when expectations are unreasonable. For example, a service manager at a car dealership told me once of a call that he received from a customer whose three-year-old car had broken down more than 1,000 miles away and demanded that the dealership provide a replacement immediately.

Illustrative Behavior 4: Follows up on customer requests to ensure that the final product or service met expectations.

Have you ever gone to your doctor when you weren't feeling well and had the doctor prescribe a medication, and then receive a call from the doctor later that evening to see how you are feeling? Or have you ever had a service call from the telephone company or a plumber and receive a call the next day to make certain that your problem was indeed fixed? If you have, you are dealing with someone who prides himself on his customer service.

Illustrative Behavior 5: Takes customer issues to the appropriate people within the organization to obtain the most accurate information to meet customer needs.

Once, in trying to refinance my mortgage, I came upon an unusual legal problem that only the bank that held my current mortgage could solve. The bank was one of the largest mortgage lenders in the country. When I called the bank's toll-free customer service number, the person on the other end had no idea how to solve the problem and offered no assistance in finding the right person within the bank to help me. It took a total of more than fifty calls from me and my attorney over a six-month period, as well as letters of formal complaint to several state and federal regulatory agencies, before I finally was connected with the right person who could solve the problem. Needless to say, none of the more than two dozen people I dealt with at this bank was competent at customer service.

> **Illustrative Behavior 6:** Gives high priority to addressing customer complaints.

Organizations and employees who are competent at customer service know that ignoring a customer's complaint can lead to lost business not just from that customer but also from many other potential customers whom the customer will tell. They also know that successfully resolving a customer complaint in a timely manner can lead to a more loyal customer who may refer other business to the organization in the future.

> **Illustrative Behavior 7:** Uses information about customers' needs as the basis of problem-solving, decision-making, and organizational action.

While it is the responsibility of the individual professional to report what she hears from customers about their needs, it is the manager's responsibility to gather such data and use it to steer her group's and the company's actions. Too often, gathering customer data is relegated to the marketing department's surveys–in actuality, everyone in the organization who interacts with customers should be gathering and reporting such data.

> **Illustrative Behavior 8:** Reminds people about the importance of the customer to the organization's success.

This is an important responsibility of managers at all levels–to keep employees at all levels aware of the importance of customer service. It is also important for managers to "walk the talk" here. For example, if a manager attends a trade show or conference and gathers information from current or potential customers, he should take the time to discuss the customers' needs with his staff upon return to the office. By showing a personal interest in excellent customer service, the manager sets the expectations for everyone else.

> **Illustrative Behavior 9:** Anticipates how plans and actions of the business will affect the customer in the short term and the long term.

Managers must always keep in mind how any decision, any plan, will affect the customer. In the early 1980s, Digital Equipment Corporation changed its business structure, realigning business units from an industry focus to a product-line focus. The changes were widespread. In making all of the plans for these changes, the company forgot one major customer-related item: Each of the former business units had its own ordering system. When the structural changes were made, there was no way to enter customer orders. It took several weeks, and many lost orders, to solve the problem.

> **Illustrative Behavior 10:** Proactively seeks feedback from customers and uses this information to make improvements in systems, processes, etc.

Many organizations hide their heads in the sand, assuming that all customer-related operations are working fine and need no improvement. At one major company, the newly hired head of marketing hired a well-known marketing research firm to conduct a customer survey to see how customers rated the company on a number of dimensions. When the study was completed, he invited all of the company's vice presidents to a presentation of the results.

The consultant started off the presentation with the finding that more than 30 percent of the customers surveyed reported that salespeople didn't return their calls and that they sometimes had to call three or four times before they could contact a salesperson. The vice president of sales replied: "That's not true. What's your next finding?" The consultant then reported that many customers complained that the service people didn't have enough training to competently fix problems. The vice president of customer service responded: "That's not true." And so it went—every finding was denied by the responsible party.

If these senior managers had a customer service orientation, they would have asked for specific names of complaining customers and would have proactively had their staffs contact each and every customer to resolve any outstanding issues. They would also have worked to ensure that their response systems were improved so that customers would not face these problems in the future.

> **Illustrative Behavior 11:** Coaches others to forge relationships with customers and add value.

This relates to the competency of coaching that was discussed in Chapter 4. Mid-level and functional managers who want their employees to focus on customer service must coach them on how to build relationships with customers and how to use those relationships to add value to the products and services that the organization provides to those customers.

> **Illustrative Behavior 12:** Understands and communicates how different departments and functional groups interact to support customer needs.

As an employee climbs the management ladder, her view and understanding of the company's business must expand beyond the functional area in which she started her career. As she develops her own understanding of the interconnectedness of various departments and functional groups within the company, she must help the managers who report to her similarly develop their own understanding, with the goal of breaking down walls so that every group focuses on how the organization, rather than just their function, supports customer needs.

Illustrative Behavior 13: Actively seeks out the customer to discuss business challenges in an effort to provide products and services that meet the customer's needs even before the customer recognizes the need as critical.

The higher an employee rises on the management ladder, the more removed he generally is from day-to-day contact with customers. In an organization that is focused on customer service, senior managers seek customer contact in order to gain and maintain the customer's perspective on the company's products, operations, and future plans. Whether through attending trade shows, industry conferences, or making specifically planned customer visits, competent senior managers continuously learn from their customers and use what they learn to inform planning and decision-making processes.

Resource Management

A competent manager clarifies the financial implications of decisions and uses resources effectively, in line with organizational policies and goals. He deploys resources in a way that is consistent with the organization's strategy and that benefits the organization, rather than advancing self-interest, and adheres to budgets. He ensures that employees' time is used effectively.

Illustrative Behavior 1: Plans how to eliminate unnecessary activities and procedures in order to improve efficiency and make better use of resources.

A manager who competently manages resources is always on the lookout for ways to make the work of her group more efficient by eliminating or streamlining activities and procedures, thus making optimal use of the resources within her group. Because something "has always been done this way" does not necessarily mean that the activity is necessary or is being done to optimize the resources of the group.

Illustrative Behavior 2: Determines priorities for different activities and plans an appropriate allocation of available resources.

With the constantly changing demands of any business, in addition to emergencies that inevitably arise, it is the responsibility of the manager to set priorities so that members of her group are focused on what is most important to the organization at any given time.

Illustrative Behavior 3: Deploys resources based on what is best for the organization versus advancing his or her own interests or agenda.

As a manager climbs the management ladder, his view of the organization must broaden beyond his functional roots. When, inevitably, each group reporting to the manager requests manpower, budgets, and other resources that total more than what is available to the group as a whole, the competent manager must consider the tradeoffs necessary to optimize the work of the entire group, showing no favoritism to any one function. At higher levels of management, the manager becomes part of a cross-functional team and must weigh the overall needs of the organization, sometimes having to concede that other groups/functions needs are greater than his own.

Illustrative Behavior 4: Monitors plans to ensure that resources are used optimally and budgets are adhered to.

While good intentions are famed as a paving material, a manager must continuously monitor the allocation of resources to ensure that all resources within her control are being used optimally and that all employees are staying within budget. Budgets and plans sometimes seem to have their own wills and often tend to get out of control. The earlier that deviations from plans and budgets are identified, the easier it will be to correct them.

Illustrative Behavior 5: Analyzes the short- and long-term financial impact of decisions.

Illustrative Behavior 6: In developing plans, considers how they will affect the business's financial strength, and seeks to maximize this impact without adversely affecting other criteria of success.

While it is good to be decisive, competent managers take the time, before making decisions, to analyze both the short-term and long-term financial impacts of those decisions. What may seem like an optimal solution to a problem that the manager faces today may well have a longer-term financial impact that dictates a different decision. In many organizations that have had a long record of high growth, there is so much money being generated that the solution to any problem is to throw people, money, and other resources at it until it is solved. So long as the organization continues in a rapid-growth mode, this may work. But if the growth of revenue and profits suddenly wanes, the organization may find itself with too many people and very inefficient use of resources.

Operational and Tactical Planning

The competent manager determines short-term objectives and action steps for achieving them, including efficient use of personnel, equipment, facilities, and other resources in order to accomplish a project or initiative. He determines how to schedule and coordinate activities among individuals, teams, and work units.

Illustrative Behavior 1: Creates realistic plans that clearly define goals, milestones, and results.

Illustrative Behavior 2: Plans in detail how to accomplish a large or complex project (e.g., identifies necessary sequence of action steps, then determines when each should be done and who should do it).

All employees must plan their work, defining goals, milestones, and the results to be achieved. For large or complex projects, these plans should include details on the sequence of action steps and, where others are involved in the project, who should do what to accomplish the end goals.

Project management is its own discipline, as defined by the Project Management Book of Knowledge, issued by the Project Management Institute. Some employees may find it beneficial or necessary to study for and achieve certification as a Project Management Professional (PMP).[1] For the purposes of the AMA competency model, project management skills and certification are encompassed under the competency of "core functional and technical skills."

> **Illustrative Behavior 3:** Understands the roles of others within the company and uses this knowledge to improve efficiency (e.g., knows whom to contact in other areas to obtain information).

No employee works totally in isolation. Employees need to develop an understanding of the roles of others, within or external to their own group, as they relate to their work and know whom they can contact in other areas to obtain information or assistance. For new employees, their colleagues or their managers should provide initial guidance, but all employees need to take personal responsibility for developing their own networks of contacts.

> **Illustrative Behavior 4:** Develops controls, checks, and balances to monitor progress against plans and ensure the accuracy of the final product.

> **Illustrative Behavior 5:** Anticipates possible delays or risks to plans and determines alternative courses of action to ensure timely delivery and results.

Two important parts of operational and tactical planning are monitoring and contingency planning. This is how the employee can ensure, as she follows her original plan, that the project or plan is on track. But given that even the best-laid plans often run into snags along the way, she must consider how to handle problems as they arise to ensure the timely delivery of the final results.

As she climbs the management ladder, monitoring of day-to-day operations against plans becomes more complicated. A first-level manager may have as many as a dozen employees each working on their own projects. A mid-level manager may have a number of first-level managers whose groups each have multiple projects. At higher levels of management, monitoring of work requires some type of reporting system, because managers at those levels cannot possibly take a personal interest in each and every project being undertaken by employees two or more levels down in the organization. This is a difficult transition for many newly appointed mid-level managers–as first-level managers, they more closely monitored the work of their individual employees and used their technical expertise to ensure that those employees were doing their work correctly. Mid-level and higher-level managers must learn to remove themselves from the technical work of the individual professional and learn to manage through others.

Illustrative Behavior 6: Involves his or her team in planning and setting priorities.

Competent managers, at all levels, involve their teams in planning their work and setting priorities. Not only does this give the manager's direct reports ownership of the plans and priorities (the plans become "ours" rather than "his"), but those closest to the actual work always have a better perspective on the abilities of their employees and the nature of the work than managers who are one or more levels removed from that work.

Illustrative Behavior 7: Determines priorities for both short-term and long-term and plans an appropriate allocation of available resources.

Illustrative Behavior 8: Evaluates the current flow of work and information across units and identifies opportunities to improve coordination and make better use of resources to accomplish projects/initiatives.

Because managers, at all levels, better understand the overall business strategy and priorities of the organization than individual employees, they must take responsibility for establishing short-term plans and priorities that help the company fulfill its goals. Of course, as the manager works to balance resource allocation with company needs, he needs to explain the reason for changes in assignments and priorities to those who will be affected by such decisions.

In one of Dan Tobin's first jobs, his manager taught him an important lesson—sometimes the manager has to make decisions and reassign priorities based on the overall needs of the business. The manager's decision to defer what he believed to be an important and interesting project was not a personal rejection of Dan's value to the organization, but was based on the priorities of the larger organization. It is a difficult lesson, and one that Dan Tobin has often taught to his own employees.

Results Orientation

Employees with this competency communicate business performance measures and clarify priorities. They work on important issues first, staying with a plan of action or point of view until the desired goal has been obtained or is no longer reasonably attainable. They recognize opportunities, act on them, and look for ways to quickly overcome barriers. They persevere in the face of adversity or opposition. They translate ideas into action.

> **Illustrative Behavior 1:** Takes appropriate risks to accomplish goals.

A results-oriented employee determines how to accomplish his or her goals, including the taking of appropriate risks if taking such risks is the optimal way to achieve those goals.

> **Illustrative Behavior 2:** Overcomes setbacks and adjusts the plan of action to realize goals.

We have all seen some people who are paralyzed when they hit a snag, for whom any setback stops all progress. Results-oriented employees quickly adjust their plans when they hit a setback and find other paths to success.

Illustrative Behavior 3: Focuses on high-priority actions and does not become distracted by lower-priority activities.

Work in many, if not most, organizations is so hectic these days that there are constant, and often competing, demands on the attention of every employee. The results-oriented employee is able to focus on high-priority actions, as defined by her own goals and the instructions from her management, and not be distracted by the constant activity surrounding her.

Illustrative Behavior 4: Challenges him- or herself and others to raise the bar on performance.

Managers at all levels have the responsibility to challenge themselves and their employees to continuously raise the bar on performance. This is not the same as some managers who are constantly "cracking the whip," forcing their employees to work longer hours so that the manager can brag about the performance of his group. Rather, the results-oriented manager constantly works with his group to find better ways for everyone to accomplish goals using tools of process analysis and project management to help all members achieve more for themselves, the group, and the organization.

Illustrative Behavior 5: Focuses people on critical activities that yield a high impact.

Illustrative Behavior 6: Develops a sense of urgency in others to complete tasks.

Too often, employees get so bogged down in day-to-day activities and routines that they lose site of which activities are most critical to individual, group, and organizational success. The results-oriented manager keeps her employees focused on those activities that are most critical to success and creates a sense of urgency for those tasks.

Illustrative Behavior 7: Holds self and others accountable for delivering high-quality results on time and within budget (e.g., models high work standards and demands the same from others, criticizes mediocre or substandard performance).

A competent manager holds himself just as accountable for delivering high-quality results on time as he holds his employees. He models the behaviors that he wants his employees to practice and doesn't abide slackers or employees who perform substandard work. This relates not just to results orientation, but also to performance management–the results-oriented manager actively manages the performance of his employees, which is not the most pleasant of duties but is an absolutely essential part of the job for any competent manager.

Illustrative Behavior 8: Gives priority to achieving results for the company or department, even if it conflicts with one's own personal goals or agenda.

It is a sign of a competent, results-oriented manager that she sometimes sacrifices her personal goals for the benefit of the company. For example, if the company is facing hard times and has to reduce the number of employees, she may recognize that it is more important, in terms of the company's long-term survival and success, for another group or function to keep employees than it is for her to protect her own employees. This is never an easy decision for any manager.

Illustrative Behavior 9: Develops a plan for execution with the team to garner commitment and buy-in.

Mid-level and higher-level managers must manage *through* other people, namely through the lower-level managers who report to him. When he develops plans *with* his team, the plans become "our" plans, rather than "the boss's plans," and the result is greater buy-in from the team members who will have to execute those plans and sell them to their own employees.

Quality Orientation

Competent employees promote organizational effectiveness by anticipating and dealing with problems. They encourage others to suggest improvements to work processes, and they persistently focus on quality, as well as on results. They determine how to improve organizational coordination, productivity, and effectiveness.

> **Illustrative Behavior 1:** Ensures the quality of the work (e.g., monitors reports, reviews complaints from customers, notices mistakes in his or her own work and in the work of others).

No organization can produce quality work unless every employee is focused on the quality of his own work and that of others in the organization. It is not enough to just notice mistakes–employees with this quality orientation take action–they work to correct their own errors and help others to correct their errors.

> **Illustrative Behavior 2:** Identifies sources of mistakes and determines a course of action to prevent their recurrence.

> **Illustrative Behavior 3:** Proactively raises critical issues that impact organizational coordination, productivity, or effectiveness, and takes the lead in resolving them.

> **Illustrative Behavior 4:** Consistently monitors the quality of products and services and the processes used to produce them.

While it is necessary for the employee to consistently monitor the quality of products and services and correct any mistakes she notices, whether in her own work or that of others, it is better to determine the cause of any error and find ways of preventing a reoccurrence. In the famed Toyota manufacturing system, known as a paragon of manufacturing excellence, any employee can stop the production line at any time to fix a problem or suggest an improvement in the manufacturing process. This is a true quality orientation.

Illustrative Behavior 5: Evaluates how well a major project or activity was done (e.g., monitors internal and external client satisfaction, asks people what went well and what can be done better next time).

It is the job of a competent manager to hold an "after-action review" on every project to help employees learn lessons about what went well (and therefore should be repeated on future projects) and what didn't go well (and the reason for any deficiencies). Too often, such a review, if done at all, is called a "post-mortem" (literally, "after death") and is conducted only when a project ends in a disaster of some type. The competent manager knows that there are lessons to be learned from every project and helps employees continuously learn in order to improve the quality of their work.

Illustrative Behavior 6: Communicates and reinforces the importance of high work standards.

Illustrative Behavior 7: Encourages team members to take the initiative to improve work processes.

The competent manager knows that he cannot be the sole monitor and implementer of quality standards in the organization. He knows that he must instill a culture that engenders an orientation to quality among all employees. The manager's job is to communicate and reinforce the importance of high work standards and to encourage all employees to hold themselves accountable.

Mastering Complexity

The AMA defines this competency as quickly integrating complex information to identify strategies and solutions, learning new concepts quickly, demonstrating keen insights into situations, assimilating large amounts of information, and narrowing it down to and articulating the core idea or issue.

Illustrative Behavior 1: Understands new concepts quickly.

Illustrative Behavior 2: Assimilates large amounts of data/information to identify what is most important.

Illustrative Behavior 3: Integrates complicated ideas and approaches to develop the best possible solutions.

Illustrative Behavior 4: Breaks down complicated problems or concepts into clear and manageable components.

The world continues to become increasingly complex and interrelated. Employees are inundated daily with more and more data. As explained in the learning model presented in Chapter 1, when data has relevance to employees' work, it becomes information. Mastering this complexity, employees must have the ability to sort through all of these data to find that which is most relevant to their work, thus transforming it into information. The next step is to start using this information to make a positive difference in personal, team, and organizational business results—when employees use this information, it becomes their personal knowledge. This is not an easy task, for it requires employees to break down this mass of data into clear and manageable components and then apply them to solve complicated problems.

Illustrative Behavior 5: Focuses others on the core message or desired result of a complex plan or idea.

Employees cannot begin this learning process unless they can recognize what is important to their work. In today's complex business processes, it is often difficult for employees to understand how their personal work fits into the larger goals of the organization and to the organization's accomplishment of those goals. It is job of the manager to help employees focus on key business issues and to explain how their work fits within the organization's complex plans and the accomplishment of the organization's mission.

Business and Financial Acumen

Employees with business and financial acumen possess the technical and business knowledge needed to make the best decisions for the organization; they understand how strategies and tactics work in the marketplace. They assess the financial implications of decisions and actions and balance data analysis with judgment and common sense.

> **Illustrative Behavior 1:** Understands how his or her role contributes to the overall success of the organization.

Every employee, at every level of the organization, needs to understand how the job he does contributes to the overall success of the organization. Without this knowledge, the employee has no context for his daily work tasks and may inadvertently make decisions that seem to make sense from his limited point of view but ultimately impact the organization adversely. It is incumbent on managers at every level of the organization to help employees understand this context and to help them develop their business acumen.

> **Illustrative Behavior 2:** Understands the key drivers of the business, including how the business makes money.

Managers at all levels need to develop their understanding of the key drivers of the business and the key indicators of business performance used by the organization so that they can make optimal decisions that ultimately affect the success of the organization. This knowledge helps managers organize the work of their employees so as to best contribute to team and organizational performance.

> **Illustrative Behavior 3:** Understands the financial impact of decisions and actions.

It is not enough for a manager to know how her decisions and actions affect her group's budget. She must also understand the interrelatedness of her group's work with the work of other groups so that she can optimize the overall effects of her decisions in terms of the financial performance of the entire organization. For example, a purchasing manager typically measures herself by obtaining raw materials at the lowest cost. But if by ordering materials from the lowest-cost supplier, she increases scrap rates because the low-cost supplier also has poor quality controls, she may be costing the organization more than by ordering the materials from a higher-cost supplier who has better quality control.

> **Illustrative Behavior 4:** Analyzes data to identify trends and issues that are important to the business and interprets the results of the analyses to make recommendations for how the organization should address the issues.

> **Illustrative Behavior 5:** Understands how internal and external business measurements are defined and influenced.

At one software company, the CFO did quarterly analyses of how the company compared with its major competitors in terms of several key performance measures. He then presented these analyses at each quarterly town hall meeting of employees as part of the company's quarterly financial results. Most employees found the comparison somewhat interesting, but never really understood what they meant.

The situation changed after providing education to the next tier of managers in a program designed to develop their business acumen. After completing this program, this group of managers not only understood what the measures meant but how they were derived and, more importantly, what they could do to improve their own and their groups' performance on these measures.

> **Illustrative Behavior 6:** Continuously learns and demonstrates an in-depth understanding and knowledge of the company's core business and how the organization operates (e.g., has a thorough understanding of overall business structure, processes, policies, functions, and their interrelationships).

Starting at the mid-management level, all managers need to develop their understanding of the organizational context of the groups they manage. Their focus at this and higher levels must change from their earlier functional responsibilities to a better understanding of the overall business. They must understand the organization's key business processes and how their group fits into those processes. One of the best methodologies for developing this understanding is to teach all managers the skills of systems thinking.

> **Illustrative Behavior 7**: Assesses existing talent base to determine whether the right mix of skills/competencies is in place to ensure the current and future success of the work unit.

One of the hottest topics in today's management literature is talent management—how to ensure that the organization recruits, develops, and retains the skills and competencies it needs today and will need for the future success of the enterprise. This is especially important for many organizations because of the current demographics of the workforce, with millions of baby boomers due to retire in the next five to ten years and fewer workers available in the next generation of the workforce to take their places. This demographic fact makes it vital that managers, starting at the mid-manager level, take seriously their responsibility for understanding and building the competencies of their employees.

> **Illustrative Behavior 8**: Has a working knowledge of profit and loss and other key financial measurements used in the business in terms of current performance, forecasting, and longer-term business planning.

This is a key component of the competency of business and financial acumen. This is undoubtedly why courses with titles such as "Finance for Non-Financial Managers" continue to be one of the most popular programs offered by AMA and many other academic and professional education providers. Financial acumen becomes an increasingly important competence as employees climb the management ladder beyond the middle manager level.

Illustrative Behavior 9: Communicates the key performance/ profit levers for the business and manages to these measures.

This behavior relates directly to Behavior 1 under this competency– unless senior managers help employees at all levels understand key performance and profit levers, they cannot expect those employees to work to optimize the organization's business results. To be effective at these senior levels, managers must continuously educate employees on this topic and communicate with them as to how they and the company are doing against these measures.

Strategic Planning

A competent manager develops and drives a shared understanding of a long-term vision that incorporates people's input and describes what the organization needs to look like and how it needs to operate in the future. He determines long-term objectives and the tactics needed to achieve them. He allocates resources according to stated priorities, making sure that accountabilities and expectations for executing a strategy are clear.

Illustrative Behavior 1: Translates company strategies into meaningful plans for the business; connects them to people's daily work.

A company's mission, vision, and goals are only as good as the strategies put in place to accomplish them. Competent managers implement strategies to meet the company's goals and help employees at all levels understand those strategies and connect them to their daily work.

Illustrative Behavior 2: Demonstrates how priorities fit into the company's overall strategies (i.e., creates a line of sight).

If managers expect their employees to work toward the company's goals and implement their plans' priorities, they must help employees have a clear line of sight–to understand how the work they are being asked to do will contribute to the achievement of those goals. If employees don't understand the strategy, they may inadvertently work so as to obviate the achievement of the company's goals.

> **Illustrative Behavior 3:** Pursues challenges that result in long-term business benefit (e.g., proposes challenging but realistic objectives).

Whether for the overall business, a functional group, a team, or an individual employee, objectives need to be challenging, but realistic. Most people like to stretch themselves beyond their day-to-day routine and enjoy a challenge. At the same time, objectives need to have some basis in reality—for example, it is probably unrealistic for a company whose sales have stayed flat for the past five years to suddenly set an objective of increasing sales by 50 percent for the next year if there is nothing new to sell. For managers to continuously set unrealistic objectives will only demoralize employees, especially if the employee's compensation is tied to those objectives. We have seen some companies that hire employees with the promise of excellent annual bonuses based on achievement of the employee's and the company's performance, only for employees to later realize that the company's management has always set such unrealistic goals that the company has rarely reached its objectives and, therefore, bonuses are seldom paid.

> **Illustrative Behavior 4:** Understands where the business is going and the strategic objectives of the company and knows how to support them.

> **Illustrative Behavior 5:** Allocates resources based on strategies and related objectives.

A competent manager understands how the work of his part of the organization contributes to the achievement of the organization's strategic objectives and plans his group's work to provide that support. Further, she ensures that all employees in her group share this understanding so that they can make decisions on a daily basis that support their achievement.

Illustrative Behavior 6: Stays abreast of changes in the marketplace and the company's position relative to competitors.

Illustrative Behavior 7: Continuously learns and demonstrates an understanding of the competitive environment, trends in the economy, and technology that may impact the business; refers to these trends in conversations; anticipates the effect of trends on the business; and uses information about trends when evaluating alternatives and making decisions.

Illustrative Behavior 8: Engages in scenario planning (e.g., assesses where the organization is today against potential changes/ conditions in the external environment) to determine the best path forward.

Strategic planning is an exercise in learning. The first task in the strategic planning process is to learn about the marketplace, customer needs, competitors, the economy, and other factors that will affect the organization's business. Next, the management team must develop a common understanding of both the organization's current position and capabilities and its readiness to meet the challenges of the marketplace. Finally, the management team must develop strategies to meet those challenges.

Because the future is uncertain, there can be no guarantee of what will emerge in the economy or the marketplace. Scenario planning is a structured exercise where the management team imagines a variety of futures, what each might mean to the company; based on what it has learned and using its best judgment, the team makes decisions as to the company's future direction.

Today's strategy is only as good as the information collected and analyzed to develop that strategy, and as information changes, each current strategy must be reassessed in light of that information and, when necessary, modified or even abandoned in favor of a new strategy based on that new information. Thus, strategic planning is not a one-time or once-a-year activity, but a continuous process.

Illustrative Behavior 9: Communicates the company's vision, values, and strategy with conviction.

Illustrative Behavior 10: Communicates business priorities to all levels of the organization.

Once the organization's strategy has been set, the competent manager shares that strategy (as well as the company's vision and values) with all employees with conviction. If the manager expects employees to work toward implementing the stated strategy, he must demonstrate his personal commitment to that strategy and lead employees in setting their work priorities so as to support that strategy.

Illustrative Behavior 11: Does not give up the long-term vision under present-day pressure; takes a long-term perspective on problems and opportunities facing the organization.

This may be among the most difficult of behaviors for many managers. The pressures of the financial community for ever-improving quarterly financial results has led many company leaders to abandon what they truly believe to be right strategies for the long-term success of the organization in favor of meeting the short-term expectations of the financial community and the organization's stockholders. It is a very difficult balancing act.

Strategic Thinking

Strategic thinking involves understanding the implications of social, economic, political, and global trends. A manager with this competency understands the company's position in the marketplace–both its strengths and its weaknesses. She takes a long-term perspective on problems and opportunities and applies insight and creativity to the development of strategies that help the organization gain or sustain competitive advantage. She proposes innovative strategies that leverage the organization's competitive position.

Illustrative Behavior 1: Prioritizes actions based on what is best for the organization.

A manager who thinks strategically keeps organizational goals in mind when setting priorities for his group and bases those priorities on what is best for the organization, even if that means that decisions he makes are not necessarily optimal for his own group.

> **Illustrative Behavior 2:** Demonstrates knowledge of customer needs and uses this information to help determine the way forward.

"Knowing the customer" is not just a responsibility of those groups within the organization that have direct contact with customers. Every manager and every employee within the organization must learn about customers' needs and focus their efforts on satisfying those needs.

A well-known industry consultant once presented to a group of several hundred employees in a high-tech company. The audience was a mix of engineering, product management, marketing, field service, sales, and sales support personnel. He asked the audience: "How many of you work in sales?" About 10 percent of the audience, those who were in the sales organization, raised their hands. "Wrong!" he shouted. "You are ALL in sales. You all have a responsibility for creating, selling, and supporting products and services that meet the needs of your customers. You all affect company sales, and if you want this company to succeed, you must always, each and every one of you, think of yourself as being in sales."

> **Illustrative Behavior 3:** Understands and drives toward increasing his or her work unit's financial performance (e.g., understands the financial impact of plans and decisions).

A manager who thinks strategically understands that her decisions affect not just her own budgets and financial performance, but may also impact the performance of other parts of the organization. This is not always easy to do because different functional groups use different standards of performance. An engineering group may measure itself on the elegance of its product design and including the latest state-of-the-art features in each product. While they may be able to do that and keep within their budget, they also need to consider how their design will affect the financial performance of other groups. For example, they may decide that the packaging for their latest product will look much more elegant if the cabinet has rounded corners without considering that those rounded corners may greatly increase the cost of manufacturing. Or the manufacturing group may build a very compact package that saves materials costs but adds hours to the time it will take a service person to open and repair the product.

> **Illustrative Behavior 4:** Demonstrates an understanding of key business drivers and product attributes within his or her department (e.g., aligns products offered with core organizational capabilities).

Gary Hamel and C. K. Prahalad view core competence as an optimal way for strategic thinkers to help the organization envision and build the future. "It is the marriage of core competence and functionality thinking that points a firm toward unexplored competitive space . . . to move beyond what is to what could be."[2] Managers who are good strategic thinkers always keep the organization's key business drivers (core competencies) in mind to ensure that their actions are aligned with the company's strategic business directions.

> **Illustrative Behavior 5:** Anticipates strategic problems and opportunities and makes strategic decisions to address them.

As a manager rises to middle management and higher on the management ladder, her focus must change from operational decisions to more strategic thinking. Competent mid-level (and higher-level) managers anticipate strategic problems and opportunities and make plans and decisions to solve those problems and take advantage of those opportunities.

> **Illustrative Behavior 6:** Continuously identifies and evaluates viable future opportunities for the business; selects and exploits the activities that will result in the greatest return.

While individual professionals and first-level managers continuously set priorities for getting their assigned tasks done, priority setting at the higher levels of management must focus on future opportunities and how to exploit those opportunities to yield the best returns for the organization and its stakeholders. This is a major shift in thinking for individuals when they are first promoted to mid- and higher levels of management.

> **Illustrative Behavior 7:** Demonstrates creative thinking to solve strategic issues (e.g., proposes innovative strategies that capitalize on the unique qualities and core competencies of the organization).

This is a whole different way of thinking about problem solving that must be mastered by higher-level managers, based on the organization's core competencies. As stated by Hamel and Prahalad:[3]

> Senior management teams compete to develop a prescient, well-founded, and creative view of tomorrow's opportunities that will spur preemptive competence-building, provide focus to those efforts, ensure consistency in investment programs, and serve as a guide to decisions about strategic alliances and acquisitions and a brake on indiscriminate and tangential opportunities.

Global Perspective

This managerial competency involves understanding the international issues facing the business. Competent managers appreciate how ethnic, cultural, and political matters influence business and integrate local and global information into decisions affecting multiple sites. They apply knowledge of public regulatory frameworks in multiple countries and make deliberate decisions about how to conduct business successfully in different parts of the world.

> **Illustrative Behavior 1:** Considers wide-ranging influences, situations, and implications both inside and outside the organiza-

tion when making plans or decisions, solving problems, or developing strategies.

As communications technologies and the increasingly complex global business environment continue to evolve, managers at all levels must consider the global range of their organization's endeavors in making any plans and decisions, developing their strategies, or solving problems. What may work in the organization's home country may be impossible to implement in another country and may contradict another culture's norms or even violate their laws. Competent managers get training and find ways of managing remote employees, allowing for differences in work habits, attitudes toward management, time differences, and so on. They work to find optimal solutions that will work globally.

> **Illustrative Behavior 2:** Recognizes emerging patterns of business on a global basis and formulates strategies in line with these trends.

Trade barriers that once protected local businesses are all but gone, and managers must widen their view of business trends and competition to the worldwide arena. Ignoring global trends and competition is almost certain to yield unpleasant, if not devastating, surprises in the future. This can be a major challenge for the new mid-level or more senior manager who has previously focused on managing a group of local individual professionals.

> **Illustrative Behavior 3:** Demonstrates an understanding of the international issues facing a company.

Competent managers work to understand the organization's international operations and issues, even if their personal management domains are local. Only by understanding the organization's worldwide issues can managers optimize their decisions to benefit the overall organization. Developing this type of understanding is why many leading companies build an international assignment into the career path of high-potential employees.

Illustrative Behavior 4: Communicates how international and political issues may impact the business in the short and long term.

Senior management in many organizations views international concerns as the sole province of senior management. Competent managers realize that decisions made at all levels of the organization may well impact the organization's international operations and, therefore, communicate with all employees about those concerns.

Illustrative Behavior 5: Implements global decisions while adjusting for local perspectives where appropriate.

When the United States dominated the world's business markets, many managers felt that their decisions and commands should be implemented worldwide, without considering local laws, customs, markets, or other issues. While the United States remains the world's dominant market power, the balance of economic power has shifted, and competent managers have become more aware of, and sensitive to, how their decisions must be adjusted for local perspectives.

Illustrative Behavior 6: Creates/validates long-term directions based on business dynamics, global trends, and the overall strategy of the company.

Strategic planning and long-term directions for any organization can no longer be the sole province of senior executives or a small team of central-office strategic planners, but must involve the organization's worldwide management team as well as global partners, suppliers, and customers. If managers do not develop this type of global orientation, they will certainly suboptimize the organization's results.

Organizational Savvy

Managers who have organizational savvy stay abreast of what is happening across the organization. They understand the effects of decisions and actions on other parts of the organization and recognize the interests of others in different parts of the organization. They understand the influence dynamics of the organization and use that information to establish alliances to achieve organizational objectives. They understand the organization's culture and norms of behavior.

> **Illustrative Behavior 1:** Approaches problems with a clear understanding of organizational and political realities.

> **Illustrative Behavior 2:** Understands how the culture of the organization impacts how the work gets done and takes this into account in planning and decision making.

In every organization, of every size or shape, there are organizational and political realities that shape organizational life and sometimes make the job of the manager easier or more difficult. A savvy manager keeps her antenna tuned to these realities so that she can find practicable solutions to the problems and challenges she faces and make realistic plans and decisions that don't violate organizational norms.

> **Illustrative Behavior 3:** Understands the goals/objectives of other departments/work units and uses this information to establish alliances and resolve issues.

> **Illustrative Behavior 4:** Understands the interdependent nature of operations and the impact of various departments/work units on workflow within the organization.

> **Illustrative Behavior 5:** Understands how his or her decisions may impact others across the organization and involves them appropriately.

While managers may vary in how well they pick up on organizational undercurrents, all managers with organizational savvy know that they need to expand their views beyond their own groups to understand the goals, objectives, and work methods of the other groups with which they work and how these form interdependencies with their own groups and others. The savvy manager, before making a local decision, also examines how that decision may affect other groups' work and involves them before making such a decision. This becomes increasingly important for mid-level and higher-level managers who, while they started their careers in a particular function or specialty, must broaden their view of the overall business in order to make optimal decisions that may well require trade-offs between competing objectives and competing subgroups.

Illustrative Behavior 6: Keeps up to date on what is happening across the organization.

Savvy managers keep their eyes and ears open to learn what is happening in other parts of the organization, as well as their own. They make it clear to the people within their own organization that they want to hear of problems or challenges before they become crises. They don't "shoot the messenger" if they hear bad news.

Illustrative Behavior 7: Proactively shares information with others across the organization based on an understanding of their priorities, goals, and objectives.

Of course, people will be more willing to share relevant information with you if you proactively share information with them, especially when it may affect their priorities or the achievement of their goals and objectives. Savvy managers know that communications flow in multiple directions and ensure they are known as a willing receptor and sender of information, rather than as an information roadblock.

Illustrative Behavior 8: Considers organizational culture and norms of behavior in making decisions.

Every organization has its own culture and norms of behavior, and the competent manager takes these into account in making decisions. Employees, at any level, who violate these norms too frequently will often find further progress in their careers stalled.

Organizational Design

Competent managers ensure that the organization's structure and systems support its strategies. They take action to optimize resources and work processes using such techniques as business process reengineering and continuous process improvement. They organize work to enhance efficiency and to drive results by appropriately grouping responsibilities and establishing linkages within their own groups and throughout the organization.

> **Illustrative Behavior 1:** Understands the importance of aligning organizational structure and strategy.

> **Illustrative Behavior 2:** Reviews organizational structure, systems, and processes to ensure they support change initiatives.

Managers know that their strategies will be easier to implement if the structure of their organization is aligned to support those strategies. Should the organization be structured by industry or by product line? Should there be a single global organization or a network of local country operations? Should services, such as information systems, human resources, or purchasing, be centralized or decentralized?

Competent managers examine the alternatives available for organizational design and choose the structure that will best support their business strategies. They also realize that the optimal organizational design for a million-dollar company may not remain optimal as the company grows or as it expands into new markets or geographies. Thus, with each major change in strategy, these managers re-examine their organizational structure, systems, and processes to ensure that they align with the new strategy, rather than continue to support an obsolete strategy. Many change initiatives have failed because organizational leadership has told people that it wants them to act in new ways, but neglected to change systems, processes, measurements, and rewards and allows them to continue supporting the old ways.

> **Illustrative Behavior 3:** Identifies key skills within the work unit and determines how to best organize the work (e.g., grouping responsibilities, establishing linkages) to enhance efficiency and coordination.

> **Illustrative Behavior 4:** Collects feedback from employees at all levels to understand what is working and what could be improved related to existing systems and structure.

> **Illustrative Behavior 5:** Identifies and implements ways to optimize resources and work processes.

Wise managers do not make changes in organization structure and processes without input from all levels and without developing a thorough understanding of current skill levels, job roles, and work processes. While no one particularly likes change, employees will generally be much more responsive to change when they feel that their voices have been heard–when employees participate in making plans, the plans become "our plans" rather than "management's plans."

> **Illustrative Behavior 6:** Creates clear descriptions of the work, roles, and responsibilities to help facilitate coordination and cooperation.

Little frustrates employees more than a manager who tells them: "Things have to change around here" and then leaves them with no details or guidance. Competent managers provide clear descriptions of the work, roles, and responsibilities of each group (if not to the individual employee level) when instituting changes. Before making the changes, they focus not only on how to achieve the organization's goals and implement its strategies, but also on how to facilitate the coordination and cooperation that will be required across the organization to achieve the goals of the change initiative. And once they have made their plans, they explain to employees exactly what changes will take place and the rationale for those changes, while supporting their employees as they work through the changes.

Human Resources Planning

A competent manager ensures the talent base is in place to meet organizational needs. He assesses current skills sets and identifies the right mix of talent to fill gaps and ensure sustained results. He accurately assesses "fit" based on the requisite skills and competencies, as well as alignment with the organizational culture.

> **Illustrative Behavior 1:** Develops clear job descriptions based on the key skills and competencies (personal, interpersonal, technical, and managerial) required for the role.

> **Illustrative Behavior 2:** Clarifies the current skills and knowledge within the work unit as well as its future needs.

> **Illustrative Behavior 3:** Considers the long-term implications of team performance and skills in order to ensure sustained results.

Human resources planning requires the manager to understand the key skills and competencies that are needed within the organization to meet its goals, both today's goals and tomorrow's. Based on the results of such planning, the competent manager then writes job descriptions that detail the skills and behaviors needed within the group. An important point here is that even if the organization requires many people with the same job description, it is rarely possible or wise to try to make all employees clones of each other. Competent managers value diversity, not just in terms of gender, race, nationality, etc., but also in terms of styles of working and thinking. They value people who approach problems from different points of view, find it desirable to have both thinkers and doers on their teams, and so on. And while current plans require just so much of skill A or competency B, it is often desirable to have extra reserves of key skills and competencies so that people can help each other out when work bottlenecks arise.

> **Illustrative Behavior 4:** Makes plans to fill development or skills gaps within the work unit.

> **Illustrative Behavior 5:** Accurately assesses talent and makes hiring decisions based on a clear picture of what is required for success in the role, as well as cultural fit.

Few managers at any level can say that they already have all of the skills and competencies within their organization to satisfy every current and future requirement. The gaps that the manager identifies may be for the group as a whole (for example, "we will be introducing a new technology that everyone needs to learn") or for one of more specific individuals (for example, "Bob and Mary are good candidates for promotion to first-level manager, but they need to learn some team leadership skills to prepare them for that role"). In many cases, this will mean working with the individuals and the human resources or training group to prepare a development plan for the group or for specific individuals. In other cases, it will mean preparing a job description for one or more people to be hired from outside the organization.

Because people cannot be described by a list of specifications, as can a machine part (if the machine part meets all of the technical specs, you know it will fit and will work), the manager must also ensure that any candidate for a position (new, promoted, or replacement) is a good fit with the organizational culture. Every organization's culture is different, and thought must be given to what makes a good cultural fit. Author Dan Tobin worked for more than a decade for Digital Equipment Corporation, which had a very unique organizational culture. He knew people who worked for IBM, Digital's main competitor and another great player in the computer industry. But people who worked for the two companies knew that each had a unique organizational culture and that success in either company could not guarantee a good organizational fit if the person were to move to the other company.

Monitoring the External Environment

Competent managers collect information about opportunities and threats in the external environment that may affect their work in the short or long terms. They analyze trends and look for circumstances that may enhance their own organization's performance.

> **Illustrative Behavior 1:** Understands industry and market trends and the impact they may have on the organization in both the short and longer term.

Gaining, maintaining, and improving competitive advantage cannot be done without understanding both the market you are serving and the other organizations against which you compete. While the tasks of gathering market and competitive information may be assigned to a specific market research function, it is incumbent on managers to study market data if they want to make better strategic and operational decisions.

> **Illustrative Behavior 2:** Analyzes data and creates benchmarks (based on research on the industry and on specific competitors) to monitor the quality of products and services and improve existing processes.

While being profitable may be enough of a measure of success for many managers, the most competent managers continually measure themselves against their industry and their competitors to see how they are doing. This may include such measures as sales per employee, return on equity, a product's mean-time-to-failure, market share, or hundreds of other possible measures. The management team must decide which measures to monitor and analyze which of their products, services, and processes measure up to the competition and which need improvement.

> **Illustrative Behavior 3:** Identifies trends and patterns in the marketplace that may positively or negatively impact the business.

> **Illustrative Behavior 4:** Takes action to mitigate threats and capitalize on opportunities in the external environment.

In monitoring the external environment, there are tons of data available. As explained in the learning model in Chapter 1, only those data that have relevance and purpose (as defined by the organization's managers) become information, and that information only has value to the organization if it is applied to the organization's work to make a positive difference in business results. Thus, managers must use external data to identify trends and patterns in the marketplace that pose threats or create opportunities for the organization and must take action to mitigate those threats and capitalize on those opportunities. If managers ignore this responsibility, all of the market data that the organization collects will have no value to the organization.

Core Functional/Technical Skills

A competent employee maintains up-to-date knowledge and skills within his field of expertise and remains abreast of developments in his field and industry. He provides guidance or counsel on technical matters related to his field. He knows how to use company-specific technology.

> **Illustrative Behavior 1:** Quickly masters new technical knowledge relevant to his or her position.

This is a vital competency for the individual professional and is the basic competency for which most employees are hired. It is also very important for the first-level manager, who must know the work of her employees and be able to coach them on the technical aspects of their jobs.

As managers climb the management ladder, their mastery of this technical knowledge must yield to their new responsibilities as managers of people and the business in general. Many technically proficient employees have failed as managers because they could not make this transition. This is also why many organizations have created separate technical career paths for technology specialists, where technically brilliant employees who have no interest in (or talent for) management can be recognized for their technical contributions to the organization without have to abandon their technical proficiency by moving onto the management ladder.

> **Illustrative Behavior 2:** Has a comprehensive knowledge of all existing computer systems and other technologies relevant to his or her job responsibilities.

There are few jobs in any organization today that are not reliant on computer or other technologies. Employees at all levels must master the use of the systems and technologies that they use in their work. As jobs change and as employees climb the management ladder, these technologies may change–for example, a computer programmer must have much more detailed knowledge of the systems he uses than does the organization's chief technology officer (CTO), while the CTO must be able to master the operational dashboard he uses to monitor performance of the company's major technical systems.

> **Illustrative Behavior 3:** Offers helpful advice and guidance when others are learning technical matters related to his or her role or function.

An employee who has key technical skills should always be willing to help peers or managers with advice and guidance when they ask for help in understanding technology. For the first-level manager, helping employees learn is a key part of the job, and individual professionals who regularly help others with advice and guidance are often considered prime candidates for first-level management positions.

Some companies are using what is called "reverse mentoring" to help senior executives learn more about today's technologies from younger staff members. "The person generally credited with introducing formal reverse mentoring is General Electric's former CEO Jack Welch. In 1999, he ordered 500 of his top managers to find workers who were well versed in the Internet and tap into their expertise. Welch himself chose a mentor and blocked off time to learn about everything from Internet bookmarks to competitors' Web sites."[4]

> **Illustrative Behavior 4:** Is knowledgeable about best practices relative to the technical aspects of his or her function/role and benchmarks against other organizations.

With the rapid advance of technology, no employee or manager can assume that he knows everything he will ever need to know about his technical specialty. Competent managers keep up-to-date on advances in their fields through a variety of methods, including continuing education, reading trade and industry periodicals, attending tradeshows and conferences, and making benchmarking visits to other organizations.

Illustrative Behavior 5: Acquires technical/functional knowledge of new areas that he or she manages to sufficient depth to be an effective manager of the overall function.

For mid-level and functional managers, it is not possible to be as technically astute as the individual professionals or the first-level managers within their groups, but they must still keep abreast of major developments in their technical or functional fields to be effective in their roles.

Summary

Competencies related to knowing and managing the business are not the exclusive province of senior managers. Starting with the individual professional, all employees have a responsibility to understand their organization's overall business goals and the major business systems with which they work and that affect them. As employees climb the management ladder, more of these competencies become relevant as more senior positions require management of various aspects of the organization's business.

Selecting for Competence

Once you have defined the management competency model for various positions in your organization, your challenge is to find the right people with the right competencies for the right positions at the right time.

Your first step is to devise strategic staffing plans for those areas critical to business success. Your strategic staffing plans should tie to the overall business strategy and help you further refine which specific competencies are most needed where. These areas might be ones that are hard to fill or where competition is great; they may be for positions where the organization needs to tap new or nontraditional sources of talent; they may be plans to find management talent by blending external hires with promotions from within.[1] Strategic plans need to focus on issues and look to the future of the organization. Not all positions need to be addressed in a strategic plan.

Once the strategic plan is in place, you have a choice in how to go about executing the plan and filling open positions in the organization: You can "buy" competencies by hiring new people, or you can "make" competencies by encouraging self-learning, providing training and development for current staff, or promoting people who possess the competencies you need or who show promise of being able to develop those competencies.

In this chapter we address selecting for competence: hiring and promoting people based on the competencies defined for a position. Subsequent chapters will address how to encourage self-learning and provide training to help people further develop the competencies valued by the organization.

Hiring for Competence

Hiring procedures are anything but easy. Sifting through resumes and participating in interviews, you search for the right candidate with the competencies you need for a particular position. It can be confusing. People can be hard to read. Couple that with the fact that candidates today are well schooled in how to present themselves. They anticipate traditional interview questions and rehearse what they think the preferred answers might be. They may look at work differently than the person conducting the interview because they are of a different generation or cultural group.

Most of us can tell horror stories of when the interview process went wrong, and, to be honest, not all future work circumstances can be foreseen in an interview. And we all know the wrong hire can be a great cost to the organization (see "The Wrong Hire").

How do you find the right person? Certainly the old way of hiring, where the interviewer developed rapport and made decisions on personal opinion or a "gut feeling," is ineffective. Today's more traditional interviewing practices too often focus on situational scenarios: asking a candidate "what would you do if . . . " A better solution is competency-based behavioral interviewing.

According to Victoria A. Hoevemeyer in her book, *High Impact Interview Questions,*[2] competency-based behavioral interviewing (CBBI) is "a structured process that combines competencies with the premise that, with few exceptions, the best predictor of future performance/behavior is past performance/behavior and the more recent the performance/behavior, the more likely it is to be repeated." This method comes closer to predicting the on-the-job performance of candidates, so you reduce your percentage of "bad hires."

Hoevemeyer describes how the CBBI process focuses interview questions exclusively on the competencies required for success in the position. Interviewers are trained to use the specific questions, and rating scales provide more objectivity than a subjective gut feeling. Questions focus on actual current and past performance, not "might do" behavior. Hoevemeyer outlines a six-step process for implementation:

1. Determine the structure for the competency model. This involves the entire organization, all positions, functions, and levels, from individual contributor to senior C-level executives.

THE WRONG HIRE

The candidate made a great impression on the interviewer: He was well groomed, well spoken, and had a law degree. He explained that the law wasn't for him; he discovered his passion for public speaking while working at his church. He wanted to hone his skills and help others do the same. The presentation training company needed polished individuals to learn their presentation methods quickly and train business executives in those skills. It seemed like a perfect fit, and the candidate was hired.

During his initial training, the trainee appeared open to learning and spent hours practicing the new methods. The only criticism was that he was too "evangelical" in his presentation style. He needed to harness his tendency to "perform" and to recognize that most business executives sought a more conservative style. He needed to focus more on coaching others to bring out their natural style that would resonate with the audiences they addressed. For several months, he was coached and trained at the headquarters office.

The second part of his training involved traveling with other staff members to co-train client groups. Once he was on the road, calls to headquarters revealed stories about his coming late to sessions or missing them entirely. He always described extravagant travel delays, unforeseen circumstances with family, etc. After many incidents, he was given a warning and counseling, but seemed unable to take responsibility for the changes he needed to make. Then co-workers began to get strange phone calls at late hours—he was double-checking program details, sometimes seeming a bit disoriented, and sometimes offering excuses for travel delays. His unreliability led to his dismissal. It later came to light that he had a substance abuse problem and was seeking rehabilitation.

CBBI may have helped prevent this wrong hire. During the interview, the manager could have asked questions about how the person handled stressful situations, how he viewed his job responsibilities, if he had ever failed to deliver what was expected of him, whether he was timely, and perhaps even how he responded to taking directions from others. Answers to those questions may have revealed some avoidance behaviors, inability to handle stressful situations well, or tendencies to shirk job obligations or be unreliable in following through on assignments. Since the nature of the job

(continued)

demanded those qualities, those answers might have alerted the hiring manager to potential problems before offering the job.

Peg Pettingell

2. Determine and define the competencies for each level. This is done independently of current or future employees and is based on technical, functional, and special skills needed for success in the positions. We described the AMA management development competency model in Chapters 3, 4, and 5 as an example.

3. Determine the interview questions pertinent to the position and the competencies you want to assess. Once developed, questions need to be used consistently among all those people doing the interviewing.

4. Develop the rating scale(s) and criteria for differentiation in ratings. Provide all interviewers with a rating scale, definitions of what the scale means, and examples of how to use it.

5. Design the organization's interview formats. For example, you may require several telephone screening interviews and face-to-face meetings.

6. Provide training to all interviewers. This training should include role-play opportunities with feedback to ensure that participants will get more comfortable with CBBI and that similar interviews will yield similar ratings and results across the organization.

An example of typical CBBI questions illustrates the value of the process. If you are seeking to hire a new manager who is action oriented, you might ask each candidate to tell you about a time she willingly took on additional work even though her current workload was heavy and how she got the job done. Or you could ask her to describe a time when others were not acting quickly enough on a critical task and she took the lead to accomplish it. The answers to either of these questions provide insight into the candidate's actual behavior. You can probe further if you need to. You then develop similar questions for the other important competencies in the position you want to fill. By the end of the interview you will have a good idea of whether the candidate does or does not possess the specific competencies you desire. By keeping a rating sheet based on the answers, you can more accurately compare candidates after all have been interviewed.

This method of interviewing can help determine both innate competencies and performance capabilities. Stories and examples of how a candidate performed in the past give valuable insight into personal values and how he or she would handle a similar situation in your organization in the future. As you listen to the candidates' descriptions, you will learn about their character and their values, as well as their performance abilities.

CBBI takes a substantial amount of time to develop and implement, but it ensures the gathering of systematic and objective performance data on the competencies you seek, resulting in a fair and accurate assessment of the competencies you want in a particular position. It increases the likelihood of hiring, or promoting, the candidate who is the best fit for both the position and the organization.

Using Tests/Certifications

In some positions, tests or certifications provide data about a candidate's abilities. This is particularly valuable in technical areas or areas where you may have limited personal experience (see "The Cisco Certified Internetworking Expert (CCIE) Certification"). A caution: Be aware that some commercial training programs train their students to pass the certification test and that achieving the certification does not automatically equate to the ability to do the job. You need to scrutinize the pass rates. With higher pass rates, the certifying company looks more successful; with higher failure rates, the company may look more rigorous. Ask questions of others in your field, or in the industry, to determine how the testing or certifying company is viewed in terms of reliability. If you use certification and testing, you need to be sure the instruments are valid and reliable and accurately reflect performance on the job.

Knowing these potential problems, you may also want to devise some hands-on way of assessing desired skills and competencies in the interview process, perhaps asking for a demonstration of a particular process or procedure or providing a problem situation for candidates to resolve. One example of this is how AMA hires its seminar faculty.

THE CISCO CERTIFIED INTERNETWORKING EXPERT (CCIE) CERTIFICATION

The Cisco Certified Internetworking Expert (CCIE) certification holds a unique place among technical certifications. While most technical certifications require only that the candidate pass a written exam, the CCIE certification requires not only a written examination, but also a hands-on lab examination that takes place at a Cisco facility. Candidates for the CCIE must demonstrate not only proficiency in designing Cisco networks, but more important, the ability to troubleshoot network problems.

In speaking with people who have taken the CCIE exam, they say that the focus is more on problem-solving techniques and speed—if you don't know the technology and how to solve relevant technical problems well enough, you will never be able to complete the full array of exercises in the allotted time. In fact, Cisco examiners generally say that they can tell, by watching the candidate work for the first hour of the exam day, whether a candidate will be able to pass the hands-on exam.

There are few parallels in the world of management education and training—we do not require people to prove their capabilities before being given a management position (a fact often pointed out by technical professionals who must prove their technical merit before being promoted on a technical career ladder).

Many people complete AMA's online application to join our faculty. They cite experience and certificates or degrees in business or training, as well as expertise in a particular subject area. Promising candidates are interviewed by phone, and then must make a face-to-face presentation to product portfolio and faculty management staff before they are "cleared" to represent the organization. AMA staff assesses the candidate's subject matter expertise and actual facilitation skills in presenting material and conducting discussions. Even if candidates have previously conducted seminars, they may not meet the rigorous

AMA standards of competence. In fact, only 10 percent of applicants meet the standards for AMA faculty positions. You could set up similar situations to test certain competencies for the positions you are filling, relating it directly to the work applicants will perform for your organization.

Promoting from Within

Most organizations find it desirable to promote their current employees to fill management openings whenever possible. It is an especially smart move now, as the competition for talent increases in a shrinking labor force. Promoting from within can decrease hiring and training costs while sending positive messages to employees. It demonstrates to employees that they can achieve goals and advance without having to change companies. It saves managers' time as it eliminates external screening and interviewing time, and it raises the company's image by offering better employment security than is usual in today's work environment. According to a 2003 study conducted by the Mellon Financial Corporation, promoting from within saves considerable time and expense as external hires take up to twice as long to reach full productivity.[3]

How can you effectively blend bringing in new talent and promoting employees from within? Some think the 80/20 rule is one to follow: 80 percent promoting from within and 20 percent hiring outside the organization. This provides good continuity and keeps promises to employees, while providing some freshness and new ideas.

Using the same rigorous screening process for internal and external candidates yields excellent internal candidates and ensures a fair and accurate assessment of abilities. An added benefit, internally, is your ability to check any stories and examples a candidate provides with other staff throughout the organization. This helps you objectify the process so that internal and external candidates have an equal chance to present their capabilities.

To ensure that the company favorite, or the employee with the longest tenure, is not the automatic hire, have the job description and competency list ready ahead of the job posting. If you discover that a candidate's skills are close, but not exactly what meets the requirements, consider training to fill the gap. That word will spread and other employees will take notice and realize the company's interest in helping its employees progress.

There are two common traps that you must avoid when promoting internal candidates. The first is the argument against an internal candidate because "he never did it before." In this case, you may not seriously consider internal candidates because they have never demonstrated one or more competencies desired for the new position. In fact, they may have the desired talent, but have never been called upon to use it in their current role. Most people tend to judge internal candidates more harshly than external applicants. The second trap is the "entitlement trap," where we may promote an internal candidate without setting clear expectations that are "owned" by the employee, i.e., what she needs to work on to "earn" the position after it is given to her.

Conducting the Interview

A thorough interview takes a minimum of 45 minutes. Keep notetaking materials on hand so you won't have to rely on your memory alone to track responses. Stick to your interview plan and ask the questions you designed, so that all candidates have an equal opportunity to be rated fairly. Study the resume, cover letter, and other assembled documents ahead of time to save time during the first half of the interview. Be sure you know the questions you cannot legally ask.

Resist your initial gut feeling and have faith in the process you put in place. Most of us like to hire people like ourselves, but good teams need a diversity of people and styles to function effectively. Keep in mind the competencies you have attached to the job requirements and focus your questions to measure those competencies. Ask the same questions of all candidates and use your rating scale to evaluate their answers.

Some companies also like to throw a "curve ball" in the interview—something abstract with no right or wrong answer—to shed light on a candidate's reasoning power, outlook, and comfort in negotiating ambiguity, competencies that you may deem important, but which are generally difficult to measure. Scott Pitasky, general manager of recruiting for Microsoft, explains that you want people who think differently from each other or you end up with a group of talented people who always come up with the same answer. One of Microsoft's questions of choice is "Why are manhole covers round?"[4] How a candidate responds to such a question reveals clues about creativity and thinking style.

Avoiding Common Mistakes

Thorough and adequate preparation can prevent some mistakes commonly made in the interviewing process:

- Talking too much: Give an abbreviated description of the company background and your job, and focus on getting the candidate to do most of the talking as he answers your open-ended questions. Remember that silence is uncomfortable; candidates will often reveal more if you are not too quick to fill the silence with another question or comment.

- Asking leading questions: Take care not to telegraph the answer you're looking for–e.g., asking a question like "You do create slides in PowerPoint®, don't you?"

- Being afraid to ask tough questions: Ask all candidates the same questions regardless of whether you think they will be comfortable answering them.

- Not giving adequate time: Take the time for a fair evaluation of each candidate, even when you are tempted to cut it short. Sometimes a nervous candidate doesn't come across well at first, but relaxes and reveals more competence as the interview progresses.

- Rating candidates against each other: Use your objective criteria and rating scale, not your feelings. A mediocre candidate can look like a superstar if he follows a weak candidate.

Hiring the right person for each job is the foundation of a successful business. The selection process is critical, whether you are hiring from the outside or promoting from within. It is also hard work. Success is more likely when you base it on a well-thought-out competency model, employ a definitive process with a common rating scale, and train your interviewers to be skilled and consistent in conducting effective interviews.

Creating a Leadership/Management Pipeline

Future needs of the organization are another issue of concern. The speed of change in business today makes it hard to predict exactly when succession shifts will occur. How can you ensure that leadership and management positions will be filled with the right people having the right skills at the right time? Growing your own talent is one way to ensure effective future leadership. The current predictions of a future talent shortage, due to generational changes in the workforce, make this approach an important part of your overall staffing strategy.

The Leadership Pipeline, by Ram Charan, Stephen Drotter, and James Noel, presents an excellent blueprint to accomplish this.[5] The book describes six critical career passages (see Figure 6.1) representing changes in organizational positions: manage self, manage others, manage managers, manage a function, manage a business, manage a group, and manage an enterprise. Creating an effective leadership pipeline ensures that your organization will have an adequate supply of high-quality candidates for both present and future leadership positions.

Charan and his co-authors explain that each passage in the pipeline requires individuals to shift their mindset and acquire new ways of managing and leading, leaving their old ways behind. The three areas of change for each passage are:

- Skill requirements: New capabilities required to execute new responsibilities.
- Time applications: New timeframes that govern how they work.
- Work values: What they believe is important, i.e., the focus of their effort.

In using this approach, your responsibility is to adjust the pipeline to meet the reality of your organization. Your challenge then becomes making sure that people in leadership positions are at the appropriate level for their skills, time applications, and values, and helping people begin to develop the appropriate skills, time applications, and values for promotion to the next level, so they are ready when you need them. Building this type of pipeline requires a specified process and a commitment to effectively manage it.

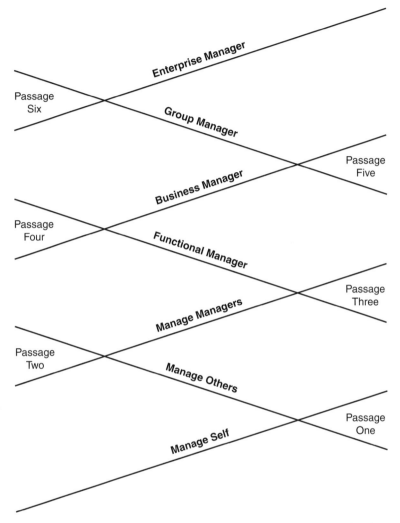

Passage
Six

Enterprise Manager

Group Manager

Passage
Five

Business Manager

Passage
Four

Functional Manager

Passage
Three

Manage Managers

Passage
Two

Manage Others

Passage
One

Manage Self

FIGURE 6.1   Critical Career Passages in a Large Business Organization

The methods presented in the book are designed to help you diagnose your current and future pipeline problems, create development plans, and manage performance with tools and techniques for coaching leaders, while dealing with succession issues, preventing leadership failures, and maintaining the flow in your pipeline. Adapting this method to your organization's specific needs can help enhance performance at all levels of management. Integrating your competency model and the pipeline provides an overall framework for people to determine what skills, time applications, and values they need to develop to be eligible for promotion to the next level in the organization. The competency model helps pinpoint skills to work on. The total framework becomes a tool for self-assessment of specific development needs, and the framework can easily fold into your overall organizational performance management and development process.

Summary

Selecting people with the right competencies for the job you need done is critical in today's business environment. An integrated approach to staffing includes an overall staffing strategy with provisions of how much external hiring versus internal promotion is desirable, a competency model that defines the skills your organization values, and an effective leadership pipeline plan with appropriate maintenance methods identified.

Your next concerns center around providing the training and opportunities for learning that will continue to help people develop within the organization to meet changing business needs. The next few chapters focus on these issues.

Developing Employees

The war for talent is heating up. Labor force forecasts predict more jobs than employees by 2008 and beyond. This war will not be a minor skirmish; in fact, Jay Jamrog of the Institute for Corporate Productivity calls current talent conditions a "Perfect Storm" that will make retention and engagement a key issue for organizational leadership in the future.[1]

Jamrog's research says skilled, educated workers are at peak productivity from age 35 to 54 and predicts the number of workers in that age category will decrease by 15 percent while demand will increase by 25 percent in a few short years. The shortage will hit the fields of management and high-tech the hardest.[2] What can your organization do now to manage the situation? You need ways to increase retention. The best way to do that is to build an environment that fosters retention and engagement in your organization. One great strategy is to encourage self-directed learning; another is to provide training for employees.

Employees want to increase their marketable skills. And research is finding that the more training they get, the more likely the employer will retain them. They stay when they feel the organization is investing in them. Let's take a more in-depth look at how you can encourage self-directed learning and provide appropriate learning opportunities so that employees can grow to meet their own personal goals and the organization's skill and knowledge requirements.

Encouraging Self-Directed Learning

We learn our way through life. We learn to walk and talk, to play with others, to love, to live compatibly with others, and to earn a living through our work. Through it all we are self-directed learners; we choose what we learn, even when we have no choice in what is being taught.

In the workforce, employees often learn by observing, such as when an employee watches a manager handle a situation and decides whether, given the opportunity, he or she would handle that situation similarly or differently. Some employees have been known to say they learned more from poor managers than from good ones—the good ones make it look easy, but when they observe a poor manager do something egregious to an employee, they think, "When I'm a manager, I'll never do that do my people!"

As Dan Tobin explained in his book of the same title, all learning is self-directed.[3] And self-directed learning is a powerful tool in the workplace. When employees take responsibility for their own learning, they improve their knowledge, competencies, and skills to do their work more effectively and to prepare for advancement. To be successful, though, they need some help and support from the organization and from their managers, coaches, or mentors. They need the organization's leaders to establish a positive learning environment where learning is nurtured and valued. They need advice and assistance from managers who are themselves committed to learning and from the training organization, as well as access to tools to enable the process.

The new generation of workers, known as the Millennials, comes to the workforce with a predisposition to self-directed learning. Their familiarity with, and extensive use of, technology in every facet of their lives has given them confidence in seeking answers. When they have a question, they "poke around" the Internet, googling the topic, asking people in chat rooms and discussion forums, and connecting with others who might have some answers. These are very independent learners.

Workers in all generations can benefit from, and become adept at, some self-directed learning. For organizations to harness an employee's natural curiosity and ability to find information, you need to provide supplemental tools, advice, and guides to independent learning. You need to provide a framework or model of what needs to be learned to align with the goals of the organization—what needs to be mastered, when, and why. For example, Dow Chemical created detailed competency models for all jobs so that employees could easily see what they needed to learn for whatever job they aspired to. You also need to assist learners in identifying what learning is done best independently, and what learning is best acquired in other ways.

Four Learning Types

Not all learning can or should be done independently. Tobin identifies four possible categories of learning types (see Table 7.1[4]):

- Dependent self-directed learning
- Dependent other-directed learning
- Independent other-directed learning
- Independent self-directed learning

Quadrant I, dependent self-directed learning, is when the employee decides what to learn. The employee is dependent on others to provide the methods, materials, and schedule for learning. For example, an organization might provide a catalog of training programs or a library of

TABLE 7.1 Four Types of Learning		
	Other-Directed	*Self-Directed*
Independent	**Quadrant III** Learning topics, methods, and materials selected by the company. Employee may have some choice as to method and schedule, but must prove mastery of the learning content.	**Quadrant IV** Learning topics, methods, materials, and schedule selected by the employee. Employee is solely responsible for what is learned.
Dependent	**Quadrant II** Learning topics, methods, materials, and schedule selected by the company, which also provides instruction. Employee is tested at end of program to prove mastery of the learning content.	**Quadrant I** Learning topics selected by the employee, but the employee is dependent on the company or another source for determining learning methods, materials, and schedules.

self-study materials. The employee determines the need for learning, but relies on the organization to determine the content.

Quadrant II, dependent other-directed learning, is when the organization mandates the learning and predetermines the requirements and the methods, materials, and schedule. This category often reflects topics demanded for legal compliance or safety regulations. Employees have no choice in the training. For example, large corporations often mandate management training for newly appointed managers; the training presents "the company way" of managing the function and employees. In many technical companies, where many employees have earned Ph.D.s in their field, most of those doctoral programs included no instruction on managing a business or leading people. Companies need to fill that gap.

Quadrant III, other-directed independent learning, is when the company determines what must be learned but leaves the method selection up to the employee. For example, when an organization introduces a new phone system, there is no choice for employees–they must learn to use it. The organization might offer training, but attendance is not mandatory, and other resources might be available, such as a printed brochure or a computer-based introductory training session.

Quadrant IV, self-directed independent learning, is when employees determine what they want to learn and how they will learn it. For example, in accepting a new project, an employee might recognize the need to learn how to create spreadsheets to monitor finances. The employee seeks out the information and the preferred resources, sets the schedule, and proceeds to complete the learning and apply it to the project at hand. His or her boss may be unaware of the employee's learning plan, being concerned only with the employee's job performance as evidenced in the overall project management.

According to Tobin, choosing the right category of learning can be done by asking two questions:

- *Is there a clear reason why all company employees, or a specific subset of employees, must master a new set of skills or body of knowledge?* A clear mandate puts learning into the other-directed (or company-directed) category as represented in Quadrants II and III. Lacking a clear mandate, employees can be made aware of the need, but decide for themselves whether to pursue the learning.

- *Is there a clear reason why the company should provide specific training to employees for these skills or body of knowledge?* There may be mandatory or regulatory reasons for a company to provide training or a contractual requirement with a client. Faced with needing to train a large number of employees, an organization might create its own training program as the most cost-effective measure.

Flexibility is the key. Allowing employees to have some choice in their learning needs, methods, and schedules, while ensuring the organization's business needs are met, is generally the best choice.

A Positive Learning Environment

"A positive learning environment (PLE) encourages, even demands, that every employee at every level be in a continuous learning mode, constantly searching for new ideas, trying new methods, sharing ideas and learning with others, and learning from others, to find new and better ways to achieve individual, group, and organizational business goals."[5]

Real learning comes when employees apply new ideas to their work, discovering what works and what doesn't. More learning occurs when they share their results with other employees and/or learn something new from the others to help them achieve better individual, group, and organizational results.

If an organization lacks a positive learning environment, employees are not encouraged, nor will they seek opportunities to learn, to use their knowledge on the job or to share with others. They will use their learning energy elsewhere or look for another job.

A positive learning environment is a powerful attraction for young professionals. They want to learn and progress in an organization and in their careers. They look for organizations that foster and encourage that learning. They like working for managers who take an interest in helping them learn and who are themselves learners. Everyone benefits from the constant sharing that occurs in such an environment.

Some examples of company policies that support a positive learning environment include tuition assistance plans, company-paid professional memberships and conference attendance, corporate membership at university libraries, and sponsorship of employees to write papers for publication and to present at professional conferences.

Learning Responsibility

In a classic book in the adult learning literature, Malcolm Knowles stated, "Every act of teaching should have built into it some provision for helping the learner become more self-directing. . . . I don't think it is healthy—or even humane—for a person to be kept permanently dependent upon a system or upon another person."[6]

How can you foster that responsibility in learners? You can help them identify their own needs, define a learning plan, find and access learning resources, and find ways to apply their learning to their work.

Your first challenge is helping employees understand the goals of the business, so they can plan their learning to help the organization and themselves reach their goals. This can start with new hire training and be constantly reinforced through company-wide newsletters, as well as sharing press releases, annual reports, and news bulletins with everyone in the organization. Leaders and managers need to reinforce everyone's contribution to the overall organization in their staff meetings and in performance reviews.

Your next challenge is helping employees recognize their current competencies and what competencies they need to learn or improve. Your organization's competency model explains competencies desired or required for each job and level of the organization. It tells an employee what the organization sees as important and provides a blueprint for skills and abilities to be developed for promotion. Employees can use that as a starting point to identify the knowledge and skills they want to learn to advance on their desired career path. Managers can be trained in how to help people assess where they are and what they need to learn as part of the organization's performance management system, as well as how to coach employees in their learning process.

Most people think they know what they are good at. And most are probably wrong. Helping people identify their strengths, so they can build on them, is an important part of supporting self-directed learning, and an important role you play in this process as will be discussed further in Chapter 9.

Peter Drucker proposed a three-pronged approach to identifying strengths.[7]

1. Do feedback analysis. When you make a decision or do something, write down what you expect to happen. Several months later compare the actual results with your expectations. Over time, this will show you where your strengths lie and where you are not competent.

2. Concentrate on your strengths. Work to improve them and look at where you need to improve or acquire new skills or fill a gap in your knowledge.

3. Discover where your intellectual arrogance is causing ignorance and overcome it. Recognize there are skills and areas of knowledge that would enhance your strengths. For example, if your feedback analysis shows that you continually fail in projects because people don't cooperate with you, perhaps improving your interpersonal skills will provide the help you need.

Once employees identify what they want to learn, you can provide learning resources. Some companies have learning guides that employees use to determine methods for a wide variety of learning needs. The guides give pointers for relevant books, articles, websites, and courses, as well as suggestions for assistance within the company from managers and peers in applying learning to the job. Employees can be paired with other employees who excel in the area of learning and get coaching from that person. Other resources might include knowledge management systems that direct employees to sources of information within the company or online.

Learning Contracts

An important part of promoting self-directed learning is encouraging the development and use of learning contracts. Learning contracts help employees organize their learning more efficiently, encourage them to be creative in developing their strategies and finding resources, and force them to provide better evidence of their accomplishments. Contracts can be simple, stated as what I want to learn, what information I need to look for, what sources I will use, how can I efficiently collect the information from the sources, how will I organize and analyze what I find, how can I report my findings, and how I intend to use the learning on the job for the benefit of me, my group, or the organization. Or they can be more elaborate, detailing the learning needs, the learning plan, how the learning will be applied to work either in an individual case, in the team, or in the organization, and how results will be measured. Plans are more likely to be followed if they are written out and shared with a manager. A sample learning contract for an employee is shown in Chapter 9.

Managers need training, since coaching and teaching employees how to learn may be a new role for them. They, too, can benefit from a learning contract–perhaps at a greater level of detail than the employee's. An example might look like Table 7.2, Sample Manager's Learning Contract.

TABLE 7.2   Sample Manager's Learning Contract[8]

Part 1: Define Learning Needs

1. The company's stated goal is to develop the use of self-directed learning by employees at all levels to reduce the cost of training and to help the company reach its stated business goals.
2. Write one goal for yourself that reflects what you need to do to support this corporate goal.
3. What specific behavior(s) do you need to adopt (or change) to meet these personal goals?
4. What new knowledge or skills do you need to acquire to enable you to meet these personal goals?

Part II: Develop a Learning Plan

5. What learning resources are available to you or can you find to help you acquire the knowledge and skills specified above?
6. What learning methods will you use?
7. Develop a schedule for the specified learning activities: "I will complete which activity by which date?"
8. How will I measure my learning?

Part III: Apply Learning to Work and Measure Results

9. How will you apply the learning to your job?
10. How will you know whether you have met your personal learning goals and whether these have helped the company achieve its stated goal in reducing training costs and enabling employees to help the company achieve its business goals?

For self-directed learning to succeed, it must be part of an organization's culture. Every employee can benefit from self-directed learning, but employees need coaching from their managers, and managers need coaching from their managers. A continuing emphasis on self-directed learning creates an environment focused on continuing learning, growth, and change.

Providing Training

Employees view training as a sign that the organization values them and their future in the organization. It is a perk that keeps on giving–training provides knowledge and skills that employees benefit from in their present job and take with them wherever they go in the future. Training upgrades personal skills for better immediate job performance and helps employees learn of new developments in a field. This is particularly valuable when employees have been out of formal schooling for some time.

From your organizational viewpoint, training is a way for you to improve staff skills and avoid the additional costs that come with having to hire new people to find those skills. In the current job market, training is a differentiator for attracting Generation Xers and the new Millennials, because they put a high value on training and seek employers who offer training. These younger generations are very self-confident learners and performers; they expect the organization to provide avenues for their self-improvement.

Training is also a way for you to fill the skill gaps that the baby boomers will leave when they retire, taking their management skills with them. Recent research by Personnel Decisions International (PDI) shows that companies will face a substantial loss in managerial knowledge as the boomers begin to retire in the next ten years.[9] In the PDI research, when boomers and Generation Xers were compared, baby boomers were more likely to be rated highly by their managers in ten out of eighteen competencies, were more likely to be rated as "knowing the business," and were rated substantially better in their ability to coach and develop others. On the other hand, Generation X managers were more likely to rate higher in self-development and in analyzing issues than their older counterparts. Many of the performance or knowledge gaps that Generation Xers have can be filled through training.

Training is flexible. You can find it being offered in many locations at many different times during the year, and it comes in a variety of forms. The training you recommend or select for a particular employee depends on the type of training needed, the urgency of the need, personal learning preferences, and the investments of time and money that are considered reasonable by the manager. Self-directed learning and some of the ways individuals learn on their own were addressed earlier. Those techniques can be effective for acquiring information and in learning processes or procedures. When it comes to interpersonal skills, practice is required for real learning and behavior change to take place, and that happens only when people interact, preferably face-to-face in a group setting. An added benefit of the group experience in traditional classroom-based training is the breadth of perspectives participants are exposed to.

The question of whether to sponsor the learning internally or externally needs to be thought through. Indeed, there are advantages and disadvantages to both (see Table 7.3). You want to weigh your decisions

TABLE 7.3   Internal Versus External Training

	Advantages	*Disadvantages*
Internal Training	• Company-specific content • Contacts within the organization • Less expense per person • Less time away from job • Immediate application of learning can be monitored • Flexible scheduling • Taught by organization staff	• No opportunity to learn how other organizations operate • No contacts or networking outside the organization • Content limited to what is known internally • Participants may be reluctant to admit weaknesses or errors
External Training	• New perspectives and content • Anonymity when developing basic or deficient skills • Networking opportunities with people in other organizations • More frequent offerings to choose from • Instructors who are expert in their fields	• General content and examples may not apply to your industry or situation • Often more costly • Schedule set by others • Time lost from job

carefully by asking several questions. Are there large numbers of employees needing the training? Can you provide it on a schedule to meet the business demand? Is the content important to, or particular to, internal operations here in the organization? Would it be better for employees to learn with other employees, or would they benefit from exposure to the way other organizations do things? Would it be appropriate for employees at different levels of the organization to be in the same learning cohort?

Let's take a closer look at group learning opportunities.

Group Learning Opportunities

Electronic Training

E-Learning was discussed earlier as an individual pursuit, but it can also be a group training experience, with interaction and practice built in. Online courses come in a variety of formats; some involve a cohort of individuals who study, discuss, and submit assignments on a schedule determined by the instructor, much like a bricks-and-mortar university class without all participants being face-to-face or in the same location. It can be done synchronously (with everyone participating at the same time) or asynchronously (with people accessing learning resources at different times).

- **University model courses** may or may not be degree-related. Some "virtual universities" provide extensive degree programs online, with scheduled "classes" (synchronous) and discussion groups supported by individual work submitted to the instructor for feedback. If classes are held synchronously, they may be recorded so that if someone cannot attend, they can review the class at a later time. Each class may last 1 to 1½ hours, with discussion boards or chat rooms for follow-up conversations and sharing of information. Assignments get e-mailed to the instructor, and grades are issued. Some courses encourage practice of skills through online conversations, simulations, or follow-up work between student partners. If a course is part of a degree program, the provider specifies the progression of required and elective courses toward a degree. However, many online colleges allow individuals to take a course without enrolling in a formal degree program as well as providing noncredit courses.

- **Webinars** are offered by various training companies and professional associations. Webinars usually focus on a single subject of interest, with one or more perspectives and/or topics presented and some limited discussion time following the formal presentation or lecture. Webinars typically last about an hour and include some polling of audience interest or knowledge and limited discussion among participants. They sometimes allow the opportunity for participants to submit questions, but they are primarily one-way communication vehicles. When presented as a series, they may incorporate "homework assignments" between meetings. Webinars can be effective for training on specific topics, particularly in fields where knowledge or perspectives are constantly changing. For example, a webinar may be used to update users on the latest version of a software product, to update accountants on the latest changes in tax laws, or introduce a new therapy method to physicians. They are typically not offered for college credit, but may be used to fulfill the continuing education requirements as set by various certification agencies.

- **Company-specific web-training courses** are often offered via electronic media because of ready availability, relatively inexpensive cost, and worldwide reach. When she was with Accenture, Peg Pettingell conducted some communication skills training courses, enabling people around the globe to come together to learn about the topic, with interaction via both voice and keyboard to ask questions, clarify points, and add comments and stories to the discussion. Practice of the skills was accomplished during "breaks" when individuals in the same location had assignments–an opportunity to interact and provide feedback. This method can be effective for some topics, but class sizes need to be kept to reasonable numbers for each class to maximize the possible interaction and discussion. Multiple sessions can be scheduled, with individual or small group assignments between meetings. People typically require initial instruction on how to use the system effectively and some technical support to ensure smooth sailing during the broadcast.

- **Discussion groups and online communities** present opportunities to learn about topics in a field of interest and are considered training when they provide more than just conversational exchange. Some professional associations maintain bulletin boards and discussion groups where members can post questions and receive referrals to good sources of information or advice from an expert, or someone who has "been there." Communities for ongoing conversation around particular topics of interest are constantly being formed. These communities are a resource and depository for in-depth information on certain topics. They can be a rich source of learning for your employees when they offer open discussions of a topic. Sometimes these include regularly scheduled panel discussions, with questions from the field, and additional sources for follow-up on the topic. Of course, the danger of unmonitored public discussion boards is that the answers provided have not been validated, so people take risks when using advice from people whose credentials or authority they have no way of checking.

- **Webcasts** offer a quick and easy vehicle for keeping people up to date on the latest information or thinking around a particular topic. They are a great vehicle for quickly updating your learning or being introduced to a new topic with minimal investment of time out of the workday. For example, recent AMA webcasts focused on the topics of internal consulting skills for the HR professional, storytelling as a leadership tool, the challenges of becoming a great leader, and the use of the MBTI instrument in the workplace. None lasted more than 45 minutes, and hundreds of people tuned in to learn the latest thinking from experts in their respective fields.

Instructor-Led Classroom-Based Training

Most organizations offer some instructor-led, classroom-based training of employees. Whether it is new hire training, training on current and new equipment or procedures, or formal instruction on a particular topic, face-to-face training helps employees do their jobs better. While online training can allow participants to get their questions answered immediately, most people prefer to ask questions face to face in a reasonably sized group where they have the opportunity to quiz the instructor and other participants. Many large organizations even operate corporate universities where they offer courses in a variety of business topics, such as management, communication, business acumen, and finance. Many of those courses are instructor-led seminars and workshops and may or may not include online support or follow-up.

Instructor-led classroom-based training offers benefits other training avenues lack. Communication is at its best when people have the combination of verbal, vocal, and visual cues to read and use in expressing their thoughts and ideas. The personal interaction of faculty and students establishes an environment for questioning, group problem solving, teamwork, practice of new skills with feedback on performance, peer-to-peer exchange and dialog, and informal networking. Training in interpersonal skills requires practice with another person; only through practice can employees develop the confidence and ability to use those skills on the job. When conversing with another person, individuals can take the necessary time to reflect and respond, hear their own opinions stated aloud, and see if they are understood when their thoughts are reflected back from another person. So much of the work in organizations requires individuals to work with others; face-to-face training provides a laboratory to learn and practice those interpersonal skills for getting the job done with minimal conflict and disruption. It also provides the opportunity to develop skills for handling situations that will occur in the next promotion level in the leadership pipeline.

There are many options for instructor-led classroom-based learning:

- **Internal training courses** offer an opportunity to learn the organization's preferred way of handling things, e.g., sales training presents its view of customers, its method of negotiating, or the organization's preferred problem-resolution tactics. Customer service training reflects a company's customer philosophy and treatment preferences. The company's preferred coaching model can be taught to all managers. Instructors can be dedicated trainers, company technical experts, or managers from within the organization. Using managers to conduct all of parts of internal training programs reinforces the importance of the topics being taught and demonstrate the importance and value placed on learning within the company. The content of this training can be developed within the company or can be provided by other training providers, such as AMA, or can be licensed from those training providers and taught by company trainers.

- **External training courses.** There are hundreds of training organizations, such as AMA, that offer face-to-face public seminars and have the capacity to customize them to your organization's particular needs. Most have catalogs or online listings and schedules offering courses in various locations multiple times over the course of a year. Some list courses by competencies, so you can match your employees' needs to the competencies the seminar addresses. All provide options for you in helping your employees get the training they need to either perform their current job or progress in their abilities and skills, so they can better succeed in their current jobs and be prepared for promotion to the next level. One of the benefits of sending employees to a public program is that they are exposed to people and ideas from other organizations. External programs can also be beneficial when your organization wants to provide training on a basic skill to a senior employee to address a competency deficit because it gives the employee some level of confidentiality (rather than having him attend an internal training program with other more junior employees).

- **Conferences.** Professional groups continuously research the "hot" and emerging topics of interest in a particular field and seek out experts to present information to their members at their annual conferences. They take great pride in being on the cutting-edge of the thinking in their respective fields. These conferences offer valuable training to attendees, in large sessions with nationally known speakers, and in small seminar-type presentations on other topics. As you look for training for future managers, check the conferences that pertain to their field of interest as an avenue for training. Additional benefits are that attendees meet other people in the same industry for networking opportunities, learn what competitors are up to, and learn of new resources they can call on to search out solutions to their problems.

- **Professional group meetings.** Many professional groups have local or regional chapters that meet periodically to hear expert perspectives on a topic particular to, or related to, their field. Usually meetings last just a few hours, but can be a rich experience with presentations by experts and questions from the practitioners present. Often the question-and-answer sessions are the better opportunity for learning, as questions tend to be very practical and real-world focused.

Future Training

The training literature is beginning to focus on concerns about meeting the needs of the Millennial Generation. This is the first generation to grow up with our advanced technology–they take it for granted. It is so much a part of their life, they don't consider it anything but a way they communicate. They are constantly plugged in and multitasking. They are easily bored if their learning is not specific to their perceived needs or if it is not paced quickly enough. In their world, when they seek an answer, they go online and find it. They share what they learn with friends, and they help friends search for information through blogs, chat rooms, wikis, and online messaging.

The training industry can expect new challenges from Millennials. They won't be content with day-long sessions of knowledge transfer, or even with video games or online courses or exercises to enliven the learning. You will need new learning models that blend and manage the many elements of knowledge transfer: face-to-face group interaction, accessibility of information online, the ease with which workers communicate directly, and the setting up and monitoring of procedures and processes to ensure these "fearless information seekers" are always up to date.

Recently, some managers said they found 20- and 30-somethings difficult to work with because they have all the answers and know how to do everything–right or wrong, effective or ineffective. You need to realize that as this generation matures into their 40s and beyond, they will realize that things are not always what they seem, that much of work takes a lot of listening and understanding of specific situations and different worker's perspectives. The key to their success will be staying open to learning and challenging what they think they know. You need to devise training programs to help them acquire that knowledge and learn to deal with optional paths of action.

What can you do now to begin developing those new models? You can begin with tying their learning opportunities to specific competencies needed for success in jobs at the levels of individual professional, first-line manager/leader, manager of managers, and executives. Knowing the competencies needed, you can help managers develop learning contracts with realistic ways to help employees apply their learning to the organization's work. You can design learning to incorporate known research findings and adhere to quality specifications that will help ensure knowledge, skill and attitude change, establishing standards based on what is known about learning. An example of standards can be found in Table 7.4, The AMA Design and Development Anchors, which guide our seminar development process. Every seminar contains these components, which are known to increase the likelihood of transfer of learning back to the workplace.

TABLE 7.4   AMA Design and Development Anchors

Anchor	Description
Value Proposition	A statement of the seminar's tangible benefits; it answers the question "Why should I attend this seminar?"
Seminar Goals	Two or three statements that describe what participants will know or be able to do to add value to their own work and/or their organization.
Learning Objectives	Clear statements of what participants will be able to do after the seminar: **Key objectives:** For each module, one objective that defines the most important behavior required of the learner **Enabling objectives:** Objectives that state the skills or knowledge learners must gain to perform the key objective
Journey Map	A visual representation of the learning path that participants will follow
Action Plan	A plan for how participants will apply what they have learned back at their workplace
Blended Learning	Pre-seminar assignments, pre- and post-seminar assignments, tune-up courses, and post-seminar resources that create a more comprehensive experience for the learner and produce a greater return on investment for the employer
Exercises	Practical, applicable, and relevant learning activities
Demonstrations	Presentations that help participants apply what they are learning in a way that motivates and engages them

(continued)

TABLE 7.4 (Continued)	
Anchor	*Description*
Appropriate Models and Frameworks	Organizing structures that help participants remember, learn, and apply new information, processes, etc.
Learner-Constructed, Guided Self-Discovery	"Do-your-own" exercises that help participants apply their learning to personal work situations
Peer-to-Peer Dialogue	Opportunities for participants to discuss and learn from one another
Practice–Safe, progressively challenging, and appropriate	Activities that give participants a chance to use new tools and processes and then get detailed feedback from the instructor and other participants
Tools and Job Aids	Practical, easy reference guides to facilitate the application of learning back on the job
Expert References	Research, quotations, citations of books and articles by well-known experts or authors

Summary

More research is needed on the learning habits and styles of the future generations of workers and on how to blend technology into learning processes to assist employees in learning the communications, interpersonal, and management skills that are so critical in working with others to achieve business goals. You need to stay open to new approaches to learning and to changing your traditional view of training. In the next chapter we address some ways to provide learning beyond training.

Management Development Beyond Training

Training, whether self-directed learning, e-learning, or internal or external classroom training, is only part of the solution to developing managers at all levels of any organization. Training can help employees build their knowledge. But what you should really be concerned with in developing the management talent to drive your organization's future is the application of learning to the job–how well your employees apply what they learn, by any means, to make a positive difference in the achievement of the organization's goals. This is the Kirkpatrick Level 3 evaluation that we discussed in Chapter 1, and it calls for the organization to provide opportunities for employees to apply what they have learned and, through that application, to develop the knowledge they will need to manage the business and its employees. This approach is often called "action learning."

Action Learning

Michael Marquardt defines action learning as "a dynamic process that involves a small group of people solving real problems, while at the same time focusing on what they are learning and how their learning can benefit each group member, the group itself and the organization as a whole."[1]

Here are a few examples of group action learning projects undertaken by organizations and the competencies that might be built or strengthened through participation in each project.

- At one company, a group of individual contributors identified as having high potential for future management roles was assigned to a cross-functional task force to make recommendations on revitalizing a longstanding product whose sales had been sagging in recent years. The individual members of the task force came from marketing, sales, finance, manufacturing, and engineering. Participation on the task force enabled each member to gain knowledge about the other functions represented in the group while doing the needed market research, competitive analysis, and product planning. The competencies that were strengthened included business acumen (broadening each member's view of the company's business beyond their individual functional silos), customer focus, resource management, problem solving, and both working as a team and team leadership.

- A group of mid-level managers was selected to manage the company's United Way campaign for the year and given responsibility for enlisting employees throughout the company to donate to this charity. Competencies developed or strengthened included influencing operational and tactical planning, interpersonal savvy, creativity, and presentation skills.

- A group of engineers was assigned to train the salesforce on a new product they had developed. This allowed the engineers to gain more knowledge of the perspectives of the salesforce and the customer, forced them to improve their presentation skills, and helped them view their new product from the perspective of customer benefits rather than from their own perspective of product features and specifications.

- A group of individual contributors from one manufacturing plant was sent to another plant to learn about new methods being used there and then to plan how to introduce the new methods into their own plant. This action learning assignment helped these employees develop their own learning skills as well as their planning and training skills. They also had to learn to influence their fellow employees to get them to adopt the new methods.

- One organization set up a task force of employees to address employee retention—what was causing some employees to leave while others stayed, and what could the company do to retain its best employees? This helped the task force members develop their listening and problem-solving skills, while learning a lot more about interpersonal savvy and how to present their findings to upper management.

While Marquardt's definition of action learning includes only group projects, there are many opportunities to use action learning with an individual. Here are a few examples:

- At one company, the comptroller for its sales division was assigned to take over the responsibilities for the manufacturing division's comptroller when she went out on a short-term medical leave. This helped the sales comptroller broaden his perspective beyond the sales silo.
- A new training manager for a marketing organization was assigned to arrange the orientation of the newly hired head of the marketing group's European operations during her visit to headquarters. This gave the training manager the opportunity to meet all of the managers in the marketing group to arrange the visitor's schedule and then to learn about the work of the marketing group by accompanying the European manager to all of the arranged meetings.
- A high-potential individual contributor was assigned to put together a task group to solve a customer problem. This assignment tested her team leadership capabilities as well as helping to develop problem-solving skills, customer focus, and interpersonal skills.
- A first-level manager was sent to an external training program on a new software application with the understanding that he would be in charge of implementing the new application upon returning from the training. This helped the manager develop competency in planning, problem solving, coaching, and innovation management. (It is often said that you must develop a much deeper understanding of a subject to teach it, as contrasted with just knowing it or using it yourself.)
- An experienced individual contributor who had made it known that she wanted to be considered for a management position was asked by her manager to work with two recent college graduates newly hired into the group, orienting them, teaching them the group's

THE WRONG PERSON FOR THE JOB

This product line was twenty years old and had been a cash cow for the company, performing well year after year—until two years ago. At that time, a new competitor came into the market, and the product line manager told everyone that it was no real threat to the success of the business. But he was wrong—sales and profits had eroded steadily over the past two years, and the competitor continued to gain market share with new innovations that the company hadn't even considered. When the product line actually lost money two quarters ago, for the first time in fifteen years, the product line manager was summarily fired.

The company's leadership team looked at possible replacements for the product line manager within the company. They selected a younger marketing manager who had been with the company only a few years, but who had shown a lot of creativity and good results in another product line, to head the troubled operation. He had been such a success in his current role, certainly he could come in and save the situation.

It would be kind to say that the new person was an absolute disaster. He came into the new job already "knowing" what was wrong and started issuing orders immediately. He also summarily dismissed several key people who had real knowledge of the problems and challenges when they disagreed with his approach. Six months later, the hemorrhaging of profits continued at an accelerating pace, some of the product line's most talented employees had left (and there were rumors that many others had their resumes on the street), and the CEO had no choice but to fire this manager. The costs to the company were almost immeasurable—not only the dollars represented on the income statement, but also the loss of momentum in the marketplace, the reputation of the product line among customers, and the worsening morale of the employees within the product line.

How could this scenario (one that has occurred in many organizations) have been avoided? What if the company had a development program for employees who had been identified as having high potential for future leadership positions? And what if, through a series of low-risk action learning assignments, the company had tested this individual to see if he had "what it takes to succeed"? If the company had proceeded in this way, it might have discovered that this promotion would be a disaster before making it and saved the company many times the cost of the development program.

operating procedures, and coaching them on an ongoing basis until they proved themselves ready to work solo. This assignment helped her develop a number of her management competencies while testing her readiness to step into a management role on a full-time basis.

These are among the many types of action learning projects that can be assigned to groups or individuals.[2] There are many benefits that organizations can accrue from these types of action learning assignments:

- These types of assignments help employees apply what they have learned through self-study, formal instruction, or just plain observation of other managers in the organization and to develop their personal competence in many areas.

- Assigning people to tackle problems that would typically be assigned to higher-level managers can bring new perspectives and approaches to those problems. Experienced managers often fall back on longstanding processes and procedures and may benefit from the input of people who aren't limited in their vision by the blinders of standard company practices.

- Action learning projects can also help the organization test employees' competence *before* promoting them. Most organizations have had more than one disaster arise from assigning the wrong person to an open management position, as described in "The Wrong Person for the Job."

- Action learning assignments can also test whether employees are willing to stretch themselves beyond their current assignments in order to contribute to the company's and their own success (see "Who Will Follow Through?").

WHO WILL FOLLOW THROUGH?

A software company created a two-year leadership development program for a group of mid-level managers who had been identified as having high potential for future leadership roles in the company. A primary feature of this program was the assignment of participants to action learning teams that were given developmental assignments to complete between each of the program's quarterly educational sessions. At the start of each quarterly session, each team presented its project to a panel of senior company executives, talking about both what they accomplished and what they had learned through the projects.

At one of these sessions, one team proudly presented its project and then challenged the executive team, saying: "Now that we've proven the concept of the new approach, what are YOU going to do to make certain that our project is disseminated throughout the company? We've worked very hard on this project and put in many extra hours over the past three months, and we want to be sure that YOU are going to do something to ensure that our efforts aren't wasted."

A second team presented its separate project, one that was equally as exciting as the first team's and produced equally impressive results. At the end of its presentation, the second team told the executive panel: "We believe that what we have accomplished on a small scale with this action learning project can benefit the company by broader implementation. So, we have already started to involve people from other business units and from other geographies, describing our efforts to them and our results— and we have found a lot of interest throughout the company. Therefore, we think that many other groups can use our project as a prototype for their own efforts. We have already told them that our team members will be happy to consult with them and advise them on any implementation issues that may arise."

Both teams had done a fine job with their assigned projects and had proven their competence in attaining the goals set for their respective projects. But the first team felt no responsibility for its work beyond completing the assignment, while the second team had already planned how to propagate its results on a larger scale throughout the company. To which team do you think the executive team will look for future company leaders?

Being Coached

You can find dozens of different coaching models, each claiming to hold the secret to success. In fact, if you search Amazon.com's book listings using the word coaching, you will find more than 45,000 listings! There are also many different organizations that offer training on coaching skills and at least a dozen different organizations that offer coaching certifications. We will not offer a different coaching model here, for the many different models that exist are basically the same. They focus on providing the coaching client (or coachee) an opportunity to self-discover solutions, eliciting solutions and strategies from the coachee, rather than imposing them, and holding the coachee responsible and accountable for execution. The International Coach Federation defines the coaching process as one that helps clients "deepen their learning, improve their performance, and enhance their quality of life."[3]

Some try to distinguish among various purposes for coaching, e.g., to deal with a problem employee, to improve a good employee's performance, or to help an employee apply what he has learned in the classroom, but the basic concepts remain the same in each situation. In terms of management development, we will focus here on helping new managers, at all levels, learn and improve their management competencies as defined by the AMA competency model.

If you recall the four-stage learning model presented in Chapter 1, knowledge is developed by applying information to one's work. The fact is that a lot of information garnered in the learning process, whether through instructor-led training, e-learning, or other self-study methods, never gets applied to people's work. Too often, people fall back on old ways of working rather than risk trying something new: "The new method I learned sounds great, but I've never used it in the real world, and while the new method promises a better result, I feel safer using the method I know–the old way may not be as good, but I am comfortable with it and I know it works." This is one of the longstanding objections to e-learning—once the employee returns to work and tries the new method she learned, there is nobody there to answer questions if something doesn't work as planned.

Coaching by one's manager is an effective way of handling this type of conundrum. This is why the learning contract described in Chapter 1 requires that the employee and manager discuss, both before and after learning takes place, how the employee will apply her learning on the job and what assistance the employee will need from the manager to support that application. This is a form of coaching built into the learning contract.

Another application of coaching to develop managers deals with helping the new manager, at all levels, learn to trust his or her instincts. Very often, a newly promoted manager instinctively knows the right thing to do, but is hesitant to follow those instincts for fear of failure. Coaching of the new manager can help to elicit those solutions and reinforce the strategies that the new manager has developed but is wary of trying.

As valuable as coaching can be in developing managers at all levels, it is neither the only nor the correct approach in all situations. There are times when a manager must *tell* an employee what to do and other times when the manager must *teach* the employee what to do. For example, when there is an emergency situation that requires immediate action, the manager may not have the time to help the employee find the right solution—the critical nature of the situation may require that the manager impose a solution. In other cases, when the manager knows that the employee doesn't have the necessary knowledge or skills, the manager may choose to teach the employee how to solve a problem so that the employee can solve similar problems in the future without relying on his manager's input. For example, a new mid-level manager may approach his boss with a problem situation and ask for assistance. A typical response in this type of situation might be: "Let me tell you how I view this type of situation, how I would handle it, and why I recommend taking this approach." This is a prime "teaching moment."

Coaching is built on trust, and the coach must be certain not to violate this trust. If there is only one solution to a problem situation, or if there are reasons why a particular solution must be imposed, the coach should make it clear that she is going to impose a solution and explain why. The worst thing a coach can do in this situation is to ask the coachee to suggest possible solutions with the coach rejecting all offered solutions until the coachee comes up with the one that the coach has in mind–this isn't coaching, it's manipulation.

Who should coach the new manager? Coaching can be done by one's manager, a trainer, a human resources manager, a colleague, or even an employee.[4] The primary requirement for a coach is that he has the opportunity to observe the manager in action and have the trust of the manager. That said, we recommend that the primary coach of a manager at any level be that manager's own manager–as explained in Chapter 9, the employee-manager relationship, at any and all levels, is the key to development.

The nature of coaching may change depending on the level of the coach and the coachee, but the basic skills remain the same. Marshall Goldsmith, widely noted as one of the leading executive coaches of our time, has written that executives often avoid coaching their direct reports for several reasons–because of the demands of other facets of their work, because they feel that their direct reports have greater knowledge about their businesses than they do, and because they fear alienating their direct reports. But Goldsmith argues that executives should also be coaches, al-beit with a somewhat different focus than lower-level managers:

> The "good news" is that while successful people tend to resist negative feedback about the past, they almost always respond well to positive suggestions for the future. By focusing on the future, executives can help direct reports be "right" tomorrow, as opposed to proving they were "wrong" yesterday. Effective coaches can generally cover what they need to say by focusing on the future (as opposed to dwelling on the past).[5]

The AMA regards coaching skills as a real key to developing managers at all levels in an organization. For this reason, the AMA recommends that all managers, at all levels, be trained on coaching skills and be held accountable for coaching their employees.

Gaining Perspective

Many organizations pride themselves on growing and promoting managers internally. While this is often an admirable practice, it is desirable, if not absolutely essential, that the company also help managers gain perspective from the outside. Just because the company has been successful doing things in the same way for a long time doesn't mean that a better method that would bring greater benefit to the company doesn't exist somewhere else in the world. Dedicated managers at all levels tend to focus inwardly and limit their perspective on what else is going on in the outside world.

So, how can managers gain this type of external perspective? We recommend the following methods:

- Reading and discussion
- Membership and participation in professional and industry organizations
- Attending conferences and tradeshows
- External benchmarking and field trips
- Attending external education and training programs

Reading and Discussion

Thousands of new business and professional books are published each year. While many offer only slight variations on old models, theories, and methods, there are new ideas offered by many, and even those that rehash old ideas often provide a fresh approach to their application. Many business, professional, and industry publications and websites review selected books in each issue. Other reviews can be found on websites such as Amazon.com and 800CEORead.com. Similarly, there are many business and professional publications and thousands of websites that focus on new ideas related to management, as well as industry and professional topics.

Your company should encourage reading outside of work and the open discussion of new ideas and approaches. Does your company maintain a company library or pay for employee subscriptions to relevant journals and magazines? Will your company reimburse employees for the purchase of relevant books? Has your CEO, having read a book with some new ideas, ever ordered multiple copies for employees and led an open discussion of the ideas (see "Have You Ever Been Caught Reading on the Job?")?

HAVE YOU EVER BEEN CAUGHT READING ON THE JOB?

In many presentations I have given to corporate groups, I have often asked the audience: "How would you feel if your CEO walked into your office and found you sitting there reading a book?"

Most people reply that they would be embarrassed to be "caught" reading, rather than "working" and would quickly hide the book. But assuming that the book had something to do with your job or the company's business (as opposed to a mystery or a romance novel), reading should be viewed as a legitimate form of employee learning. A good CEO in this case might ask: "What's that you're reading? Any good ideas we should be considering for our company? Would you recommend that I read it, too?"

At one company where I headed employee development and organizational learning, I purchased several copies of a new business book that I thought could benefit the company and sent them to the CEO and a few other officers with a note. A week later, the CEO called me and said that he really liked the book and could I buy copies for all of his direct reports and then lead a discussion of key ideas from the book at one of his staff meetings a few weeks later. Another time, I sent a new book to a division head who, after reading it, asked me to put together a discussion guide that he could use with his division management team. (Of course, there were times when I did this and got no response from the people to whom I had sent the book—not every idea that rings true for you will appeal to everyone else.)

Dan Tobin

Almost every woman we know belongs to a reading circle–a group of local women who meet once a month to discuss a book that the group chooses and everyone reads. In fact, these reading circles and groups have become so widespread that many publishers provide discussion guides for popular books on their websites, and some have even started publishing discussion guides as an appendix to the book itself. Business book publishers have been lax in providing similar discussion guides for their books, although some e-publishers[6] sell study guides for selected best-selling business books. The New York chapter of ASTD has a book club whose members "share insights we gain from articles, books and life experiences."

Membership and Participation in Professional and Industry Organizations

There are professional and industry organizations for virtually every type of industry and profession. These organizations publish journals, magazines, and newsletters, usually have annual meetings or conventions, have websites with many resources, and often have local chapters around the country or the world that meet on a regular basis. They provide opportunities for members to exchange ideas and learn from others; host educational sessions and presentations on new ideas, methods, tools, and processes; and host trade shows where members can see the latest products and services from a wide array of vendors. Many of these resources are provided free to nonmembers, and some associations allow nonmembers to attend meetings and conventions for an additional fee. It is usually easy to find such associations—just put the name of your industry or profession and the word "association" into a search engine and scan the results.

These types of associations provide many opportunities for learning. Even if your organization provides many internal training programs, it is always good to look for new ideas on the outside. Membership in these types of organizations helps employees network with their fellow professionals, find out what's working or not working for others, and discuss their own ideas in a safe environment. Many of these associations also have active discussion boards that can be very helpful when you want to find a source or an answer to a question because you can draw on the knowledge of many people with many different levels of experience (see "Teaching in Brazil").

Active participation in a local chapter or a national association can also help to develop competencies that you may not have the opportunity to develop in your job—competencies such as organizational abilities, leadership, and teamwork.

Does your company pay for employees to join relevant industry and professional associations? Do you reimburse employees for meeting

TEACHING IN BRAZIL

In the mid-1990s, I was invited to present a series of workshops in Sao Paulo, Brazil. Never having been to South America, I didn't know what to expect in terms of my audience, how American ideas would be received in Brazil, or how to work with the simultaneous translation that would be used for the seminars.

I turned to a training and development discussion forum hosted by Pennsylvania State University to which I belonged to gather more intelligence. I posted a note about my assignment and asked the 6,000+ participants from around the globe for advice. Within 48 hours of posting my note, I had more than a dozen responses. Some were from members in Brazil who told me about the Brazilian business community to which I would be speaking. Others came from Americans who had given seminars in Brazil and offered some practical advice. On the subject of simultaneous translation, I heard from several people who had worked with translators and also from two people who did simultaneous translation. All of the advice enabled me to be more effective in the seminars I presented.

It should be noted that I did not know any of the people who responded to my request, but that they were, through this discussion forum, part of my professional network and were willing to share their knowledge and wisdom with another member of the profession, asking only that I continue my participation in the forum and offer my knowledge to answer questions from others.

Dan Tobin

fees or expenses to attend a national conference? Do you allow employees to take time from their regular work to do work for the association? There can be many benefits from doing so.

Attending Conferences and Tradeshows

There are thousands of conferences and tradeshows each year, covering a myriad of topics and technologies. Attending such events can provide many learning opportunities for your employees:

- At conferences, they will be exposed to many different ideas and see how others have been implementing them.

- At tradeshows, they will see how your own organization presents itself to the public (assuming that your organization is participating) and, by working at the company booth, hear the questions and reactions of current and potential customers.

- Employees also can visit the booths of your organization's competitors, see what they are offering, and hear the reactions of the buying public to your competitors' products and services.

- By presenting at a conference or tradeshow, your employees can test their own ideas, develop speaking skills, and test the reaction of current and potential customers to new ideas for products and services.

- By speaking with other participants who have similar experience and interests, employees can build their own professional networks that can offer ideas and advice in the future.

- By bringing back to the workplace the new ideas they have garnered from their participation in such events, employees can help others learn as well, extending the benefits beyond themselves.

External Benchmarking and Field Trips

Benchmarking became very popular over the past several decades as part of the quality movement. Organizations of every size have conducted benchmarking visits to measure themselves against industry "best practices" (see "A Note on Best Practices").

Some organizations have created benchmarking groups whose sole purpose is to conduct benchmark studies of others in their own industry or in other industries, and sometimes within their own organization, to find ways to improve performance and results. In other organizations, such benchmark studies are assigned to the groups that will be affected by changes, and in yet others, the studies were assigned to groups of high-potential managers. We prefer the latter approach, because benchmark studies can provide valuable learning to high potentials (whether individual contributors or managers who are candidates for higher-level positions) by exposing them to ideas and methods outside the organization. Being part of a benchmarking team can help to develop a number of

A NOTE ON BEST PRACTICES

AMA avoids using the term "best practices." To state that one method or model is a *best* practice implies that a scientific study has been done to prove that this method or model is superior to all others that exist—and that just isn't the true in most cases. Further, just because a method or model works well in one organization doesn't necessarily imply that it will work best for all organizations in all circumstances. For these reasons, American Management Association, in creating instructional materials for its many programs, prefers to use the term "excellent practices."

competencies, including perspective, problem-solving, decision-making, teamwork and team leadership, and influencing skills.

Field trips can also be a valuable learning experience, opening employees' minds to new ideas and approaches. You can organize your own field trips or use the services of a company that organizes such field trips. One such organization is New York-based FutureThink, a consultancy that provides education, best practices, and field trips on innovation. FutureThink describes its organized field trips within New York in this way:[7] "To think out of the box, get out of the office. Take a full-day innovation immersion in New York City. You'll get first-hand interaction with the innovative sites and experiences that are shaping the business landscape."

Attending External Education and Training Programs

While there are many benefits to be gained from company-driven education and training programs, designed specifically for the organization's employees and given by company trainers, there are also benefits to occasionally sending employees to external programs. The benefits include:

- Exposure to new ideas and approaches from the external training organization.

- The ability to try out new skills in a safe environment where the participant doesn't have to worry about exposing ignorance or offering a novel idea that might embarrass him or her among peers in his or her own organization.

- The ability to learn from the experiences of other participants from a wide variety of organizations, both within and without the participant's own industry.

- Building personal and professional networks that can provide advice and reinforcement beyond the time spent in training.

Summary

In this chapter we have discussed a wide variety of development methods that extend beyond formal training programs. As will be discussed in the next chapters, many of these approaches to management development require the active participation of both employees and their managers. Further, there are new roles that will be defined within the management development process for organizational leaders, the human resources group, and the training group.

C H A P T E R

The Role of the Manager/ Employee Relationship

Most managers understand their responsibility for developing their employees. The role of manager as developer is widely recognized and written about in the management literature. It is a core management responsibility that is vital to the manager's and the organization's success.

In *Managing for Excellence,* Bradford and Cohen[1] identify several benefits of the manager as developer role. First, it increases the probability that assigned tasks will be completed at a higher level of excellence, as employees seize new opportunities, uncover problems and difficulties early, share knowledge, and feel a commitment to the decisions made. Second, it increases feelings of responsibility by employees, not only for the task at hand, but for the success of the unit as they participate in management decisions. Third, employees become more motivated as they gain a sense of influence and power over their work. Those benefits are impressive and very desirable, which explains why "developing employees" generally appears on every management position description at every level of the organization.

Managers who develop employees effectively also reap their own benefits. They enhance their reputation in the organization. Other managers look to them and their department when seeking qualified staff. The manager becomes known as the "go-to" person for high-quality staff. His or her subordinates are seen as high performers. A senior partner in one of the world's largest accounting and consulting firms once told Dan Tobin that his personal measure of success has always been how many of the junior associates whom he hires eventually become partners in the firm.

Managers also make themselves more promotable when they develop their staff. In looking for candidates for promotion, senior managers observe who has someone ready to take their place, with minimal disruption to the operation of the unit. If a manager feels threatened by competent employees or is fearful of becoming obsolete when he develops an employee, the manager is, in reality, closing down his own chance for promotion. While some managers hoard knowledge, feeling that knowledge is power ("If I can't be replaced, I can't be fired"), more savvy managers recognize that developing their employees can improve their own careers ("If you can't be replaced, you can't be promoted").

Employees like working for managers who help them develop their skills and progress in the company. Employees are generally more motivated, more loyal, and trusting of a manager who has a reputation for developing employees.

Most organizations reinforce the developer role by holding managers accountable for their employees' performance through a performance management system that includes recommendations for performance improvement. The system generally ties to advancement and compensation. Whether an individual manager actually develops direct reports depends on the organizational culture, the manager's comfort level in doing so, and the rapport that exists between the manager and the employee.

Establishing the Relationship

The relationship between the manager and the employee is the key to all successful development. No one knows an employee's strengths, weaknesses, and developmental opportunities as well as the employee and his or her manager.

Effective development requires that a manager recognize the competencies needed for success in a position and focus time and effort on evaluating each individual, determining strengths and weaknesses, and helping the employee to develop those competencies for the benefit of the employee, the work unit, and the organization. The individual employee, in turn, must be open to suggestions and willing to take on the challenge of learning.

As they work closely together over time, the manager observes the employee in a variety of situations and forms ideas and opinions about performance and potential. The manager can test those assumptions and discuss them with the employee. The employee, in turn, grows more secure in trusting how the manager assesses his or her strengths, weaknesses, and potential. The relationship develops as the lines of communication and trust build over time.

The ideal relationship is a partnership between manager and employee, focusing on how best to use the individual's talents to the benefit of the employee and the organization. As the employee grows and assumes more responsibility, he or she partners more with the boss, helping him or her, in turn, becoming an even better manager.

Organizations must support this partnership approach in tackling challenges, solving problems, and achieving common goals. This support is becoming increasingly important as organizations begin to lose baby boomer managers and replace them with Generation X managers. Generation X managers come to the table with a more collaborative approach to management. As a group, Generation X managers are more collaborative by nature, and they expect to accept responsibility for their relationship with their own boss and with their employees. Organizations need to embrace this mindset and support more collaborative partnership arrangements in getting work accomplished.

What does an effective partnership relationship look like? According to *Influence Without Authority* by Allen Cohen and David Bradford,[2] partners stay loyal to the partnership's objectives–objectives that they set collaboratively and whose importance they agree upon. True partners place the good of the organization ahead of their own good, working for mutual benefit by temporarily setting aside personal interests. Partners value and take advantage of their differing skills and perspectives, setting aside egos and capitalizing on the strengths of each partner. Effective partners tolerate each other's foibles and don't assume that bad behavior comes from bad intentions but rather from misinformation or misguided views. They are willing to give the partner the benefit of the doubt and trust in the partner's decisions.

Partners share vital information and speak up to avoid costly mistakes. Partners don't let partners make big mistakes. They help each other identify and seek new opportunities. They are constantly aware of the other and looking out for what is in the best interest of the partnership. In an effective partnership each person realizes that each has a stake in making every member of the partnership as productive and successful as possible.

Identifying Strengths

Traditionally, managers were encouraged to identify the strengths and weaknesses of their employees and devise ways for those employees to overcome their weaknesses. In that way the employee would grow in skills he or she did not have or that needed improvement. Performance reviews briefly cited strengths and focused on areas that needed work, proposing development plans, timelines, and assignments that included things like courses, books, and workshops to help the individual change and grow his or her skills and capabilities. For some this was effective, for others a disaster. Consider the employee who was weak in organizational skills, took several courses and endeavored to improve, but no matter how she tried was unable to keep project files organized. The employee was extremely creative in her approaches to projects, but could not organize the details. Should the manager terminate the employee because she could not master organizational skills and lose the benefit of her creativity?

In the new workplace, where partnership is the preferred mode of operating, managers begin by recognizing the competencies needed for effective performance in a position. The first section of this book defined the competencies for individual professionals, first-level managers, mid-level managers, and functional managers. Knowing the competencies needed at different levels in the organization helps managers pinpoint the target—what will help each individual perform and succeed in a position and what additional competencies that individual will need to develop to progress to the next level of the organization. Remember, some competencies are innate—they are what we hire or promote for—and some can be developed. Once a person is hired, or promoted into a position, the manager's job shifts from identifying the competencies a person brings to the job to helping her develop or improve more competencies and determining how best to use those competencies in the job at hand.

Once a manager knows what is desirable in a position, the manager looks to what is unique about each individual and tries to capitalize on it. According to Marcus Buckingham, in *The One Thing You Need to Know*, great managers figure out the best way to transform talents into performance.[3] There is a growing realization that you will never change what is not changeable in an individual. Instead, managers need to identify the individual's strengths and focus their efforts on how best to utilize those strengths for the benefit of all–the individual, the team, and the organization.

Buckingham sees the first talent required of a manager as an instinct for coaching, and the second as the ability to perceive individual differences. A great manager works with employees, challenging them to identify, practice, and refine their innate strengths and turn them into performance, or rearranges the environment to take full advantage of those strengths, while bolstering each employee's self-assurance and confidence.

Weaknesses can't be ignored entirely, because if left unaddressed, they can undermine strengths. Managers can provide training, support, and coaching to help employees address weaknesses to mitigate their effect, or work out partnering arrangements that compensate for the weakness.

How can you help managers perceive an individual's strengths? Certainly they need sharp observation skills coupled with careful thought. Those behavioral skills are trainable, but the thought takes more work. The brain research on executive skills, reviewed in *Smarts* by Chuck Martin,[4] can help. Executive skills are defined as those skills that help you make decisions about what information you should focus on and how you will manage your behavior. The research says every individual is hardwired to be stronger or weaker in certain executive skills. This is not a new concept. We have long believed that no one person can be strong in all competencies or skills, but that each person shows preferences for certain ways of operating and is more successful in some areas than others. There are numerous instruments–e.g., DISC and MBTI–that try to pinpoint preferred personality style differences and how best to take advantage of them in the workplace.

This brain research says that executive skills are not dramatically changeable by the time you become an adult. So, constantly focusing on weaknesses and working to overcome them can be self-defeating. Knowing your stronger skills, you can identify jobs that play to your strengths and situations that are more likely to result in failure. The research advocates focusing on using your strengths, before addressing the weaknesses. And even then, realize that you can mitigate the effect of the weaknesses, but will never really change your hardwiring. Martin's book provides a validated instrument for determining individual strengths–it can be a valuable tool for managers to identify their own and subordinates' strengths.

Armed with that knowledge, a manager can plan how best to use those individual strengths and work with subordinates to minimize the effect of their weakest skills. So, the first step in helping managers develop the partnership relationship is helping them recognize the strengths and weaknesses of their direct reports. From there, you help them develop plans for capitalizing on the strengths.

Holding a Development Discussion

When should a manager talk about development with a subordinate? Although often combined with a performance review, a fruitful development discussion can be held anytime. It is often even more effective when it is separated from the performance review process. However, in today's business world, making it part of the regular review is common practice.

Either the manager or the employee can initiate the discussion. Both will want to prepare some thoughts beforehand, and they need to set aside adequate time for the discussion. They may want to complete an assessment instrument, similar to those mentioned previously in *Smarts,* so they have a common vocabulary around strengths.

A neutral location–not someone's office, but perhaps a small conference room, a restaurant, or other comfortable seating area–emphasizes that both will be contributing equally to the conversation. If done as part of the regularly scheduled review or goal-setting process, the discussion may be in one or the other's office, and it may take several meetings to cover everything.

The manager begins by asking the employee how she sees her career developing, what she would like to be doing that is different from her current responsibilities, and how she sees her contribution to the organization in the future. The manager listens and encourages the employee to state personal goals and aspirations.

CAREER DEVELOPMENT COACHING

As a communication specialist in an organization of educators and health professionals, Peg was in conflict about her future career direction—should she abandon communications and pursue a health professional career? Would she be able to add more value to the staff of the organization if she had that nutritional science degree?

She approached her boss for consultation. Over lunch one day, they discussed Peg's strengths and her current role in the organization, possible scenarios of future roles she might play, and how she might prepare for those opportunities.

The director spent a lot of time asking questions and sharing her perspective of Peg's strengths. The conversation resulted in Peg's decision to pursue a degree in adult learning and training, which was an area of interest for her, and an area that would add valuable depth to the organization's staff abilities.

The director's patience, her careful questioning, and her knowledge of Peg's strengths were invaluable in helping make the critical career decision.

The manager then contributes what she sees as the individual's strengths and discusses them with the employee. This leads to a joint discussion of how those talents might be better applied in the work of the organization. They may review the business goals of the work group and the organizational goals and discuss how all may integrate. The manager and employee may identify learning opportunities to be incorporated into the employee's development plan to help the employee prepare for more responsibilities and greater contribution to the organization (see "Career Development Coaching").

Determining a Course of Action

Developmental needs of each employee then are blended into the overall employee development plan and also with the goals and objectives of the organization and the work unit. An effective way to do this is with a learning contract, as outlined in *The Knowledge-Enabled Organization* by Daniel R. Tobin[5] and discussed in Chapter 1. Tobin specifies five steps in developing a learning contract: (1) determining the company's business goals, (2) determining the business unit goals, (3) determining individual employee goals, (4) assessing employees' current knowledge and skill levels and comparing to needs, (5) developing employee learning goals and contract.

The manager is responsible for knowing the company goals and the business unit goals and for setting goals with each individual employee for his or her contribution to the work unit. The manager and employee work together to agree on individual goals, work roles, and the competencies required. Our previous discussion on identifying strengths is a helpful exercise for step 4—helping both to see any gaps that need to be filled, skills that need to be developed, and learning experiences that will be helpful. (A variety of learning experiences will be discussed later in this chapter as an example of how to prepare an individual contributor to become a manager.)

The learning contract is unique to each employee and specifies measures of learning achievement, how the learning will be applied on the job, and the business results expected (see Figure 9.1).

The learning contract specifies the gaps identified, the learning methods the employee will use, a schedule for the learning activities, how the learning will be measured, how the learning will be applied to the job, and the business results expected.

Too often, organizations fail to assess what was learned through a development activity, unless there is certification involved. For all development activities, the measures of learning must be applied to the employee's job and specified in the learning contract. Managers must also recognize that the application of what was learned will take time and will require continued practice to master. The employee may need coaching from the manager throughout the process. Because the contract is directly tied to business goals, the learning activity should lead to a positive change in business results as specified in the learning contract.

Preparing to Become a Manager

Perhaps the biggest development challenge is in helping to prepare an individual professional to become a manager. It can be a daunting task

Employee: _____ Manager: _____

Period Covered: _____, 20__ to _____, 20__

Business Goal(s):

Employee's role/responsibilities in meeting goal(s):

Competencies needed for specified role/ responsibilities:

Gap between current and desired competencies:

Learning Plan to Fill Gaps:

Methods:

Schedule for learning activities:

Measurement of learning achievement:

Application of learning to job:

Business results expected:

FIGURE 9.1   Sample Learning Contract

and requires thoughtful preparation, communication, training, and coaching.

Once a manager identifies the employee's strengths and examines which skills need to be developed for the first-line manager role, there are many developmental activities available to the manager to help improve the employee's performance and capabilities. There are formal avenues like training–study programs, seminars, e-learning courses, workshops, and conferences. And there are other avenues, less formal and often overlooked, that are very effective in developing competencies. Those include delegated responsibilities, coaching arrangements, mentoring relationships, job rotations, and developmental assignments. In most instances, a combination of learning techniques combined with coaching is most effective in helping employees develop new skills and competencies. Let's take a closer look at these avenues.

Developing Skills and Competencies

Self-Study   This learning pursuit is undertaken by individuals on their own and may be as simple as a literature search online or e-learning courses when they are asynchronous and involve individual learning pursuits. You might recommend this to an employee when the individual needs to acquire facts or deepen his general knowledge and understanding of a topic. Self-study works best when the plan includes follow-up discussions and/or opportunities to practice and use what was learned. For example, if a person has never run a meeting, you might recommend she research how to set an agenda, how to craft an e-mail to notify potential participants, etc. Then you might delegate the task of running the next staff meeting to this individual, coach her through the process, and offer feedback after the meeting.

Formal Instruction   This could be any class, seminar, workshop, or conference—an event where the individual is involved with other learners and goes through a learning experience with them. Any one the 3,000 AMA public seminars offered during the year on a variety of the professional skills or management topics would provide an interactive learning experience and an opportunity to meet and learn with people from a variety of industries. Of particular note: Several AMA courses offer an online learning contract, along with pre- and post-assessments to measure knowledge gained in the course (Level 2 evaluation). "Presentation Training" gives an example of an interactive learning experience.

Coaching   This is an important technique for managers. Coaching offers employees specific advice about how to do a task, providing feedback on performance, and, in many cases, assisting the employee in discovering how to solve a problem or improve his own performance. Coaching is an important element in all developmental assignments, helping ensure the employee's success in applying learning to the job.

Developmental Assignments   Delegating tasks or projects and involving employees in developmental projects are powerful ways to

PRESENTATION SKILLS TRAINING

Early in her career, Peg Pettingell was a communications consultant with a nonprofit organization. Primarily responsible for news releases, press relations, press events, and slide show presentations, she had little experience presenting in front of groups. In her yearly performance review, her boss proposed that she attend a two-day seminar on presentation skills. The expectation was set that she would learn the techniques and share them with the rest of the staff.

The training included eight videotaped presentations with individual feedback sessions. Participants included directors (her boss's level in the organization) and other communication specialists from similar organizations around the country. When the session began with the assignment of introducing yourself by telling a humorous story, Peg was panicked. Luckily, she survived the assignment. Through the subsequent training, she received excellent coaching and valuable stress-coping techniques and ended up thoroughly enjoying the training.

Coming back to the staff, she learned to operate a video camera and designed a learning session complete with coaching feedback sheets for partnering exercises. Peg conducted the staff training, and became the "resident expert" on giving presentations for the organization. Her communication skills expanded, and the organization gained valuable training while providing her with an opportunity to learn and grow not only her presentation skills, but her training skills as well. Both of these areas played a large role in her later career choices.

develop staff competencies and bring fresh ideas to projects. Most employees enjoy new challenges and see them as growth opportunities. They welcome the attention it brings to their abilities and recognize that it can help them progress in their career. Learning by working on and contributing to a real-world project can be more exciting and involving than attending a class or reading about someone else's experience. In making such developmental assignments, you want to recognize the need to stay involved, monitoring what is happening, continuing to coach the individual, and providing any necessary support through the assignment. What might qualify as a developmental assignment?

- *Researching a new approach.* One manager wanted information on a new software package and asked an employee to do the research and compare it to what was currently being used in the company. The employee eagerly did the comparison and, once the decision was made to purchase the new software, became the in-house "expert" for orienting other staff. Meanwhile, he learned how to evaluate and compare the software packages with respect to the company's specific requirements–a valuable skill for future managers.

- *Representing the work group on a cross-functional team.* One manager was asked to serve on a task force to streamline the internal sales order-taking process and delegated the responsibility to one of her customer service representatives, who brought a very practical orientation to the project. The employee also gained a perspective of how her unit fit into the overall process and met people who would be helpful when questions arose. It also helped the employee start to build her in-company network–something that would benefit her when she later became a manager.

- *Coaching other employees on a process the employee is particularly good at.* One employee might be assigned to train a new hire. Another could share a method or technique he developed or perfected because it has proven to be more efficient than the method being used by others. Not only does this benefit others, but helps the employee develop his skills in innovation and personal leadership.

- *Providing opportunities to present to higher level management in the organization.* Rather than personally make your annual update at your manager's next staff meeting, you might bring an employee to share one aspect of the job that she is doing particularly well. This visibility to upper management is an opportunity for the employee to begin building rapport with higher-ranking people and gaining a comfort level with them. This comfort level will be valuable as she progresses up the management ladder.

- *Recommending an employee for a temporary management assignment.* In one company it was a temporary assignment that gave the employee a "taste" of what it means to manage while another manager was out on sick leave; in another instance, it was a "trial" to see if the employee was indeed ready to take over, a temporary arrangement that would become permanent if the employee did well in the new role.

- *Arranging for an employee to join another work group to learn how it does something.* One organization uses this method to increase understanding across functions and to develop people so they can fill in when a crunch occurs in another part of the organization.

- *Volunteering your group for a new assignment.* This can be a learning opportunity for the entire group, as well as a chance to showcase your group's potential abilities in a new area. An example of this is shown in "The Web Newsletter."

These are but a few of the many types of developmental assignments you can use to help your employees grow their competencies and their careers. All require managers to continue monitoring and coaching employees as they go through the process. When you establish an assignment and specify a learning contract for the experience, you should build in sufficient opportunities for the interchange, such as weekly conferences, telephone updates, e-mails, etc., and make them an integral part of the learning process.

You may also want to assemble a group of managers who are facing the same developmental issues so they can share ideas and approaches that are working or have worked for them in the past. Having regular sharing sessions provides employees with opportunities to brainstorm ideas on how to handle situations can be invaluable to them. Remember that employees can also learn a lot from each other.

Helping the Boss

For real development to occur, the organizational environment has to support it. Managers need to be comfortable encouraging employees to speak up, to disagree, to press for their own needs, and to help in problem solving. If the manager listens to and encourages that kind of interaction, the team, the individual employees, and the organization as a whole will benefit. These guidelines hold true across all levels of the organization.

THE WEB NEWSLETTER

The service line of the consulting firm was expanding, and teams around the globe were engaged in new and different types of projects. They posted project results to the firm's knowledge network, but lacked a vehicle to let other teams know what was learned.

Sarah recognized an opportunity for her communication team to provide a valuable service and learn about web-based communication skills at the same time. Team members wanted to expand their skills in this area, but had not pursued it to date. Sarah volunteered her staff to design and write a monthly newsletter highlighting special projects around the globe. The newsletter would "advertise" the projects and point interested teams to the in-depth project information on the knowledge network.

Sarah had to bring her team up to speed on web design and writing for the web. She shared a resource publication and developed a protocol for how the newsletter would approach the content. She then made assignments and coached each individual through the first few issues, emphasizing the differences in writing in web-style, helping to format their work to be brief, punchy, and compelling, yet full of the most significant information on each project.

Within a few months Sarah had a viable newsletter up and running. It was widely read by the 3,000 consultants in the service line, as well as by employees in other service lines who had heard about the newsletter and wanted to know what other teams were doing. Soon, project teams were approaching Sarah to feature their project in the next issue. At the same time, Sarah's staff became known as accomplished web-communicators and was asked to assist other groups as new web material was developed for client sites.

Peg Pettingell

What is often missing in these conversations is how employees, particularly managers, learn to relate to and develop relationships with their bosses. How to keep the communication going is a constant challenge. Everyone needs to reassure the boss that he knows what he is doing. Managers need to think of what their boss needs to know and tell her before she asks. Sincerity and integrity are valued. So is caring about what happens in the work group and doing your best to use your skills and expertise to best advantage. At the same time, managers need to be open with their bosses about what they need to succeed.

Some general guidelines:

- Deliver bad news in the context of what you are doing to fix the situation.
- Don't join the fray of boss-bashing; instead always give your boss credit for what he or she does well.
- Don't lose your cool. When frustrated or angry, say so, but don't blow up or explode. Display your emotional intelligence. Avoid whining. Focus on fixing things you want to change and ask for the boss's help in changing them. Bosses appreciate a positive focus and will be more receptive to your ideas for improvements.

Summary

The partnership relationship between manager and employee redefines the nature of the traditional boss-subordinate relationship and will be much more acceptable to the new-age workforce in the years ahead. Those who see this partnership, both upward and downward in an organization, as a growth opportunity for all will be favorably received and will achieve the most success going forward.

The relationship between manager and employee is critical in determining how to develop an employee. No one knows better than the manager and the direct report what is needed and how best to accomplish the task. Development is needed at every level of the organization, and people look above them in the hierarchy of the organization for direction and support. Managers at all levels who receive good support from their bosses are more likely to provide support to their employees.

CHAPTER

10

The Role of the Organizational Leadership

What roles should the organization's top leaders (here defined as the CEO and C-level executives) play in developing management talent? We have identified six major roles for leadership to play in developing managers.

1. Linking people to strategy and operations
2. Developing the leadership pipeline through continuous improvement, succession depth, and reducing retention risk
3. Teaching in the organization's management development programs
4. Dealing with nonperformers
5. Linking HR to business results
6. Building a positive learning environment throughout the organization

Linking People to Strategy and Operations

In too many organizations, strategy is determined at the top of the house, by senior executives, perhaps with the aid of a strategic planning group, who then publish these strategies in the broadest terms to the general workforce. In many of these organizations, the great majority of employees have only the most peripheral view of what these strategies are and, worse, cannot tell you what their personal role is in helping the company to achieve those strategies. As the old saw goes, if you don't know where you are going, any road will do. So employees keep doing what they have been doing, and do little to help the company achieve its goals beyond doing business as usual.

In more enlightened companies, the strategy development process involves as many employees as possible, from every level, every business unit, and all locations. When this more inclusive planning process is completed, employees better understand the organization's strategies, and the strategic plan becomes "our plan" rather than "their plan." Employees throughout the company understand the strategies, what they must do to help the company succeed, and through the company's success ensure their own success.

Jack Stack took this even further in his company, developing what he called "The Great Game of Business." Stack states his business philosophy as

> The best, most efficient, most profitable way to operate a business is to give everybody in the company a voice in saying how the company is run and a stake in the financial outcome, good or bad.[1]

Stack educated *every* employee in his company on how to read the company's financial statements and on how the decisions they made in their jobs affected the company's financial results.

The role of organizational leadership is to lead the strategy development process and then to align all parts of the organization with the stated strategies. For short-term strategies (0–2 years), this may mean moving people into new jobs and responsibilities or hiring from the outside. In many successful companies, such as General Electric and Honeywell, leaders such as Jack Welch and Lawrence Bossidy have established a rigorous evaluation process for current managers/leaders and those in the organization's leadership pipeline. This process not only measures key competencies, but also the business results that each person has achieved.

Developing the Leadership Pipeline

Bossidy and Charan describe the need for a leadership pipeline:

> Meeting medium- and long-term milestones greatly depends on having a pipeline of promising and promotable leaders. You need to

assess them today, and decide what each leader needs to do to become ready to take on larger responsibilities. . . . Nothing is more important to an organization's competitive advantage."[2]

If this sounds like a lot of work for senior executives, it is–Bossidy states that done right, the CEO will devote 20 to 40 percent of his or her time dealing with issues of people and talent to ensure that the organization has the right people in the right jobs, while Jack Welch has stated that he spent approximately 30 percent of his time as GE's CEO dealing with personnel issues.

Without the right people in the right jobs, change is improbable, if not impossible, and the job of the leader, according to B. Joseph White, is to effect change. "To be a great leader, you have to be successful at *achieving change*–important, consequential change in the results for which you are responsible. Making change successfully is a leader's greatest challenge."[3] And change is accomplished by *people*. Technology, for all its capability and promise, can enable change (make it possible) and facilitate change (make it easier), but technology cannot cause change (make it happen). People make change happen, and if you don't have the right people with the right skills in the right jobs, aligned with the organization's strategy, change will not happen.

Bossidy's approach focuses the organization's leaders on succession planning for top positions and on development of a relatively small pool of high-potential talent. He then requires organizational leaders in various business units and geographies to conduct similar reviews and write similar development plans that reach deeper into their own organizations.

In his book, *Bench Strength*,[4] Robert Barner distinguishes between two types of talent development strategies: "foundation" strategy and "capstone" strategy. A *foundation* strategy provides at least a minimal amount of management development for all levels of management in the organization. After all, it is a truism that employees "join organizations and leave managers," so there is merit in ensuring that all managers at all levels of the organization have a chance to learn and develop basic management skills. A *capstone* strategy focuses attention and resources on a smaller group of employees who have been identified as having high potential for future leadership positions in the company (typically at more senior levels and often tied to the organization's succession planning efforts).

There are advantages and disadvantages to both approaches, as shown in Table 10.1. We believe that the wiser path is to develop an approach to management and leadership development that encompasses both strategies, providing basic training and development for all managers in the organization while providing a supplementary program for those in the high-potential pool.

Whether you opt for a capstone strategy, a foundation strategy, or a hybrid approach, it is important that these development programs have the active participation of the organization's senior leaders. For example:

- During Jack Welch's reign as General Electric's CEO, he was scheduled to teach in its leadership development programs several hundred times, and he missed only one session—and that was when he was hospitalized.

- At Amoco's Management Learning Center, the company's vice chairman presented to, and held a discussion with, each class, requiring his attendance one morning a week for forty weeks a year.

- When Larry Bossidy first took over as CEO of Honeywell, he spent as much as 40 percent of his time on personnel issues and continued to spend 20 to 30 percent of his time on talent issues.

TABLE 10.1   Advantages and Disadvantages of Foundation and Capstone Strategies

Talent Development Strategy	Advantages	Disadvantages
Foundation Strategy	• Provides at least some training and development for all managers at all levels • Sends the message that good management and leadership skills are important at all levels of the organization	• Lessens the focus on top performers • Requires a large investment to reach all managers
Capstone Strategy	• Supports succession planning for top positions • Helps retain top talent • Improves visibility of top performers	• Members of the high potential group may become elitist • You may overlook some solid performers

In each of these cases, the company's top leadership didn't just *say* that developing employees is important, they *demonstrated* its importance by taking the time from other responsibilities to devote to developing the next generation of managers/leaders who would build the company's future. In too many companies, top executives abdicate this responsibility to the human resources and training groups. While these groups can do a lot to provide the training and tools to develop employees, as will be discussed in the next two chapters of this book, there is nothing that can replace the role of the company's top executives in building what we call a *positive learning environment* as we will discuss later in this chapter.

Teaching in the Organization's Management Development Programs

While the decisions made in the types of talent review sessions held by Welch, Bossidy, and many other corporate leaders is important, these sessions are not visible to most employees. To best demonstrate the importance of developing the organization's leadership pipeline, the organization's leaders must make their commitment visible, and there is no better way of doing this than by teaching, and participating in other ways, in the organization's management and leadership development programs. As mentioned above, Jack Welch and other top GE managers spent a significant amount of time teaching in GE's leadership development programs. When the organization's leaders make themselves available in these programs, they demonstrate a real commitment to the organization's next generations of leaders and emphasize the importance of learning.

Dealing with Nonperformers

If an organization is going to be successful, it must deal with people at all levels who are not performing to company standards. Whether a person is not performing because he has been promoted beyond his level of ability, whether a person doesn't have the competencies needed for a particular job, or whether there are other factors involved, ignoring such problems does not make them go away. Whether the solution is to demote an individual back to a job where she had proven her competence, to provide training or coaching to a person to improve his competence, or to dismiss that employee from the company, nonperformance must be addressed if the organization is to perform at optimal levels. These types of decisions are never easy, but they are a major responsibility of the organization's leadership.

Too often, nonperformers are ignored and left in their jobs because their managers lack the courage to deal with them. It is never easy to tell people they aren't making the grade, that they are going to be demoted or, worse, lose their jobs. But leaving a nonperformer in place not only hurts the business, it also damages the morale of the people who work for and with the nonperformer. How often, when after tolerating poor performance for too long, a decision has been made to terminate such an employee, do leaders hear the many people who have been performing well and taking the time to compensate for the lack of performance of the poor performer say "What took so long?"

Linking HR to Business Results

In many organizations, the HR group is given sole responsibility for developing the leadership pipeline and managing employee performance. Bossidy and Charan argue for a greater role in these processes for the organization's senior leaders. So where does this leave the HR organization? Their answer is that it makes the HR organization even more important. By linking these typical HR functions directly to the organization's business results, it makes HR "more important than ever, but its role must change radically. . . . In this new role, HR becomes . . . a far more powerful force for advancing the organization than it was in its typical staff function."[5] In Chapter 11, we will deal with this changing role of the HR organization.

Building a Positive Learning Environment Throughout the Organization

An organization that has a positive learning environment (PLE) "encourages, even demands, that every employee at every level be in a continuous learning mode, constantly searching for new ideas, trying new methods, sharing ideas and learning with others, and learning from others, to find new and better ways to achieve individual, group, and organizational goals."[6]

Organizational leaders who become teachers and who create individual development plans to guide the learning of employees are certainly consistent with this definition of a PLE. Additionally, organizational leadership can promote the development of a PLE by:

- Modeling learning behaviors
- Actively seeking talent from every part of the organization
- Becoming mentors and coaches
- Encouraging creativity and innovation
- Helping employees learn from their own experiences, both positive and negative

Modeling Learning Behaviors

Organizational leaders need to devote time to their own learning and to make their learning visible to the rest of the organization. Some examples:

- Many CEOs and C-level officers spend time talking with major customers. At one company the CEO, returning from a customer visit, called a meeting of the product development group, telling them what he had learned from the customer about how they use the company's products and the customer's ideas for both new products and modifications of current company services, leading a discussion of future product and service directions. (It should be noted that the CEO made it very clear that he was not issuing orders to do what this customer wanted, but only opening up a dialogue based on what he had learned. Many CEOs have learned from hard experience that often when they ask a question, many employees consider it an order, and that was not their intention.)
- A vice president of engineering attended a conference and was very impressed with the presentation of a new engineering technique being used at another company in a different industry. Upon returning to the office, he briefed his staff on what he had learned and asked them to assemble a group of people to visit the other

company to learn more about the innovation and to see if their company could benefit from adopting it.

- On a fairly regular basis, AMA CEO Ed Reilly will send out an article he has read to various employees asking them to read it and then discuss it with him: Is the topic of the article relevant to the AMA's business? What are we doing in this area? Is it worth our learning more and adopting or adapting the recommended approach to our business?

- At Whirlpool Corporation, the company's senior leadership established a corps of innovation mentors and coaches to help employees develop and test new ideas.

- By encouraging cross-functional teamwork, international assignments, job rotation, and building of technology-enabled employee forums, organizational leaders can help to extend learning beyond the classroom and encourage the cross-fertilization of new ideas.

In many organizations, the action learning projects being done as part of high-potential leadership development programs are presented to senior executives (and sometimes to members of the board of directors). This not only encourages participants in these programs to do outstanding jobs on their projects, it also helps the senior executives learn more about the ideas arising from lower-level employees with whom they would not routinely interact. It gives the executives a better view of the next generation of leaders from organizations and geographies not in their regular line of sight and sends the message loud and clear that the development program and the results of the action learning projects are valued by the organization's senior leaders.

Actively Seeking Talent from Every Part of the Organization

Good ideas are not the sole province of any organization's executive staff, nor do all solutions have to flow from the organization's headquarters location. If an organization hopes to develop the best management and leadership talent, it must look to every part of the organization, every functional area, every level, every worldwide location, as potential sources of talent, and must devote as much energy and attention to talent residing in remote locations as to that located at the organization's headquarters.

Very often, organizations that are hidden from the view of company headquarters tend to run their own shows. The remote managers feel that as long as they deliver results in terms of production, sales, profit margins, for example, they can safely ignore any mandates from the company's headquarters. In some cases, this is the right way of running things—especially for foreign subsidiaries where the working culture and local regulations may be very different from that of the headquarters country. But in most cases, this local focus may optimize local results, but hurt the overall organization. For example, local managers may hide high-potential employees from the rest of the company for fear of having them recruited away from the local operations. While this may help the local operations in the short run, it may not benefit the larger organization in the longer run.

While the executive team can conduct talent reviews for their direct reports and perhaps one more level down into the organization, they should also require that every functional area and geography conduct similar reviews that reach deeper into their respective organizations. We have seen many organizations "require" this type of action, but few that tie measures and rewards to its accomplishment. Too often, as long as an executive is "making his numbers," the softer measures of management and leadership development are allowed to falter.

Remember—what gets measured and rewarded gets done. At one company, where the CEO's mandates for talent reviews and development plans were stymied by mid-level managers, she issued an order that any manager who did not fulfill these responsibilities would receive no stock options for that year—that certainly got people's attention.

Becoming Mentors and Coaches

By acting as mentors to more junior employees, organizational leaders help educate those employees about the company's history and culture while learning more about the younger generation and encouraging them to build their careers within the company. Preserving the organization's culture and memory will become even more important over the next decade when so many baby boomers will be retiring and many organizations will have to quickly develop a new cadre of managers from a younger generation.

Coaching generally involves a person's direct reports. To properly coach someone, the coach should be able to observe that person's performance on a regular basis. Coaching focuses on improving performance by helping the employee better understand what he doesn't know that he doesn't know, i.e., areas of unconscious ignorance, as well as discovering areas of competence of which the employee may not be aware (unconscious competence). Coaching does not impose a solution, but helps the employee to discover her own solution and to learn from her own experiences, both good and bad. When the organization's top executives do coaching themselves, they establish an expectation that coaching will take place at all levels of the organization, and this certainly helps to establish a positive learning environment throughout the organization.

Encouraging Creativity and Innovation

Throughout history, creativity and experimentation have been the original forms of learning—trying out new ideas and methods to discover what will work and what won't work. Does your organization promote creativity or stifle it? If you want to nurture creativity, you need to rid the organization of phrases that block new ideas and replace them with those that encourage them, such as those shown in Table 10.2.

You also need to break complex problems down into simple solutions made up of manageable steps. FedEx executive Tom Schmitt and his colleagues have written an exceptional book on the topic[7] in which

TABLE 10.2 Changing the Nature of the Dialogue	
Instead of saying . . .	*Say . . .*
That's a dumb idea.	That's an interesting idea. Tell us more.
That doesn't sound feasible.	How would you see that working?
That will never work here.	How could we make that work here?
We'd need too many resources from other parts of the organization to make that work.	What resources would we need to make that happen, and how do you think we can get them?
You'll never be able to do that.	How can we help you get that done?

they recommend asking simple questions that lead to simple solutions. For example,

- What would have to be true for us to lower production costs for this product by 50 percent?
- What would have to true for us to sign up 5,000 new customers next year?
- What would have to be true for employee turnover to be zero?
- What would have to be true to produce accurate financial statements within two days of month's end?
- What would have to be true for customer service to respond to each customer call within 3 seconds?

If your company's leadership continually asks these types of questions, they will encourage employees and managers at all levels to keep thinking about how to better manage the organization's business, how to keep employees and managers challenged and engaged, and how to create the company's and their own future.

Helping Employees Learn from Their Own Experiences

Some managers are better than others in helping employees learn from their experiences (see "Take Risks but Don't Fail"). Many management training programs include sections on how to hold a performance discussion with an employee who is not doing well. Most organizations have detailed procedures that must be followed in a corrective action situation, starting with counseling and coaching by the employee's manager, followed by a verbal warning, a written warning, and, finally, termination if the employee fails to correct his errant behavior or improve his work product. A lot of this effort is mandated by the organization's HR group, which tries to protect the organization from wrongful discharge lawsuits.

Much less time is spent in these types of programs on how to help successful employees get even better at their work, even though research has shown that this is a much better investment of the manager's time in terms of the expected results.

"TAKE RISKS BUT DON'T FAIL"

I once worked for a manager who encouraged his people to take risks to help the business grow. If you took such a risk and were successful, you were handsomely rewarded–promotions, stock options, large raises, bonuses–all were available if you had a spectacular success.

But what if the risk turned out badly–you failed or your project wasn't particularly successful? If you were only partially successful, you might continue working in the group, but it would be clear, from the manager's behavior, that you were no longer among "the favored few." If you failed, you were almost shunned by the manager, and it quickly became evident that you should look for new employment outside the group. Depending on your track record in the group, he might give you a decent recommendation and a few kind words upon your departure.

So, who took risks in this group? The people who tempted fate were those who had confidence in their own ideas and abilities, were willing to bet that they would win, and felt that even if they failed they could find work elsewhere.

But by instituting this (unwritten) policy, the group manager lost a lot of opportunities for even greater success. First, there were many people in the group who had great ideas, but weren't willing to take a risk. Second, those who took risks that were only partially successful were shut off from the group manager and basically none of their future ideas were heard or acted on. But most important, the group manager made it impossible for the unsuccessful employee or others, including himself, to learn from the failed or less than fully successful initiative.

Dan Tobin

When is the most common time that a senior manager will call for a *post mortem* review of a project? The answer comes from the phrase "*post mortem*," meaning "after death"–it takes place after a disastrous result or an unsuccessful project. What went wrong? Why did you fail? Too often, these types of reviews are used to assign blame, rather than to learn from experience.

Learning has to be a continuous process–what did we learn from any project, successful or unsuccessful? What can help us avoid disaster next time, but also what went right that we want to build on? Even if a project is successful, there is always something that can be learned to ensure better results the next time. If you think back to the four-stage learning model presented in Chapter 1, wisdom comes from adding experience and intuition to knowledge. Through "after-action reviews" we can help people distill the wisdom they have gained from almost any experience, be it successful or unsuccessful. And the key tool for distilling this wisdom is dialogue.

What the manager in the "Take Risks But Don't Fail" story lost through his actions was the ability to learn from experience, both for himself and for the employees who took the risks. There was never an after-action review, even if the risk produced an exceptionally good result.

In Chapter 3, we repeated the oft-told the story of the "million-dollar mistake" by a high-potential at IBM. When Mr. Watson told the employee that he wasn't going to fire him because he had just invested $1 million in his education, he should have followed that statement by asking the employee what he learned from that mistake to see if IBM had gotten value from the investment. This is why after every NASA mission, successful or unsuccessful, the first post-mission activity is to debrief the participants–to learn while people's memories are still fresh.

Learning from one's mistakes and successes is a vital part of a positive learning environment, and it is the organization's top leadership that must set the example by asking the questions to help employees, and the organization as a whole, learn from experience.

Summary

For an organization to be truly successful in creating a management/leadership pipeline, the organization's leaders must create a positive learning environment that fosters learning at every level. Further, they must take a personal role in identifying and grooming future leaders, making this a priority for senior executive meetings, and set an example for learning and development by their own teaching, coaching, and mentoring others.

CHAPTER

The Role of the Human Resources Group

I want bigger margins than anybody else, and to accomplish this we have to have great people and train them better and faster than everybody else. We need to have educational programs that are focused on key business issues and problems, the things that matter. HR's role is to help me solve these problems.

Larry Bossidy[1]

In today's business literature, "talent management" is a very hot topic. It has been the subject of many global surveys, dozens of books and articles, and many training programs. Some define it as succession planning; others as developing high-potential employees. Some companies have invested millions in buying and developing systems to keep track of talent.

Every company pays at least some lip service to the concept. Some, like Larry Bossidy, see it as an executive responsibility. Others, such as Ram Charan, Stephen Drotter, and James Noel writing in *The Leadership Pipeline*, say that it is a responsibility of all levels of management, starting with the board of directors and continuing down to the first-line manager.

For many, talent management is the prime responsibility of the human resources and training organizations within a company. In its highlight report on talent management, the Institute for Corporate Productivity[2] paints an "ideal scenario" of the future where "talent management becomes highly integrated and spreads to all levels of the organization."

Talent management processes, tracking of talent, and talent-related strategy are interwoven with business strategy and everyday management functions. Functionally and philosophically, all the once-disparate areas that comprise talent management have been brought together. Talent management is an umbrella that covers recruitment, retention, and engagement. Also, functions such as performance management, training and development, leadership development, and succession planning . . . have been wrapped into talent management.

These and other affected functions, such as workforce planning, talent acquisition, and retention initiatives, are reciprocally tied into talent management's recordkeeping and reporting. Line managers and HR personnel can easily see data on all aspects of talent management, per employee or broken out by group. All the areas that affect talent are part of a comprehensive talent strategy and are leverage[d] to work together.[3]

University of Michigan professor David Ulrich defines the vital roles that the HR group must play in any organization, and the HR practices that will "ensure that people and organizations perform at their best."[4] These roles include:

- Coaching Organizational Leaders: Ulrich argues that HR leaders are in a prime position to coach the organization's leaders on their behaviors and their actions. "HR players are in the ideal position to do executive coaching because they are outside the career politics (e.g., not after the senior leader's job), have training in the human side of the business, which enables them to observe unintended consequences, and offer insights not often shared with the business leader."[5]

- Acting as the Organizational Architect: "They help turn general and generic ideas into blueprints for organizational action," says Ulrich. "They help identify choices not evident to the business leader about how organizations might be better governed. They come to the management meeting understanding business realities and organizations and ensure that dialogue . . . focuses on the right issues."[6]

- Facilitating Action: Having a good blueprint is not enough. HR needs to go beyond the role of architect and actually facilitate the changes in structure and behavior defines by the blueprint. Ulrich states: "HR facilitation has a legacy in organization development work of HR. In OD work, HR professionals would help groups identify their charter and then learn how to collaborate to accomplish their charter. While some of the traditional OD work has been downplayed, the need to facilitate teams, organizations, and alliances continues."[7]

Key Roles of HR in Management Development

There is no one model that will work for every organization. If there were a perfect model, there would be one book on the subject, one guru, and every organization's HR group would support company leadership in exactly the same way. Let's focus some of the key roles that the HR organization can play in terms of management development in your organization. These include:

- Succession planning
- Identifying internal management talent
- Leading talent reviews
- Planning for developmental assignments
- Coaching

Please note that the topic of management training is covered in the next chapter. In many organizations, management and leadership training are a function of the HR group, while in others they are the responsibility of a separate training group.

Succession Planning

In many, if not most organizations, succession planning efforts encompass only top-level positions–the CEO and other C-level officers and perhaps the heads of major business units. While these are important jobs for which to have succession plans, your succession planning process should be aimed at creating what Charan and Drotter call a "leadership pipeline." The idea of a pipeline is that you want to keep the pipeline as full as possible to ensure that your organization has the management and leadership talent ready for any eventuality–a sudden departure of a key staff member, a sudden surge in business, the acquisition of another company, and so forth. This means that you have to delve deeper into the organization in looking for talent, not only to provide for quick and orderly succession at the top of the organization, but also to create a management and leadership infrastructure that will carry the business forward over succeeding years.

One common error to avoid in succession planning is to model each successor as a clone of the incumbent. This is all too easy to do–you start looking for successors who match the competencies of the person who currently holds the job. A better approach is to do a modified 360-degree analysis of each key job. Ask the incumbent what competencies or qualities he or she feels are important to the job today and which will be important in the future. Also ask board members (for C-level jobs), peers, and subordinates to specify the competencies they feel are and will be important to the job. The competency profile you derive from this type of exercise may be very similar or very different from that of the incumbent. This may not reflect the quality of the job that the incumbent has performed, but rather that requirements change over time. Several years ago, General Electric's chief learning officer talked about how different current GE CEO Jeffrey Immelt is from his predecessor, Jack Welch. While Welch has become an icon of business leadership, Immelt's style and method of operation are very different. The CLO stressed that this was not to say that one was better than the other, but that both were very effective in their roles. In fact, he said, in the history of General Electric, every new CEO has been very different from his predecessor, and each person has been "the right one for the business at that time."

The second vital part of the succession planning process, beyond identifying the competencies needed for each position, is to identify candidates for each position, judge them fairly, and derive development plans for each individual to prepare for eventual promotion.

The third vital factor in succession planning and management is to extend the process beyond C-level positions. As stated by the Institute for Corporate Productivity:

> Managers at all levels of an organization have to look for talent, but they are reluctant to give up their most effective employees. The fear of losing these people is justified, as many companies move promising candidates into "developmental" positions. Colgate-Palmolive

identifies its future "stars" after their first promotion from an entry-level position, and immediately puts them into a rotational program. Employees on the leadership track at GE are expected to move every two to three years. These rotational programs involve real assignments, in contrast to short-duration exposures.[8]

Identifying Internal Management Talent

The leaders of many organizations measure management success almost exclusively on the basis of numbers: Did the business unit "make its numbers" in terms of sales, profits, units manufactured, quality statistics, and so forth? While most leaders pay lip service to the many competencies identified as being critical to management success, they don't have regular opportunities to observe many of those competencies, especially those we identified in the categories of knowing and managing yourself and knowing and managing others.

The HR organization, on the other hand, has a much more comprehensive view of many of these management competencies. HR works with employees at all levels and sees and hears on a daily basis how well managers are doing in managing themselves and their people. HR hears employees' complaints about their managers and conducts exit interviews with employees who are leaving. They see, on a daily basis, which groups are being managed well and which have higher-than-average turnover, which individual professionals are excelling at their jobs and are showing potential for management positions.

And while the organization's top executives deal on a regular basis with their direct reports, HR has a broader view into lower levels of the organization. So, in many ways, HR is in a better position to identify management talent at all levels of the organization than are top executives.

All of these factors put HR in a prime position to identify management talent throughout the organization and to lead talent reviews by top executives. HR can identify candidates who may be "protected" by their bosses—those who are producing numbers but may be hurting the organization through their lack of communications and interpersonal skills, and those with high potential for more senior positions but who are hidden from top management because their managers don't want to lose the benefit of having them in their own groups.

This is not to remove responsibility for identifying talent from managers at all levels of the organization. No one in the organization knows an individual employee's capabilities better than his or her manager. But to make this work effectively, managers at all levels must be measured and rewarded, at a substantive level, on how well they choose and develop their employees to prepare those with the greatest potential for higher-level positions.

Leading Talent Reviews

Talent reviews are formal meetings where the organization's leaders review the management talent in the organization and make decisions such as:

- Who is ready to be promoted?
- What does the organization need to do to develop the next generation of managers and leaders? This can be done in terms of specifying the types of training programs the organization wants to offer to employees, but should also include critical reviews of each management candidate and what each of those individuals needs to do to prepare for his or her next management position.
- Which managers, at all levels of the organization, just aren't working out as hoped? In some cases, the solution may be to provide additional training or coaching to remedy problems. In other cases, the recommendation may be to move the person to a different role, while in the most extreme cases the solution may be to terminate the person.

Doing thorough talent reviews is time consuming. Jack Welch has often been quoted as saying that he spent up to half of his time as GE's CEO developing people. Larry Bossidy has stated that he spends up to 30 percent of his time on personnel matters. If your organization wants to be effective in ensuring that it has the management talent it will need to succeed, it must recognize that this is a vital function and demand this type of attention from the organization's senior leadership.

HR's role in conducting talent reviews is to collect information on each employee who will be reviewed and to present that information to the organization's leadership team in formal talent review sessions. A common tool for collecting such information is the use of 360-degree evaluations keyed to the management competencies most critical to the organization. An important point to make here is that data collected through the 360-degree evaluations and the talent review process itself should not be used to do a performance review, but rather should be viewed as a tool to help plan for the development of the individual employee (see "The Numbers Don't Matter").

THE NUMBERS DON'T MATTER

On my first day of work at a high-tech company, I was called in by my manager, the senior vice president of human resources, and given my first assignment. "More than a year ago," she told me, "we developed a plan to do 360-degree evaluations for the top 150 people in the company below the executive committee level. We have an evaluation form and a process all defined. The problem is that Harry (the company's founder and CEO) has never felt comfortable with the project, so we never got started. I want you to go see Harry, find out what his objections are, and solve the problem so we can get started on this."

I made an appointment to see Harry the next day. "Have you seen all of the e-mails I sent on this?" he asked me. No, I hadn't. "Let me forward them all to you. Read them and then we can get together tomorrow to discuss them."

An hour later, I had printed out all of his e-mails. Harry was an engineer, and what he was trying to do was to perfect the formula. The 360-degree evaluation would yield a score of between 1 and 5 for each participant (to two decimal places). Harry's dozen or so e-mails dealt with adjustments to the raw evaluation score. If a person had exceeded his goals for the past year, should we increase the overall score by 0.25? If he had missed his goals, should we subtract 0.2 from the score? Should we give a fractional boost to a person's score if she had been with the company for more than ten years? There were more than twenty different suggestions for these types of adjustments.

When I met with Harry the next day, he asked me my reaction to all of his e-mails. "You make some very good points," I said. "But what you didn't recognize in all of it is that the numbers don't matter."

(continued)

He was shocked by my statement. "What do you mean the numbers don't matter? Why are we doing all of this if not to generate a score for each person?"

I replied: "Harry, let's say that we were able come up with the perfect formula and, at the end of the process, have a rank-ordered list of all 150 people, based on their weighted scores. The day after we complete the project, a member of your executive staff leaves the company for whatever reason. Will you look at the rankings and say 'Person A has the top score of all 150 people—4.63. The next person on the list has a score of 4.52 and the rankings go down from there. Therefore, we will automatically give the open job to Person A'?"

"Of course not," Harry replied. "There are a lot of other factors that will go into the decision on who gets the job."

"So," I said, "the 360-degree evaluations will give you some good information that can be used to evaluate candidates and to plan for developing people in their areas of weakness, but the overall scores don't really matter. There is no perfect formula that will take the place of your and your team's judgment."

We started the project the next day.

Dan Tobin

At the conclusion of the talent review process, the HR group should also work with the individuals identified as high potentials and their managers to write a development plan for each person. This development plan may include training, coaching, developmental assignments, and other methods discussed elsewhere in this book.

Planning for Developmental Assignments

In Chapter 8 we discussed the use of action learning projects in developing management talent. Developmental assignments take this approach a step further by rotating high-potentials through a series of assigned jobs to further develop their business acumen, familiarize them with various aspects of the organization's business, and, in the case of international assignments, bring them an appreciation and understanding of the ways the organization conducts its business in different cultures. The difference here is that the employee is assigned to a real job for a period of a year or more, rather than adding an individual or group project to his or her current responsibilities.

A number of large corporations do this on a regular basis. Earlier we mentioned the General Electric and Colgate-Palmolive programs. In other companies, a financial development program or a marketing development program may rotate high-potentials through a variety of assigned positions to enable them to learn the full breadth of each discipline as practiced in the organization. At the same time, the organization carefully watches each individual's job performance to see that each one is adaptable enough and learns quickly enough to take on each new role and to ensure that employees are not promoted beyond their capabilities.

The role of HR in this type of program encompasses a number of tasks:

1. First is the identification of high-potential employees who should be considered for placement in the rotation program. As stated earlier, many managers try to hide and hoard talented employees, rather than offering them up to other parts of the business, and this behavior sometimes requires HR to take responsibility for candidate identification.

2. Second, while the employee's manager will monitor the results of each assignment in terms of business goals, HR is often in a better position to monitor the employee's performance in terms of the "softer" side of management responsibilities. And this type of feedback will prove invaluable when the organization does its talent reviews and succession plans.

3. Third, HR can help executives identify opportunities for developmental assignments. HR may know before company executives when an employee is planning to take an extended medical or personal leave, thereby creating an opportunity for a developmental assignment. And by monitoring the leadership pipeline, HR may suggest internal candidates for open positions thereby saving the organization the time and expense of searching for an external hire.

Coaching

In an ideal world, managers at all levels of the organization would actively coach all their employees. But many times, managers do not have the time, interest, or capability to act as the employee's coach on all possible issues. Certainly, in terms of legal issues such as discrimination and harassment, HR is the logical place for an employee at any level of the organization to seek coaching and advice. Further, because HR as a profession is more attuned to "the people side of the business," HR staff can be effective coaches on communications and interpersonal skills, as well as on HR processes such as performance reviews. Exactly which of these coaching roles is right for your organization's HR group depends on a number of factors, such as how proficient managers within the organization are at coaching their employees themselves and the role that your HR group has chosen to take within the organization.

One area in which your HR group should regularly provide coaching is on development plans. For example, many commercially available 360-degree surveys generate individual reports that can exceed 50 to 100 pages. Your HR group should take responsibility, not just for administering the surveys, but also for coaching employees on how to interpret their personal reports and how to use them to plan for their own development. And, further, by examining the overall survey results across all employees, HR can counsel senior management on the needs to stress competencies for which there are widespread low scores.

Developing General Managers at McKesson

McKesson Corporation is a $75 billion diversified healthcare company that includes businesses ranging from pharmaceutical distribution, hardware manufacturing, software products, and integrated data services. Concerned with the need to develop numerous general managers who could manage large segments of its business, McKesson defined the general manager role to include "wide variations in accountabilities, functions managed, and competencies required, ranging from:

- Leaders of stand-alone strategic business units . . . with accountability for all facets and functions of their business, to
- General sales and distribution managers . . . to
- Product GMs, managing business strategy, complex product planning, and development and customer fulfillment."[9]

The HR organization, working with the company's executives, set a series of objectives to guide the development of a proactive general management program:

- "Differentiate the nature and scope of the varied kinds of GM roles presently existing in the company.
- "Identify competency-based (and other) criteria for selecting leaders into those varied roles.
- "Provide a rationale for effective movement of key talent through experiences that grow GM leadership breadth and depth.
- "Assure that the education curriculum provided is clearly targeted to the needs of general managers."[10]

Through an intensive, highly structured eight-step process, McKesson created a series of "development maps" for general managers to "provide a structure for top executives to use during talent management sessions to guide development planning."[11] The process includes the following steps:[12]

1. Engage top leaders in defining the nature of GM work and future development needs in the business.
2. Use the archetypes model to define basic GM job families.
3. Define the intellectual complexity requirements, motivational profile, and competencies needed in the GM job family.
4. Map current GM roles to the experiences grid: terms of scale versus strategic complexity or other factors most critical to the business.
5. Map critical competencies to the experiences grid to demonstrate which roles are most likely to develop them.
6. Adapt the development roadmap to guide effective talent movement across the enterprise.
7. Adopt a set of principles to guide strategic talent management and flow.
8. Align all talent-management practices around the road maps and experience grids.

An example of one of McKesson's development roadmaps is shown in Figure 11.1.

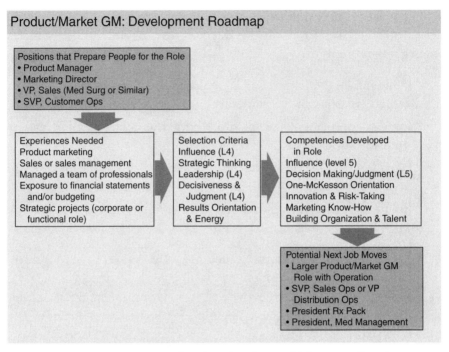

FIGURE 11.1 McKesson Product/Market General Manager: Development Roadmap[13]

It should be noted that this type of talent management study requires a huge commitment of time and resources. But even if your organization cannot make this type or size of commitment, asking the right questions regarding job roles, competencies, and development plans is a primary role for your HR group in helping your organization develop the management talent it will need for the future.

Summary

An organization's human resources group plays a key role in developing managers for current needs and for the future. The relatively new concept of talent management defines multiple roles for the HR group, from recruiting new talent to developing existing talent to coaching employees at all levels to help them succeed. To do this, HR needs to better understand the organization's business, its future goals, and its short- and long-term strategies. HR must become a true strategic partner by demonstrating how "people issues" are keys to organizational success.

CHAPTER

The Role of the Training Group

In previous chapters, we have emphasized the key roles in management development as belonging to the employee and his or her manager, the organization's leadership, and the organization's human resources group. So what is the role of the training group?

We are past the point in time when the training group sat in a corner of the human resources organization offering individual skills courses out of a catalog or just provided an e-learning platform that contained a menu of canned e-learning programs bought from a vendor. While these roles will still exist to some extent, we need to redefine the role of the corporate training group to better meet the management development challenges facing the organization.

The competencies described in the first section of this book, for individual contributors and all levels of management, apply as much to the members of the training group as they do to employees in every other function of the organization. Training staff members need to understand the organization's business and its major business processes, just as all employees do. But they also need to work with the human resources group and the organization's leaders to better understand employees' learning needs and how those learning needs apply to the company's business goals.

Members of the organization's training group need to develop more of an action orientation and view their roles as extending beyond the classroom and the e-learning platform to the successful application of learning to the employees' work. People who have long called themselves "trainers" need to change their basic orientation and now think of themselves as *learning facilitators*, as described in Table 12.1 and "Sharing Your Learning."

This is not to say that learning facilitators should not provide generic training programs on management skills as part of the organization's management development program. There is a definite place in the management development program for such generic management programs, especially when a group of employees has recently been promoted to new management positions at various levels of the organization. First-time first-level or mid-level managers need to get a basic

TABLE 12.1 Comparison of the Roles of Trainers and Learning Facilitators	
Trainers	*Learning Facilitators*
A trainer determines what others need to learn, develops a training program to transmit the required knowledge and skills, and provides the training.	A learning facilitator helps employees identify their personal learning needs and assists them in finding ways to satisfy those learning needs.
A trainer develops training programs.	A learning facilitator provides a variety of learning methods to help the employee meet personal and organizational goals.
A trainer presents the training he or she has developed.	A learning facilitator enables individual and organizational learning from a wide variety of sources.
A trainer creates generic training programs for large audiences.	A learning facilitator tailors learning solutions to meet individual learning needs.
A trainer is focused on the acquisition of knowledge and skills.	A learning facilitator is focused on the application of knowledge and skills to the job.
A trainer is focused on the goals of the training program.	A learning facilitator is focused on the goals of the employee and the organization.
A trainer's responsibility ends when the employee leaves the classroom or when he or she makes available an e-learning or other self-study program.	A learning facilitator's responsibility ends when the employee has completed a learning activity AND has successfully applied that learning to his or her work.
A trainer measures success by how satisfied the employee is with the training experience.	A learning facilitator measures success by how effectively learning is transferred to the job to make a positive difference in individual and organizational business results.

SHARING YOUR LEARNING

Some years ago, I presented a session on "knowledge sharing" at a conference of training professionals. Just prior to my breakout session, there was a general session given by a futurist who was a marvelous speaker in which he presented many unique and valuable ideas.

I opened my session by asking how many people had attended the previous session. Almost all of the 200 people in my session raised a hand. Next, I asked, "How many of you thought that the ideas that the speaker presented could have value not just for yourself, but also for your organization's CEO and other organizational leaders?" Almost all the hands were raised again.

Then I asked, "How many of you are planning to buy the speaker's book or a recording of the speaker's session to give to your CEO?" Two hands were raised from the 200 attendees.

The people in the room were training professionals, whose job was to spread knowledge in their organizations. And yet only 1 in a 100 was going to take this opportunity to do so. If they thought of themselves as learning facilitators, rather than as trainers and training managers, many more would have taken the initiative to share their learning more widely with their organization's leadership.

Dan Tobin

---

orientation to the responsibilities of their new jobs and the expectations for their new roles within the organization and start building the skills required to succeed in those new roles.

Some generic skills must be taught to all people involved in the management development process. For example, if the organization is introducing a new performance management system, all managers need training on how to use the system. This type of training provides an opportunity to also reinforce more basic management skills, such as giving feedback.

There is also a role for generic e-learning programs on basic individual and management skills. With the continuing pressure within organizations to reduce time away from the job for training, there are certainly ways of using e-learning to provide information on a wide variety of knowledge and skill areas. At the same time, it should be noted that e-learning programs do not provide the most effective training on behavioral skills or motor skills. For example, you can obtain information on how to ride a bicycle from a variety of media and watch videos of people riding bicycles, but you cannot say that you can ride a bicycle until you get on one yourself and practice. Similarly, there are a number of vendors in the market who sell e-learning programs on presentation skills. Certainly, there are some basic topics on organizing presentations, rules for creating visuals, and even demonstrations of effective presentation techniques that can be provided through e-learning. But most training professionals know that the most effective way of improving presentation skills is for the learner to practice those skills in front of a live audience and to videotape the practice sessions so that each learner can view and critique his or her own performance.

Many organizations buy a library of e-learning courses on various business, professional, and management skills and make them available to all employees as a *supplement* to live training. In this way, when there are no classroom sessions available, employees who need to immediately learn about a given topic at least have a resource they can use. It may not be as effective as an instructor-led class, but at least it is something that can help the employee. It is also a way to enable employees to explore learning topics that are beyond their current responsibilities–for example, it is a way for individual contributors to start learning about management skills before they become eligible to enroll in a management training program, or for a first-level manager to start learning about the strategic planning process even though people at this level don't have responsibility for strategic planning. Many global organizations also like to make these types of e-learning programs available to employees in countries where the number of staff is too small to justify bringing a live training event to that country. By providing a library of e-learning courses to these remote employees, the training group can make at least some learning resources available to all worldwide employees.

But despite the enthusiasm of some e-learning zealots, it is not true that all types of training can be done via e-learning just as or even more effectively than in a classroom. We have seen examples of e-learning companies that sell their services, saying that they can take any classroom program and convert it to e-learning with the promise of the same or better learning outcomes. A common erroneous assumption made by many companies is that they can take a week-long classroom program, convert it to e-learning, and magically eliminate the need to have employees spend any time taking that training. Perhaps in the far future, when we implant chips in employee's heads and download them from the Internet, this might be possible, but today, this is the work of science fiction, and the few science fiction stories that have included this strategy in their plot lines almost always end in disaster.

New Roles for the Training Group

To effectively develop managers, there are a number of new roles and methods that the AMA recommends for organizational training groups, including:

- Training employees and managers on their respective roles in the management development process.
- Developing learning guides to help employees and their managers identify the full range of internal and external development methods and opportunities available to them as they write the employee's development plan and learning contract.
- Coaching employees and managers on how to find and utilize this wide variety of learning resources and methods.
- Customizing externally sourced training.
- Working with company management to define and oversee action learning projects.
- Following up beyond the classroom or e-learning platform to help employees apply their newly acquired knowledge and skills to their jobs.
- Taking a more active role in the classroom and reinforcing learning by challenging employees when they are not actively applying what they have learned.

Training on Roles in the Management Development Process

Throughout this book, we have described how an organization's management development efforts require new roles for employees and their managers, for the organization's leaders, and for the human resources group. A prime role for the training group is to help all of these players learn about, and acquire the knowledge and skills required, for these new roles. Some examples include teaching

- Managers how to hold development discussions with their employees who aspire to management.
- Coaching skills to managers at all levels of the organization.
- Human resources staff and managers at all levels of the organization about the wide variety of learning methods and activities available to help develop management talent and how to choose among the many alternatives.
- The organization's leaders how to interpret results of 360-degree reviews to evaluate management talent and what to do with the results of such reviews.

Developing Learning Guides

It is no longer sufficient for your training group to publish an annual catalog of the courses you offer to employees. When your responsibility was simply to provide training, it was enough to let people know what seminars you were offering when and where and how to enroll. But in your role as a learning facilitator, your responsibility extends beyond the formal programs you offer in your classrooms to include e-learning resources, reading lists, directories of expert resources both within and without your organization, and the pointers to other learning opportunities as described throughout this book. To do this, you must widen your own learning resource networks both internal and external to your organization.

You also have to decide on which methods you want to recommend. For example, which of the 200,000 book listings on Amazon. com on the topic of leadership do you want to recommend to your organization's employees? If they want to learn the "secrets of leadership," there are books promising such secrets from exemplars of leadership ranging from Attila the Hun to Colin Powell, from Billy Graham to Santa Claus, from H. J. Heinz to Jack Welch, from Abe Lincoln to Elizabeth I. Rather than letting your employees randomly choose their own learning paths, your learning guides should reflect the leadership philosophy of the organization.

The learning guide may also offer tips on how to find a coach or a mentor within the organization, how to tap into an internal community of practice, or how to join the national or local chapter of a local professional society. It could include a calendar of events, including not just your training schedule, but also of local meetings and training events of interest, relevant college courses offered locally, and so forth.

The learning guides should open the eyes of employees and managers to the many learning opportunities that are available to them, beyond the organization's formal training programs, and help them plan for their own and their employees' development.

Coaching Employees and Managers on How to Identify and Use Learning Resources

As managers work with their employees who aspire to a management career, the training staff can coach those managers on how to identify and use a wide variety of learning resources to help prepare employees for those careers. Management development will no longer be limited to sending employees to an internal or external management training program, but may include a wide variety of developmental activities and assignments that can help employees test their interest in a management career, prepare newly assigned managers for their newly acquired responsibilities, and improve the skills of existing managers. The learning guides we just discussed can be a great resource for this purpose, but if the organization has always relied on the training group to provide guidance on which courses to take, it will take time, and coaching from your training group, to teach them how to choose from and best utilize this vast array of learning resources and methods.

Customizing Externally Sourced Training

Many organizations purchase training programs from external vendors, such as the AMA, and have the vendors' faculty conduct the training programs. This represents a substantial portion of AMA's business. In many cases, the program is bought intact, i.e., the organization may have had one or more people attend an AMA public program and found it so valuable for those people that they decide to bring it in-house to reach a wider employee audience. In those cases, the AMA sends the materials to the organization and an AMA faculty member arrives to teach the class just as it was taught in the public seminar setting.

In many other cases, the organization purchasing the training program from the AMA will ask us to customize the program for them. Some examples:

- For a Fundamentals of Finance seminar, the organization may ask the AMA instructor to use the organization's own financial statements as examples in the class so that participants develop a better understanding not just of financial principles, but also of the organization's own financial position.
- In teaching a class for first-time managers, the organization may ask the AMA instructor to include the organization's own performance management forms in the section on doing performance reviews.
- In teaching a class on making sales presentations, the organization may ask the AMA instructor to have participants practice their own sales presentations, rather than using generic examples.

As learning facilitators, your training group should work with external vendors to ensure that, as much as possible, their generic training programs are tailored to your company's specific learning requirements and business goals.

Defining and Overseeing Action Learning Projects

We have advocated the wide use of action learning projects for both individuals and teams as a method of management development. Your training group can work with your organization's management and human resources staff to define and structure these projects to maximize both the benefits to the company and learning by the participants. For example, the training group might write a guide to working on an action learning project, develop templates for reporting progress on those projects, and develop an action planning booklet to facilitate the employees' transfer of their learning into their regular work roles.

Further, your learning facilitators can act as coaches to the participants in these action learning projects to help them succeed and to transfer the learning from the projects to their regular jobs. For example, if the action learning project involves a team of employees, a learning facilitator may attend some team meetings and provide just-in-time learning on topics ranging from running meetings to team problem solving techniques to how to ensure involvement of all team members in the project.

Following Up to Ensure Application of Learning

In the old training paradigm, the responsibility of trainers ended when the training session ended. With the AMA's recommended approach, the learning facilitator's responsibility continues beyond the formal training activity to help ensure that learning is transferred to the participants' jobs. When employees are in an internal or external classroom, taking an e-learning program, or conducting self-study, they often don't know what questions to ask because the material is new to them, and they have never tried to use what they are learning in their jobs. When they return to their jobs and try out their newly acquired knowledge and skills, new questions will inevitably arise. Your learning facilitators can help speed the application of learning to the job by scheduling a formal follow-up session several weeks after the completion of the selected learning activity and being available to employees to answer their questions on an as-needed basis—for example, through holding regular "office hours" when they will take calls, by promising a 24-hour turnaround on e-mail inquiries, or by monitoring a participants' discussion forum.

At the AMA, we have begun to hold virtual follow-up sessions for selected seminars. Several weeks after participants complete an AMA seminar, they are invited to participate in a web-based conference with the instructor. In this session, the instructor may reinforce learning, ask the participants to report on the progress they have made in implementing what they learned in the formal classroom, lead a discussion of challenges the participants have faced as they have implemented what they learned, and answer participants' questions—especially those questions that they didn't even know to ask when they were in the classroom. Your organization's internal training group can provide a similar service for in-house training programs and work with external vendors to arrange for the same type of follow-up for externally sourced training. Feedback from such sessions may also be incorporated into the original seminar—for example, if most participants have experienced difficulties in applying one particular piece of learning, it may be advantageous to revise that portion of the original seminar. You can also use this type of follow-up exercise to help participants form an internal network for exchange of tips and other information, enabling employees to coach each other on what they have learned and their experiences in applying that learning on the job. This type of activity, usually supported by an intranet-based discussion board, can also help employees extend their personal networks within the company beyond the limits of their functional silos or their geographic bounds.

Challenging Employees to Apply What They Have Learned

Learning facilitators need to take more responsibility for ensuring that the content they deliver actually results in the desired behavioral change. This means that they have to extend their view from what happens in the classroom to what will subsequently take place when the training participants return to their jobs. This can be difficult to accomplish and may move your training staff outside their zone of comfort. "Team Training" describes a training scenario.

The trainers in this true story knew that they could conduct the training program they were hired to do, but they also knew that no matter how good the instruction they provided, there would be no change in the participants' behavior back on the job. They therefore took it on themselves to challenge the group's manager—something that most trainers would not see as part of their job description. In this case, the participants' behavior was not going to change unless their manager's behavior changed first. In other cases, the trainer may sense that the behaviors he or she is seeking to change just aren't being accepted by the training participants themselves (see "I Want to Fail Them All").

In this story, the college instructor could not do what she felt was right, because it wasn't her job to change the students' long-held prejudices. But in a corporate setting, the responsibility of the learning facilitator is different. If the learning facilitator finds that the employee's beliefs, attitudes, or behaviors may cause harm to the organization, she must take responsibility to challenge the participant. If this relates to a manager's bigotry or sexism, and the manager is allowed to continue with prejudicial and unfair attitudes and practices, the organization can

TEAM TRAINING

I once met two trainers from a Fortune 500 company. Their specialty was training of intact work teams on how to better function as a team. They had recently received a request from the head of an information technology group to give their three-day program to that manager's team.

On the first morning of the training, they started out by asking: "What is your greatest challenge to working together as a team?" There was no response.

Then they asked: "What do you like best about working as part of your team?" Again, there was no response.

Next, they asked: "What are your team's goals?" No response.

Finally, they asked: "Do you think of yourselves as a team?" One participant bravely spoke up: "We aren't a team. We're a bunch of people who work for the same manager, each on our own tasks as assigned by our manager. We don't have team goals, just individual projects. We've never met together as a group, never mind as a team, before today."

Many trainers at this point would have continued to teach their three-day program, telling the participants how much more productive they could be if they functioned as a team and telling the participants to get from it as much value as they could. But these trainers understood that unless the manager started treating her employees as a team, they would never be a team, so they did something that most trainers wouldn't dare to do–they sent the entire group back to their offices and went to meet with the manager to explain that if she wanted her employees to work as a team, she needed to treat them as a team, and that before she could send her employees to team training, she would have to attend a team leader's training program.

Dan Tobin

be held legally liable for the actions of the manager. Even if the problem behavior is not a matter of law, the learning facilitator must challenge participants who are blatantly (or even covertly) violating the company's standards. The problem could be with communication styles, interpersonal behaviors, or writing performance reviews–no

" I W A N T T O F A I L
T H E M A L L ! "

For a number of years, I taught in a graduate management program for working adults. One day, I received a call from a newer faculty member whom I was mentoring.

"I've got a problem," she said. "I'm teaching a class on diversity, and I want to fail everyone in the class." She explained that she was teaching the class in a small industrial town and that the students were all from the area, which had union-dominated blue-collar industries and few minorities.

I asked if her students were meeting the requirements of the class. "They've done all the required work, written all the papers, made all the presentations. But they're a bunch of bigots!" she told me. "Not one of them deserves to pass the course."

I explained to her that it was unlikely that she would be able to change lifelong beliefs over the course of eight weekly classes. "If they've met all the requirements, you don't have any choice but to pass them," I told her.

"But they're a bunch of bigots!" she shouted. "They don't deserve to pass a class on diversity!"

"I understand what you are saying," I told her, "but from the college's point of view, they've met the requirements. And even though the college faculty and administration would support your conclusions, they would feel that they had to pass them all if they met the requirements of the course. The problem with their bigotry is not yours to solve–it belongs to the students, their families, their community, and their employers."

Dan Tobin

matter what the subject, the reason the company is providing the training is so that employees will conform to company standards, and if it becomes clear in the classroom that an employee is not willing to do so, it is the responsibility of the learning facilitator to challenge the employee and, if necessary, report the problem back to the employee's manager or to the HR group for further action.

This is not a common behavior for trainers, and it may be very uncomfortable and difficult for them to do, especially if the offender is of a higher rank in the organization than the trainer. Before trainers can feel confident in doing this, they must feel assured that their actions will be backed up by their own management, by the HR organization, and by the company's leadership.

The Shoemaker's Children

There is an old tale of the shoemaker who is so busy making shoes for his customers that his own children go barefoot. Similarly, many training groups are so focused on the learning needs of their customers that they fail to recognize and act on their own learning needs. To be successful in making the needed transition from training to learning facilitation will require learning and reorientation of many trainers, and training managers, who have lived with the old model for many years.

A Note on Evaluating Training Groups

A number of training associations and consultants, including *Training Magazine* and the American Society for Training and Development, publish annual statistics on training within organizations. Some typical statistics that these surveys collect and compare on a year-to-year basis include:

- Company expenditures on training, overall and per employee.
- Number of days of training per employee per year.
- Number of trainers in the organization, total and per employee.
- The ratio of in-house versus external training expense.
- The percentage of the training budget spent on classroom training versus e-learning.

The challenge of trying to interpret these statistics is that they tell us nothing about the effectiveness of the training, whether the right people are receiving the right training, and whether they are actually applying it to their work to improve business results. In *The Knowledge-Enabled Organization*,[1] Daniel Tobin asserts that more than half of the money spent by organizations on training programs is wasted because what the employees learn in those programs never gets applied to their work. But these are the statistics that are collected, because they are relatively easy to measure. Albert Einstein once said: "Not everything that can be counted counts, and not everything that counts can be counted."

Will the changes recommended in this book on how organizations should develop their management talent increase spending? Probably. But following these recommendations will also ensure that the organization has the management talent it needs to help the company survive, grow, and prosper. The use of the learning contract described in Chapter 1 will ensure that the learning employees undertake will be tied directly to organizational, team, and individual business goals, and that what gets learned also gets applied to the employees' work to make a positive difference in business results.

Summary

In order to meet the ongoing need for management and leadership development, the role of the organization's training group must change. Rather than thinking of themselves as trainers whose responsibilities end once the student leaves the classroom or completes an e-learning program, members of the training group must redefine themselves as learning facilitators. Learning facilitators work with employees from the time that a learning need is defined to the time when it is successfully applied to the employees' work. Successful learning facilitation is not measured by how many employees completed a class or how many hours of training are provided to each employee, but whether employees at all levels are able to meet their individual, group, and organizational goals.

The Future of Management Development

How will future efforts at developing management talent differ from those that are used today? What will be the effects and requirements of the looming shift in the age cohorts within organizations? Will technology advances change the way that management development happens? How will the roles of organizational leadership and human resources and training groups change over the coming years?

In this final chapter of the *AMA Guide to Management Development,* we will try to address these questions based on the AMA's own experience as well as the views of a number of management thinkers and consultants with whom we have conferred.

Changing Demographics and the Loss of Corporate Memory

In 2006, the United States reported that over the course of the last century, the number of people aged 65 and over grew from 3.1 million in 1900 to 35 million in 2000.[1] Globally, it is predicted that by 2050 more people will be over the age of 60 than under the age of 15. These population shifts will impact the future workforce.

The U.S. Bureau of Labor Statistics predicts talent shortages as the baby boomer generation retires. Walter McFarland and Kate Morse of Booz Allen Hamilton report:

> Facing a shortfall of as many as 10 million workers, the U.S. workforce will encounter a talent drought of epic proportions by the end of the

decade, according to the Bureau of Labor Statistics and the Employment Policy Foundation. A recent survey of 150 Fortune 500 companies found an average expectation of 33 percent turnover of executives within the next five years, while one-third do not believe that they will be able to find suitable replacements.[2]

While many organizations are focused on the need for succession planning and leadership development programs in order to replace senior executives who will retire in the coming years, the loss of knowledge that these executives will take with them as they retire is only the tip of the iceberg. Stefanie Smith[3] discusses other problems that will inevitably arise from the loss of knowledge and corporate memory:

> They are the programmers who know the intricacies of computer networks and legacy integrations. They are the salespeople who have sustained relationships with key customers over decades. They are the accountants reporting to the controller who know how complex expenses and transactions are classified for the auditors. They are the administrators who know how to handle recordkeeping that appears arcane and intricate to the executives to whom they report.

These types of knowledge are tacit in nature and, as explained in the four-stage learning model presented in Chapter 1 of this book, cannot be taught in the classroom, but can be transferred through dialogue and discussion of the older generation of employees with the younger generations. This reinforces the arguments made in Chapter 10 concerning the role of organizational leadership in developing managers—only by actively participating in management development programs, including classroom training, coaching, and mentoring, can the organization's older generation of leaders effectively transfer their tacit knowledge to younger generations.

The Rise of Technology

The younger generations have grown up using technology. They constantly use instant messaging (IM) from their computers, their cell phones, and their Blackberries. They play complicated games in virtual worlds. They use these electronic communication methods to build and maintain incredibly large personal networks. Having grown up watching *Sesame Street,* they become easily bored if they do not have something new and exciting to view on a continuous basis, so they can easily become bored with the repetitive tasks of many entry-level jobs and frequently change jobs and employers to find new challenges. They do not fear the next generation of technology, as do many in older generations, but eagerly await it and become impatient if the organization is slow to introduce technical innovations. They rely on the Internet, on Wikis, and discussion forums to quickly find answers to their questions, and they welcome this type of collaboration.

But can all of this technology replace traditional, instructor-led management training? Some e-learning zealots have claimed that e-learning is *always* more effective than instructor-led training, and there are a number of companies whose business is converting instructor-led training to e-learning. And many companies have jumped at the chance to replace centralized instructor-led training to e-learning because of the opportunity to reduce costs—no more travel expenses, no more instructor salaries, no expensive classrooms to maintain. But many of these companies have made some poor assumptions about e-learning and have learned difficult lessons because of those *false assumptions,* such as:

- *Anything that can be learned in the classroom can be learned online.* E-Learning is best at transmitting factual knowledge, but less effective at building skills. So, while e-learning can be effective in teaching people the basics of reading a financial report, it is much less effective at teaching presentation skills or interpersonal skills.

- *Converting instructor-led training to e-learning means that employees do not need dedicated learning time.* We have seen many companies that have converted a five-day classroom program to e-learning and then assumed that employees no longer need dedicated learning time—they can learn it on their own time, when they have a lull in their work or access the e-learning program from home on weekends and evenings. There have been successful court suits where exempt employees have claimed that employers are forcing them to dedicate many hours away from the office to learn work-related information and skills, and they should be paid for this time. Also, many younger-generation employees are seeking a better work–life balance than the older generations and resent being required to use their leisure time on work-related learning. There is also an important dynamic that takes place in a dedicated classroom where the instructor and the students are focused on a specific learning agenda for an extensive period of time. This dynamic cannot be effectively replicated with short bursts of e-learning.

- *Statistics on the rate of return of e-learning don't generally focus on the right part of the ROI equation.* Many studies have been done that show that there is a great rate of return on investments in e-learning. Rate-of-return analysis, at its simplest, is the ratio of benefits to costs: $ROI = Benefits/Costs$.[4] Most of the ROI studies of e-learning have focused on the reduction of costs, which will always raise the value of this ratio. Throughout this book, we have emphasized that organizations should focus on the benefits of management development, and most e-learning ROI studies have assumed that benefits will remain constant while costs are reduced.

This is not to say that management development in the future should not take advantage of new technological applications that can further the management development effort. For example, the American Management Association has already introduced several technology-based supplements to selected programs:

- For most of its top-selling programs, AMA-Complete offers computer-based pretests and posttests (to measure knowledge acquisition) as well as tune-up courses that reinforce learning from the classroom experience. We also offer other online resources, including supplementary materials and online tools for selected programs.

- AMA's recently introduced seminar designed to build business acumen is centered on a sophisticated business simulation that helps participants learn about the interrelatedness of business functions in planning and operations.

- AMA has created its first online community to serve people who have taken its MBTI (Myers-Briggs Type Indicator) programs. This community also includes a series of blogs.

- AMA has started to offer *virtual follow-up sessions (VFS)* to its corporate customers to help reinforce classroom learning and to assist learners as they apply their learning after their classroom experience.

• AMA has started a very successful series of webcasts and podcasts to inform participants of new trends and ideas in the management field. Because these sessions are limited to 60 to 90 minutes, they are used to inform people, rather than to train them.

While many of AMA's technology-based applications are designed to appeal to more tech-savvy learners, we also recognize that the younger generation's reliance on technology as their primary means of communication has also created other problems in the workplace. Several years ago, AMA introduced a new program titled "How to Communicate with Diplomacy, Tact, and Credibility." This seminar was originally planned as an advanced-level communications program for people who were already good communicators but wanted to hone their skills, but this was not the audience it attracted. We found that many organizations were sending to this seminar relatively young employees who, although they had excellent technical skills, were poor communicators who tended to offend others with their bluntness. Rather than seeking out this seminar, many of the participants were sent to the seminar and had no idea why they were sent–they had no idea that their interpersonal communication skills were lacking or that others in their workplace found their communication styles offensive. We quickly redesigned the seminar to meet these needs, and it quickly became one of the AMA's top sellers.

So evolving technologies will continue to expand opportunities for collaboration and knowledge sharing, it cannot totally replace formal learning experiences, whether in the classroom or on the job.

Rapid Management Development Through Action Learning

Because of the rapidly changing demographics of the workforce explained earlier in this chapter, there is a great need to accelerate the development of younger generations for more senior management and leadership positions. While there will always be a need for formal educational programs to help prepare these younger employees for these responsibilities, *action learning* will become an increasingly important method of development.

In Chapter 8, we discussed the use of action learning to help employees apply what they have learned in the classroom (and through other means of education). Action learning must, in the future, be used and supported to help ensure successful development. In many organizations faced with large numbers of retirees, younger employees are promoted and then left to "sink or swim"—it is assumed that the best employees will succeed in their new responsibilities, and those who don't survive will be let go and replaced with other promising candidates. Few companies can afford this type of random experimentation, because the cost of failure extends beyond the loss of a bright young employee—it can have a major effect on an organization's overall business results and on the overall morale within the organization. While many younger employees are eager for these types of promotional opportunities, even the highest potential employees fear failure, and many have a tendency to want to succeed on their own, waiting to ask for help until they are so over their heads that it is too late to save them.

The most forward-thinking companies will use two strategies to help ensure the successful development of younger generations for more senior-level positions. First, they start developing these people early through comprehensive leadership development programs that combine many modes of learning including classroom learning, action learning, coaching, and mentoring. These types of programs help fill the leadership pipeline and also act as a screening method. Observing participants as they take part in action learning projects can reveal those who have the best characteristics for leadership before they are promoted, thereby improving the chances of successful placement in more senior-level jobs. These programs can also be effective in helping the next generation of leaders to build their organization-wide support networks so that key relationships are already in place when they are promoted. After the first session in a leadership development program at a small high-tech company, where several dozen high-potential mid-level managers from around the world were brought together for a three-day educational session, participants noted that even if there had been no educational component to the program, enabling these people to meet each other and discuss the company's business from their various functional and geographical perspectives would have provided a great return on the company's investment in the meeting.

The second strategy for ensuring the success of younger generations in leadership positions is to provide mentoring, coaching, and other support for them during their first months in their new positions. Rather than just letting these newly promoted employees to sink or swim, these more forward-thinking organizations provide in-water support and instruction.

In many cases, these types of promotions are to replace someone who has just retired (and the demographics cited at the beginning of this chapter forecast that this will be an increasing trend over the coming decade). Surveys of baby boomers say that most would like to phase-in their retirements–they do not want to stop working totally. One promising strategy is to retain the newly retired senior manager to be a part-time mentor and coach to the newly promoted replacement. In this way, the new manager will have the benefit of extending his or her learning from the experience of the retiree, a sounding board for his or her new ideas, and a coach who has knowledge of the specific business along with the players, customers, suppliers, and so on.

Changing Roles

With the trends in demographics, new approaches to management development, and technology playing a larger role, some parts of the organization will need to adjust or change their responsibilities. The first of these is the human resources (HR) group. We asked several leading thinkers[5] how they believe that HR and training groups will have to change in the future to meet these emerging needs.

- Professor Richard Boyatzis of Case Western believes companies will rise and fall on the strength of their HR groups. He sees the world moving to a place where people will be the biggest differentiator for companies; HR groups can help by providing more effective inspiration, motivation, and guidance of the organization's human capital and talent.

- McGill University professor Henry Mintzberg thinks HR groups need to pay attention to all candidates, not just those designated as "high flyers," and see that potential candidates get the individualized training they need. He suggests an example–www.Coaching Ourselves.com.

- Jay Jamrog, research vice president at the Institute for Corporate Productivity (I4CP) believes that HR needs to change the way it looks at the value it adds to the organization. HR directors need to develop an integrated talent management suite of offerings so they get the right people in the right positions, and they need to tell the story of what they're doing–lining people up to execute the strategy of the organization.

- University of Michigan professor David Ulrich stresses that HR needs to integrate training programs with compensation, appraisal, and staffing programs. All materials and programs need to align to the business strategy and customer expectations.

Another organizational group that will be affected by the changing environment is the training organization.

- Babson professor Allan Cohen feels that training organizations need to "move beyond the smiley face theory of training." They need to understand their organizations' business and the complexity of what people actually do. He sees the soft skills as more relevant than ever, blending the need for speed and the need to have full input into making the hard business decisions, with the need to pay attention to people's growth.

- David Ulrich thinks trainers need to pay more attention to strategy (how training matches where the company is going), technology (how training is delivered), and finance (how will the company make money from the training). He sees line managers as the ones who should judge the long-term value of the work; they should also model the behaviors being taught in training.

- IMD (Lausanne, Switzerland) professor Michael Watkins wants to see more use of what the literature tells us about how to develop expertise, which is keeping people immersed for longer periods of time in order to become expert. Training programs are useful, but companies need to commit to putting young leaders into business positions and keeping them there for longer periods of time–giving them time to live with the consequences of their early decisions.

- Jay Jamrog feels there are some standardized kinds of training programs that will continue to be needed, but that companies are going to want much more specific customized training as well. He sees soft skills as critically important for future leaders–the challenge being to figure out how to measure and reward those softer competencies of developing people and giving them the incentives to do their jobs well.

- Marshall Goldsmith sees training organizations being held more accountable for results as opposed to process and activity. He thinks executives will be much more involved in putting together the content of management development programs.

- McGill University professor Henry Mintzberg thinks training organizations will do more by doing less. They will do less formal training while playing more of a learning facilitation role (see Table 12.1) to enable managers to learn through their own experiences.

A Final Word

There is no doubt management development will be different in the future. And we have no pat recommendations for how best to do it. As Generation X and the Millennials take the places of retiring baby boomers, management development programs need to adapt to their learning and work preferences. Their high comfort level with technology and their increased ability to multitask will prompt changes we can only guess at now. We know they are different from their predecessors; we need to learn how to harness their strengths. We need to explore new learning approaches.

One huge difference the new generations bring to the workforce is their ability to work with others to develop their ideas. Through their online collaborations, they have shown that peer production can be a powerful tool for dramatically increasing the speed with which problems can be uncovered and fixed.[6] They demonstrated this with projects like the development of Wikipedia and Linux.

Their affinity for social networking is a force we need to harness.[7] This will have big implications for management in general and for management development programs in particular. We need more research on how to help them collaborate and innovate even more effectively and efficiently; we need to learn how best to tap their talents and to manage them effectively.

Now is the time to think and plan how to adapt management development approaches to accommodate the new generations who will become the future business leaders of tomorrow. We hope the perspectives in this *AMA Guide to Management Development* will spur your thinking and help you in that process.

Appendix

The AMA Management Development Competency Model

Knowing and Managing Yourself

Emotional Intelligence/Self-Awareness

Analyzing and recognizing one's own strengths and weaknesses, attitudes, and feelings; maintaining a clear, realistic understanding of one's goals, capabilities, and limitations; seeking feedback about one's effectiveness and making changes in response to it; being attuned to one's inner feelings, recognizing how these feelings affect one's behavior and job performance, and expressing one's feelings and reactions appropriately.

Illustrative Behaviors	Individual Professional	First-Level Manager	Mid-Level (Manager of Managers)	Functional Manager
1. Proactively solicits both positive and constructive feedback on his or her performance.	X	X	X	X
2. Adjusts his or her behavior in response to feedback.	X	X	X	X
3. Recognizes feelings and concerns heard in conversation to address the other person's expressed and underlying needs.	X	X	X	X
4. Understands his or her personal preferences for making decisions, solving problems, and working with others; recognizes when his or her preferred style may not be the most effective approach given the situation.	X	X	X	X
5. Asks questions that create an atmosphere in which the other person feels comfortable discussing the situation and sharing concerns.	X	X	X	X
6. Expresses his or her feelings and reactions in a calm, clear manner.	X	X	X	X
7. Communicates tactfully even when others are unhappy or confused.	X	X	X	X
8. Coaches others on the importance of self-awareness and how to become more self-aware.		X	X	X

A PDF file of the AMA Management Development Compentency Model, as well as other information about the book, is available at:
www.amacombooks.org/go/AMAGuideMgmtDevelop

Self-Confidence

Acting on the basis of one's convictions rather than trying to please others; being confident in oneself; having a healthy sense of one's capabilities without being arrogant.

Illustrative Behaviors	Individual Professional	First-Level Manager	Mid-Level (Manager of Managers)	Functional Manager
1. Clearly and appropriately states his or her opinions and perspectives, even if others disagree.	X	X	X	X
2. Exhibits confidence and conviction when presenting his or her ideas and perspectives, both verbally and in writing.	X	X	X	X
3. Demonstrates a willingness to take on challenging new projects or assignments.	X	X	X	X
4. Quickly and candidly informs others when he or she cannot fulfill a request, and the reason for it, and problem-solves an alternative.	X	X	X	X
5. Admits when he or she is wrong or someone else has a better solution and is willing to change direction or reorient his or her actions as necessary.	X	X	X	X
6. Demonstrates confidence that his or her plans and decisions will be successful.	X	X	X	X
7. Is willing to delegate tasks or assignments that team members may be able to perform better than him- or herself.		X	X	X
8. Takes responsibility for making difficult or unpopular decisions.		X	X	X

Self-Development

Seeking feedback about one's strengths and weaknesses; initiating activities to increase or enhance one's knowledge, skills, and competence in order to perform more effectively or enhance one's career; learning new information or ideas and applying them effectively; keeping up to date in one's knowledge and skills; and learning from successes and failures.

Illustrative Behaviors	Individual Professional	First-Level Manager	Mid-Level (Manager of Managers)	Functional Manager
1. Routinely asks for feedback on his or her performance and uses both positive and negative feedback to enhance performance.	X	X	X	X
2. Receives feedback in a constructive manner.	X	X	X	X
3. Probes for concrete examples and suggestions to improve his or her own performance.	X	X	X	X
4. Consults relevant sources (e.g., appraisals, reports, videos, customer feedback) to get insight into his or her own performance.	X	X	X	X
5. Is self-critical; can name both strong and weak points about him- or herself.	X	X	X	X
6. Learns from both successes and failures.	X	X	X	X
7. Initiates project debriefs to clarify learnings—both what worked well and what could be done more effectively in the future.	X	X	X	X
8. Seeks both formal and informal development opportunities.	X	X	X	X
9. Demonstrates a desire to perform above and beyond the requirements of his or her position (e.g., enthusiastically takes on tasks outside of daily responsibilities to learn and grow).		X	X	X
10. Coaches others to focus on self-development.		X	X	X
11. Builds a culture that encourages learning and continuous improvement.				X

Building Trust and Personal Accountability

Keeping promises and honoring commitments; accepting responsibility for one's actions; being honest and truthful when communicating information; behaving in a way that is consistent with espoused values; and assuming responsibility for dealing with problems, crises, or issues.

Illustrative Behaviors	Individual Professional	First-Level Manager	Mid-Level (Manager of Managers)	Functional Manager
1. Admits when he or she does not know an answer and takes the necessary measures to locate required information.	X	X	X	X
2. Treats confidential information with respect and integrity.	X	X	X	X
3. Takes the initiative to provide all relevant information, even when communicating about a problem, mistake, or other difficult situation (e.g., is clear and direct).	X	X	X	X
4. Accepts responsibility for mistakes and failures and learns from them (e.g., does not "point fingers").	X	X	X	X
5. Keeps promises and honors commitments.	X	X	X	X
6. Demonstrates consistency between his or her words and actions.	X	X	X	X
7. Backs up and supports team members in difficult situations.	X	X	X	X
8. Handles work-related problems and issues in a confident and decisive manner.	X	X	X	X
9. Is willing to hold tough discussions with others about taking responsibility for their own actions and decisions.		X	X	X
10. Sets an example by behaving in a way that is consistent with the organization's values and principles.		X	X	X
11. Asks open-ended, nonevaluative questions about work-related problems to encourage people to respond and provide a more complete picture of the situation.		X	X	X

Resilience and Stress Tolerance

Continuing to perform effectively when faced with time pressures, adversity, disappointment, or opposition; remaining focused, composed, and optimistic; bouncing back from failures or disappointments.

Illustrative Behaviors	Individual Professional	First-Level Manager	Mid-Level (Manager of Managers)	Functional Manager
1. Projects credibility and poise under difficult or adverse conditions.	X	X	X	X
2. Maintains progress (while maintaining quality) when handling multiple tasks and projects, even under stressful situations or when faced with competing deadlines.	X	X	X	X
3. Is patient, tenacious, and resourceful when seeking information to satisfy a request or complete a project.	X	X	X	X
4. Sees issues and problems through to completion.	X	X	X	X
5. Handles contacts with internal and external customers with a high degree of professionalism (e.g., maintains a calm disposition even when others are upset, does not convey impatience or annoyance).	X	X	X	X
6. Treats all people with respect and equity, even when under pressure.	X	X	X	X
7. Finds ways to overcome or eliminate barriers that are hindering achievement of his or her goals.	X	X	X	X
8. Views failures and mistakes as an opportunity to learn.	X	X	X	X
9. Quickly responds to unforeseen changes in the business.		X	X	X
10. Keeps team members calm and focused in uncertain or complicated situations.		X	X	X

Action Orientation

Maintaining a sense of urgency to complete a task; seeking information rather than waiting for it; making decisions in a timely manner regardless of pressure or uncertainty; making decisions quickly when called upon to do so; acting decisively to implement solutions and resolve crises; not procrastinating; being tough and assertive when necessary while showing respect and positive regard for others.

Illustrative Behaviors	*Individual Professional*	*First-Level Manager*	*Mid-Level (Manager of Managers)*	*Functional Manager*
1. Makes timely decisions based on the best available information (e.g., is not overcome by "analysis paralysis").	X	X	X	X
2. Has the confidence to make decisions in uncertain circumstances.	X	X	X	X
3. Balances information gathering and analysis activities with an urgency to take action and "drive it forward."	X	X	X	X
4. Tackles problems or conflict head-on; does not procrastinate.	X	X	X	X
5. Avoids distraction from less critical activities.	X	X	X	X
6. Clarifies priorities and objectives to swiftly accomplish tasks.	X	X	X	X
7. Takes the initiative to identify and solve work-related problems.	X	X	X	X
8. Coaches others to be decisive.		X	X	X
9. Checks to ensure priorities and objectives are clear among team members.		X	X	X
10. Refocuses team members on the "big picture" when they appear to have lost sight of it.			X	X

Time Management

Allocating time appropriately among people and projects to ensure that both internal and external client needs are met; reprioritizing daily tasks as each day progresses to ensure that newly emerging, urgent issues are resolved while not losing sight of longer-term projects; balancing his or her workload when involved in multiple projects.

Illustrative Behaviors	Individual Professional	First-Level Manager	Mid-Level (Manager of Managers)	Functional Manager
1. Shifts attention quickly to respond to the unexpected and simultaneously make progress on planned activities.	X	X	X	X
2. Understands what is required to get things done and establishes/implements an effective course of action (e.g., establishes appropriate deadlines and meets them).	X	X	X	X
3. Plans each day's work to complete time-sensitive issues before deadlines.	X	X	X	X
4. Takes ownership for delivering results on multiple projects or initiatives.	X	X	X	X
5. Gathers the necessary information to effectively prioritize work (e.g., urgency and importance).	X	X	X	X
6. Prioritizes and organizes a complex workload while maintaining focus and staying on track.	X	X	X	
7. Reallocates his or her time to ensure the completion of his or her own assigned work/responsibilities as well as helping others perform effectively.		X		
8. Establishes and maintains systems and files to help resolve pending issues and problems in a timely manner.	X	X	X	
9. Delegates appropriately to ensure that he or she is focused on longer-term strategic projects.			X	X
10. Reprioritizes work efforts based on changing situations and emerging issues (e.g., is responsive to organizational, systems, and/or market changes).			X	X
11. Effectively balances his or her focus on both strategy and operations to achieve optimal results.				X

Flexibility and Agility

Adjusting one's behavior to new information or changing circumstances; remaining open to new ways of doing things; experimenting with new methods; and working effectively in an unstructured or dynamic environment.

Illustrative Behaviors	Individual Professional	First-Level Manager	Mid-Level (Manager of Managers)	Functional Manager
1. Adapts his or her behavior in response to new information or changing circumstances.	X	X	X	X
2. Is open to new methods, ideas, or approaches.	X	X	X	X
3. Works and collaborates effectively in unstructured or dynamic environments.	X	X	X	X
4. Adjusts the original objective or plan to allow the best possible results.	X	X	X	X
5. Demonstrates a willingness to embrace new systems, processes, technology, and ideas.	X	X	X	X
6. Stays focused and keeps his or her team focused during times of uncertainty or change.		X	X	X
7. Coaches others to be flexible and adapt behavior to various situations.		X	X	X
8. Understands that ambiguity is a normal part of doing business and communicates this to people in the work unit/ function.		X	X	X
9. Anticipates changes in the internal and external environment (e.g., organizational, market, products, and systems) and adapts accordingly.			X	X
10. Uses new ideas to reengineer work processes or make changes in how resources are allocated within the function.				X

Critical and Analytical Thinking

Regularly questioning basic assumptions about the work and how it gets done; identifying underlying principles, root causes, or facts by breaking down information or data and drawing conclusions; applying sound reasoning; understanding the complexity of certain issues and crystallizing the components of the issue to make it more manageable; and understanding the implications of data/information.

Illustrative Behaviors	Individual Professional	First-Level Manager	Mid-Level (Manager of Managers)	Functional Manager
1. Challenges established thinking, processes, or protocols with company success in mind.	X	X	X	X
2. Quickly and systematically analyzes the root cause of work-related problems before taking corrective action.	X	X	X	X
3. Recognizes and communicates the implications of data/information.	X	X	X	X
4. Is able to clearly frame a problem, identify and collect the necessary data, and make recommendations for solving the problem.	X	X	X	X
5. Takes complex issues or problems and breaks them down into manageable components.	X	X	X	X
6. Understands how data and recommendations may impact other functions and departments.			X	X
7. Relates problems to one another and to strategic objectives to recognize opportunities for dealing with several related problems at the same time.			X	X

Creative Thinking

Reexamining traditional strategies and practices; proactively looking for new ideas and ways to improve products, services, and work processes; looking at problems and opportunities from a unique perspective; seeing patterns and themes that are not immediately apparent to others; taking time to refine and shape a new idea so it has a higher likelihood of success.

Illustrative Behaviors	Individual Professional	First-Level Manager	Mid-Level (Manager of Managers)	Functional Manager
1. Suggests ways to improve processes and create efficiencies (e.g., is willing to question current approaches in the interest of maximizing efficiency, suggests better ways to do the work).	X	X	X	X
2. Demonstrates creative approaches to solving problems and generates innovative approaches.	X	X	X	X
3. Demonstrates creative approaches to locating and applying information to meet internal and external customer needs.	X	X	X	X
4. Proactively identifies ways to improve current workflow and procedures to better meet internal and external customer needs (e.g., challenges the status quo).	X	X	X	X
5. Recognizes patterns or themes in data/information that may not have been readily apparent (e.g., looks for relationships among issues/problems rather than assume they are distinct and independent).	X	X	X	X
6. Solicits input from others who have unique or vastly different perspectives when shaping an idea or plan.		X	X	X
7. Coaches others to think creatively and encourages brainstorming when solving problems or making decisions.		X	X	X

Knowing and Managing Others

Oral Communication

Conveying ideas and opinions clearly to others; projecting credibility, poise, and confidence even under difficult or adversarial conditions; speaking enthusiastically and using vivid language, examples, or anecdotes to communicate a message; making use of unambiguous language, gestures, and nonverbal communication; considering the needs of the audience and how it is likely to react; talking to people in a way they can understand; listening attentively to others; and using appropriate grammar and vocabulary.

Illustrative Behaviors	Individual Professional	First-Level Manager	Mid-Level (Manager of Managers)	Functional Manager
1. Uses effective listening skills to identify important information in conversations and to engage people (e.g., pays attention to orally communicated facts and details, discerns and responds to the feelings and underlying messages of others, paraphrases, asks relevant open-ended questions).	X	X	X	X
2. Clearly articulates ideas, opinions, and information so others understand them.	X	X	X	X
3. Uses the appropriate medium (e.g., voice mail, face-to-face, one-on-one, team meeting) depending on the nature of the information being communicated.	X	X	X	X
4. Adapts his or her communication strategy to the audience.		X	X	X
5. Ensures that people are provided with clear, timely, and accurate information about issues that may affect their work.		X	X	X
6. Exhibits confidence and enthusiasm when presenting information.			X	X
7. Effectively facilitates group conversations in order to clarify issues and establish direction.			X	X
8. Delivers presentations to both small and large groups in a well-organized, clear, and articulate manner.			X	X
9. Understands when "skip level" communication may be appropriate and necessary (e.g., stays in touch with front-line employees without diminishing the authority of his or her direct reports).				X

Written Communication

Expressing ideas and opinions clearly in properly structured, well-organized, and grammatically correct reports and documents; employing language and terminology appropriate to the reader; using appropriate grammar and punctuation.

Illustrative Behaviors	Individual Professional	First-Level Manager	Mid-Level (Manager of Managers)	Functional Manager
1. Uses language that is clear to the reader.	X	X	X	X
2. Writes documents free of grammatical or punctuation errors.	X	X	X	X
3. Presents ideas or opinions clearly and succinctly in writing.	X	X	X	X
4. Uses e-mail as an appropriate medium (i.e., understands when a face-to-face or telephone conversation would be more effective).	X	X	X	X
5. Writes with a logical structure (e.g., introduction, supporting information, conclusion).	X	X	X	X
6. Breaks down a complex concept so that is easily understood by the target audience.	X	X	X	X
7. Uses examples that are suitable and relevant for the target audience.	X	X	X	X
8. Places material in a broader organizational context, pointing out connections and relationships.			X	X

Valuing Diversity

Demonstrating respect for individual differences (including cultural differences and diverse ways of thinking or approaching issues); establishing a climate in which all people can be comfortable and productive; evaluating the work of others in a culturally neutral way; selecting and developing people in multiple cultural settings; communicating effectively with and in multiple cultures; understanding how culture influences people's behavior; adapting one's style and behavior to meet cultural norms and expectations; and taking advantage of unique cultural knowledge, capability, or information to develop or enhance products or services.

Illustrative Behaviors	*Individual Professional*	*First-Level Manager*	*Mid-Level (Manager of Managers)*	*Functional Manager*
1. Relates effectively with people of diverse backgrounds (both cultural backgrounds and those who have different ways of thinking or approaching issues).	X	X	X	X
2. Adapts his or her style and behavior to meet cultural norms and expectations.	X	X	X	X
3. Reaches agreement with people who share different opinions.	X	X	X	X
4. Includes people of diverse backgrounds in his or her informal network.	X	X	X	X
5. Challenges others who make racial, ethnic, or sexually derogatory comments.	X	X	X	X
6. Coaches others on how cultural norms and expectations influence behavior.		X	X	X
7. Demonstrates a respect for individual differences by creating an environment in which people can be themselves.		X	X	X
8. Evaluates team members' performance in a culturally neutral way.		X	X	X
9. Leverages unique cultural knowledge, capability, and/or information to develop or enhance products and services.			X	X
10. Appreciates the contributions of different functions across the organization and involves them appropriately and in planning and decision making.			X	X

Building Teams

Facilitating the constructive resolution of conflict; increasing mutual trust; encouraging cooperation, coordination, and identification with the work unit; encouraging information sharing among individuals who do not know each other and who may represent different cultures; including others in processes and decisions regardless of geographical distance or location; finding creative ways to minimize the effects of different time zones on the quality and frequency of interactions.

Illustrative Behaviors	Individual Professional	First-Level Manager	Mid-Level (Manager of Managers)	Functional Manager
1. Acts on opportunities to collaborate across the organization, regardless of geography or cultural differences.	X	X	X	X
2. Proactively helps team members both within and outside of his or her group.	X	X	X	X
3. Shares credit for successes with team members (i.e., gives credit where credit is due).	X	X	X	X
4. Solicits and offers feedback on how people could work most effectively together.	X	X	X	X
5. Encourages frank and open discussion of a disagreement.		X	X	X
6. Encourages cooperation and teamwork among people who depend on each other to get the work done.		X	X	X
7. Coaches people to partner with colleagues across the organization, regardless of cultural differences or geography.		X	X	X
8. Recognizes conflicting priorities across the organization and initiates joint problem solving to determine the best course of action for the organization.			X	X
9. Encourages and facilitates cross-unit cooperation and coordination.			X	X

Networking

Socializing informally; developing contacts with people who are a source of information and support; maintaining contacts through periodic visits, telephone calls, correspondence, and attendance at meetings and social events.

Illustrative Behaviors	Individual Professional	First-Level Manager	Mid-Level (Manager of Managers)	Functional Manager
1. Relays relevant experiences and passes on knowledge unselfishly.	X	X	X	X
2. Maintains contacts with people in other areas of the company or in different organizations who can be useful sources of information or resources.	X	X	X	X
3. Does favors (e.g., provides information, assistance, political support, or resources) to maintain good working relationships with people whose cooperation and support are important.	X	X	X	X
4. Attends meetings and social events to continually solidify and grow his or her network.	X	X	X	X
5. Uses his or her network to solve problems efficiently and effectively.	X	X	X	X
6. Actively designs his or her network in anticipation of future needs or plans (e.g., has clear goals in mind when building his or her network).	X	X	X	X

Partnering

Identifying, building, and managing internal and external partnerships that add value to the company; initiating and leveraging opportunities to work with others across the organization to maximize individual and organizational effectiveness; working effectively across organizational boundaries to accomplish a shared objective; developing networks and alliances across the organization to build influence and support for ideas.

Illustrative Behaviors	Individual Professional	First-Level Manager	Mid-Level (Manager of Managers)	Functional Manager
1. Builds relationships with colleagues in other functional groups (e.g., proactively shares knowledge and best practices with people in other groups, understands the objectives of other functional groups and their effect on the company's success).	X	X	X	X
2. Readily shares information, knowledge, best practices, and ideas with people across organizational units.	X	X	X	X
3. Asks consultative questions of customers, colleagues, managers, and others to identify business needs and solutions.	X	X	X	X
4. Forms alliances with people in different organizational units to work toward mutual objectives.	X	X	X	X
5. Coaches team members to consult with other departments/work units in solving problems and making decisions.		X	X	X
6. Manages external partnerships according to agreed-upon plans and standards.		X	X	X
7. Identifies and builds external partnerships that add current or future value to the company.			X	X

Building Relationships

Being skilled at detecting and interpreting subtle clues, often nonverbal, about others' feelings and concerns; displays empathy and sensitivity to the needs and concerns of others; and supports others when they are facing difficult tasks; enjoys dealing with people and working with people of diverse styles and backgrounds.

Illustrative Behaviors	*Individual Professional*	*First-Level Manager*	*Mid-Level (Manager of Managers)*	*Functional Manager*
1. Seeks out people and actively shares information instead of waiting for others to connect with him or her.	X	X	X	X
2. Promptly returns all forms of communication to others including e-mail, voicemail, and more traditional forms.	X	X	X	X
3. Displays empathy when a person is dealing with a difficult problem or situation.	X	X	X	X
4. Understands and adapts to the different working styles, personalities, and cultural backgrounds of the people he or she works with.	X	X	X	X
5. Offers to provide advice and support when a person is facing a difficult problem or issue.	X	X	X	X
6. Listens actively to detect both verbal and nonverbal cues in conversation.	X	X	X	X

Emotional Intelligence/Interpersonal Savvy

Being attuned to how others feel in the moment, sensing the shared values of the group, and using that insight to do and say what's appropriate; understanding others' feelings, motives, and reactions and adapting one's behaviors accordingly; appreciating the effect of one's behavior on others; being at ease when approaching others during social occasions; making and maintaining a favorable impression; and mingling effortlessly with others.

Illustrative Behaviors	Individual Professional	First-Level Manager	Mid-Level (Manager of Managers)	Functional Manager
1. Demonstrates awareness for others' feelings and adapts own behavior accordingly.	X	X	X	X
2. Encourages others to speak or share their perspective on a situation.	X	X	X	X
3. Is attentive to others' needs.	X	X	X	X
4. Is at ease in social situations; makes others at ease.	X	X	X	X
5. Intuitively detects and avoids potentially problematic situations before they take place.	X	X	X	X
6. Shows empathy for others' problems and concerns.	X	X	X	X
7. Knows when to talk and when to listen.	X	X	X	X
8. Understands how others may perceive his or her words and actions, and that his or her intent may not always yield the desired impact.	X	X	X	X
9. Helps team members develop the ability to take into account others' concerns and perspectives.		X	X	X

Influencing

Using techniques that appeal to reason, values, or emotion to generate enthusiasm for the work, commitment to a task objective, or compliance with a request; using appropriate tactics to change a person's attitude, beliefs, or behaviors.

Illustrative Behaviors	Individual Professional	First-Level Manager	Mid-Level (Manager of Managers)	Functional Manager
1. Talks in a persuasive manner about the importance of achieving tasks or objectives.	X	X	X	X
2. Describes a clear and appealing vision of what can be accomplished with a person's cooperation and support.	X	X	X	X
3. Develops enthusiasm for a task or project by appealing to a person's needs or values (i.e., accomplishing a challenging task, beating competitors, doing something never done before).	X	X	X	X
4. Adapts style or approach to meet the other person's style.	X	X	X	X
5. Explains the benefits of the task objectives to others.	X	X	X	X
6. Demonstrates willingness to incorporate input from others.	X	X	X	X
7. Listens to others' points before making his or her own points.	X	X	X	X
8. Does not rely primarily on his or her position power to influence others.			X	X

Managing Conflict

Recognizing the potential value of conflict for driving change and innovation; knowing when to confront and when to avoid a conflict; understanding the issues around which conflicts revolve; identifying the goals and objectives of the parties involved; finding common ground; looking for win/win solutions; and seeking agreement on a solution and eliciting commitment to making it work effectively.

Illustrative Behaviors	Mid-Level Individual Professional	First-Level Manager	(Manager of Managers)	Functional Manager
1. Tries to understand another person's perspective during a discussion or disagreement (e.g., does not rush to refute each point the person makes, listens attentively, paraphrases the other person's point of view).	X	X	X	X
2. Wins concessions without damaging relationships (e.g., creates "win/win" situations, makes appropriate compromises).	X	X	X	X
3. Modifies his or her proposals or plans to deal with concerns and incorporate suggestions to reach a compromise that benefits the business.	X	X	X	X
4. Challenges people in a way that is constructive and nonthreatening.	X	X	X	X
5. Confronts and facilitates conflict in a way that helps people engage in conversation to yield a better solution.	X	X	X	X
6. Understands when conflict should be confronted and when it should be avoided.	X	X	X	X
7. Identifies the likely source of a conflict before taking action.	X	X	X	X
8. Coaches others on how to resolve conflict in a constructive manner.		X	X	X

Managing People for Performance

Setting clear performance targets and gaining a person's commitment to accomplishing those targets; checking on the progress and quality of the work, providing specific feedback on a regular basis that enables others to understand what they have done well and how they can improve in the future; and addressing performance problems by gathering information and setting goals for improvement in a fair and consistent manner.

Illustrative Behaviors	Individual Professional	First-Level Manager	Mid-Level (Manager of Managers)	Functional Manager
1. Sets goals that are clear, specific, and measurable (i.e., quantifiable or verifiable).		X	X	X
2. Conducts periodic performance meetings with direct reports to review progress against goals and ensure that goals are relevant and realistic.		X	X	X
3. Provides balanced, specific feedback on a regular basis.		X	X	X
4. Addresses performance problems in a timely and fair manner by clearly defining where expectations are not being met.		X	X	X
5. Develops a sense of commitment in others to meet challenging, yet realistic, performance targets.		X	X	X
6. Holds first-level managers accountable for managing others (not only for technical work).			X	
7. Holds people accountable for achieving their performance goals.		X	X	X
8. Offers tangible, realistic suggestions for how people can enhance or improve their performance.		X	X	X
9. Ensures that goals are aligned with organizational strategy and objectives; clarifies and communicates cross-functional/departmental interdependencies.			X	X

Clarifying Roles and Accountabilities

Communicating with others to make clear what is expected of them; conveying expectations about timelines and the quality of employees' work; and helping people understand how their roles relate to the broader objectives and success of the organization.

Illustrative Behaviors	Individual Professional	First-Level Manager	Mid-Level (Manager of Managers)	Functional Manager
1. Clearly explains expectations about the quality and timeliness of a task or project.	X	X	X	X
2. Specifies a date or time when a task or project should be completed.	X	X	X	X
3. Explains how one's role relates to the broader objectives of the company.		X	X	X
4. Explains what objectives or aspects of the work have the highest priority based on the current business environment, organizational initiatives, strategy, and other parameters.		X	X	X
5. Sets task goals that are clear and specific (e.g., quantitative targets to be attained in the next quarter or year, activities to be completed by a given date).		X	X	X
6. Tailors instructions to a person's skills, experience, level of confidence, and other needs.		X	X	X
7. Takes the initiative to meet with a person who is not meeting expectations to clearly define what is expected and why it is important for the business or work unit.		X	X	X
8. Coaches others to convey expectations about the quality and timelines of projects and tasks.			X	X

Delegating

Assigning responsibilities to direct reports and giving them the authority to carry them out; maintaining the proper level of involvement without abdicating or micromanaging; assigning tasks that are a good fit with a person's capabilities; assigning tasks for development and providing guidance to ensure success; debriefing assignments to reinforce learning.

Illustrative Behaviors	Individual Professional	First-Level Manager	Mid-Level (Manager of Managers)	Functional Manager
1. Gives clear instructions (content, deadlines, decision-making authority) on delegated tasks and projects.		X	X	X
2. Clearly communicates the desired results of the delegated assignment.		X	X	X
3. Delegates assignments designed to meet direct reports' individual development or career goals as well as assignments that enable better time management.		X	X	X
4. Provides ongoing coaching and support without micromanaging delegated assignments.		X	X	X
5. Debriefs delegated tasks and projects to identify key learnings and provide both positive and constructive feedback.		X	X	X
6. Coaches managers on the importance of effective delegation for developing and retaining talent.			X	X
7. Systematically reviews own responsibilities and identifies opportunities to delegate projects or initiatives to ensure he or she is focused on strategic issues.				X

Empowering Others

Giving people the authority, information, resources (e.g., time, money, equipment), and guidance to make decisions and implement them.

Illustrative Behaviors	Individual Professional	First-Level Manager	Mid-Level (Manager of Managers)	Functional Manager
1. Provides people with the information they need to do their jobs well.	X	X	X	X
2. Allows direct reports to make important decisions and implement them without prior authority.		X	X	X
3. Presents an assignment in general terms and allows others to determine action steps for implementation.		X	X	X
4. Encourages others to come up with solutions or ideas on their own; acts as a sounding board when needed.		X	X	X
5. Demonstrates confidence in people's capabilities; gives people the benefit of the doubt.		X	X	X
6. Ensures people have the resources they need to accomplish a task or objective.		X	X	X
7. Asks people in the work unit/function for feedback on the extent to which they feel empowered to make decisions.			X	X

Motivating Others

Setting high standards regarding quality and quantity of the work; displaying commitment to the organization and enthusiasm for its products and services; conveying confidence in others' capabilities; appealing to others' unique needs, motives, and goals to motivate them to achieve; and celebrating others' successes and praising them for a job well done.

Illustrative Behaviors	Individual Professional	First-Level Manager	Mid-Level (Manager of Managers)	Functional Manager
1. Sets high standards for performance.		X	X	X
2. Models excellence and enthusiasm for the work.		X	X	X
3. Speaks positively and enthusiastically about the organization's products/ services and future direction.		X	X	X
4. Inspires others to a greater effort by setting an example in his or her own behavior of courage, dedication, or self-sacrifice.	X	X	X	X
5. Identifies and appeals to individual needs and motives.	X	X	X	X
6. Establishes challenging, yet realistic, performance goals that tap into people's interests and motives.		X	X	X
7. Rewards and recognizes others for a job well done.		X	X	X
8. Uses others as a sounding board for generating ideas and plans; acknowledges their expertise or perspective when asking for their opinions.		X	X	X
9. Coaches others on ways to motivate.		X	X	X

Coaching

Providing others with the opportunity to develop new skills; clarifying expectations; offering instructions and advice; and providing support and feedback to enhance performance.

Illustrative Behaviors	Individual Professional	First-Level Manager	Mid-Level (Manager of Managers)	Functional Manager
1. Explains why he or she thinks a person's performance is good.		X	X	X
2. Offers to provide advice or assistance when a person needs help with a difficult task or problem.		X	X	X
3. Provides extra instruction or coaching to others to help improve job skills or learn new ones.		X	X	X
4. Encourages people to create a personal development plan.		X	X	X
5. Provides feedback both on the spot and through periodic meetings to monitor progress against goals.		X	X	X
6. Helps people understand the impact of their behavior on their peers, the work unit, the customer, and others involved.		X	X	X
7. Makes him- or herself available as a resource to his or her direct reports (e.g., provides information, helps to remove barriers to their effectiveness, acts as a sounding board to generate ideas).		X	X	X
8. Is patient and helpful when giving complicated explanations or instructions.		X	X	X
9. Offers helpful advice on how people can advance their careers.		X	X	X

Developing Top Talent

Consistently attracts, selects, develops, and retains high performers; raises the performance bar for his or her work unit or team so that it consists of top performers; providing people with the opportunity to develop new skills, carry out challenging assignments, and accept new responsibilities; and holding people accountable for their performance.

Illustrative Behaviors	Individual Professional	First-Level Manager	Mid-Level (Manager of Managers)	Functional Manager
1. Does not tolerate mediocre or poor performance; swiftly addresses performance problems.		X	X	X
2. Ensures continuous and open lines of communication and feedback.		X	X	X
3. Gives coaching and support to improve team and individual results.		X	X	X
4. Makes maximum use of the different talents of team members.		X	X	X
5. Raises the bar for performance within his or her work unit by setting challenging objectives and measuring performance against them.		X	X	X
6. Provides people with the opportunity to develop new skills and accept new responsibilities.		X	X	X

Knowing and Managing the Business

Problem Solving

Identifying work related problems; analyzing problems in a systematic but timely manner; drawing correct and realistic conclusions based on data and information; and accurately assessing root cause before moving to solutions.

Illustrative Behaviors	Individual Professional	First-Level Manager	Mid-Level (Manager of Managers)	Functional Manager
1. Anticipates potential problems and takes actions to prevent them.	X	X	X	X
2. Quickly and systematically analyzes the causes of work-related problems before taking corrective action.	X	X	X	X
3. Works to see all angles and perspectives on a problem or issue before drawing conclusions or moving forward with plans or decisions.	X	X	X	X
4. Identifies the appropriate tools, resources, and expertise across the organization to develop the best solution to resolve a problem or issue.			X	X

Decision Making

Generating and evaluating alternatives before making a decision or taking action; considering the risks associated with an option and selecting the option that has the best balance of risk and reward; encouraging input from others when it is appropriate; standing by decisions without reconsidering unless information or circumstances make it necessary to do so; evaluating the effectiveness of decisions after they are made.

Illustrative Behaviors	Individual Professional	First-Level Manager	Mid-Level (Manager of Managers)	Functional Manager
1. Anticipates the consequences of decisions.	X	X	X	X
2. Involves people appropriately in decisions that may impact them.	X	X	X	X
3. Makes decisions, sets priorities, and chooses goals based on risks and rewards.	X	X	X	X
4. Quickly responds with a back-up plan if a decision goes amiss.	X	X	X	X
5. Proactively identifies and prioritizes the key issues involved to facilitate the decision-making process for his or her team or group.			X	X
6. Sticks to a decision even when faced with resistance or opposition (e.g., stays confident in the decision, does not give in or falter).			X	X

Managing and Leading Change

Putting opportunities and threats to the organization in context and clarifying how the organization needs to be different and why; communicating a vivid, appealing picture of what the organization needs to look like in the future; clearly communicating the need for change and gaining people's commitment; putting a realistic plan in place to achieve the desired outcome and ensure it is resourced adequately; preparing people to adjust to change; keeping people informed about the progress of change; and celebrating successes.

Illustrative Behaviors	Individual Professional	First-Level Manager	Mid-Level (Manager of Managers)	Functional Manager
1. Defines clear targets and milestones for change efforts and gains people's commitment to them.		X	X	X
2. Proactively identifies and addresses causes of resistance to change.		X	X	X
3. Clearly communicates the rationale for and benefits of proposed changes.		X	X	X
4. Provides clear, timely, and accurate information about a change.		X	X	X
5. Answers questions related to the impact of the proposed change directly and with candor.		X	X	X
6. Solicits people's feedback about how a change effort is progressing and how people are doing.		X	X	X
7. Adapts own behavior to support organizational change; acts as a role model for others.		X	X	X
8. Determines a plan to introduce and manage a change in line with the company's strategy and available resources.			X	X
9. Evaluates systems and processes to ensure that they are aligned with and supportive of change efforts.			X	X
10. Gains the commitment of first-line and mid-level managers early in the change process.				X
11. Ensures that the necessary resources are available in the function or work unit to implement change; revises plans if needed to reflect available resources.				X

Driving Innovation

Fostering a climate that encourages creativity and innovation; allowing others to challenge and disagree; taking prudent risks to accomplish goals; assuming responsibility in the face of uncertainty or challenge; championing new untested ideas and building support among stakeholders; celebrating and learning from failures; building and maintaining open channels of communication for the sharing of ideas and knowledge.

Illustrative Behaviors	Individual Professional	First-Level Manager	Mid-Level (Manager of Managers)	Functional Manager
1. Recognizes and rewards others when they suggest innovations and improvements.		X	X	X
2. Allows others to question and positively challenge ideas and issues.		X	X	X
3. Takes calculated, prudent risks to achieve important objectives.		X	X	X
4. Takes prompt action to implement a promising idea.		X	X	X
5. Fosters an environment where people feel "safe" taking risks (i.e., acknowledges that mistakes and failures occur and focuses on learning from them rather than placing blame).		X	X	X
6. Provides forums for team members to share ideas and knowledge and brainstorm new approaches.		X	X	X
7. Creates and reinforces a culture of being proactive and taking initiative to improve existing processes and procedures.			X	X
8. Sponsors innovative approaches to new business/markets that improve current results/performance.				X

Customer Focus

Demonstrating a concern for the needs and expectations of customers and making them a high priority; maintaining contact with customers, both internal and external to the organization; using an understanding of customer needs as the basis for decision making and organizational action.

Illustrative Behaviors	Individual Professional	First-Level Manager	Mid-Level (Manager of Managers)	Functional Manager
1. Responds to a customer's inquiry or problem in a timely and effective manner.	X	X		
2. Conveys realistic expectations to internal and external customers.	X	X		
3. Effectively manages customer expectations (e.g., reshapes incorrect/inappropriate assumptions, establishes realistic timeframes, pushes back as necessary).	X	X		
4. Follows up on customer requests to ensure that the final product or service met expectations.	X	X		
5. Takes customer issues to the appropriate people within the organization to obtain the most accurate information to meet customer needs.	X	X		
6. Gives high priority to addressing customer complaints.	X	X	X	X
7. Uses information about customers' needs as the basis of problem-solving, decision-making, and organizational action.		X	X	X
8. Reminds people about the importance of the customer to the organization's success.		X	X	X
9. Anticipates how plans and actions of the business will affect the customer in the short term and in the long term.			X	X
10. Proactively seeks feedback from customers and uses this information to make improvements in systems, processes, etc.			X	X
11. Coaches others to forge relationships with customers and add value.			X	X
12. Understands and communicates how different departments and functional groups interact to support customer needs.				X
13. Actively seeks out the customer to discuss business challenges in an effort to provide products or services that meet the customer's need even before the customer recognizes the need as critical.				X

Resource Management

Clarifying the financial implications of decisions; using resources effectively and in line with company policy and goals; deploying resources in a way that is consistent with the strategy and that benefits the organization rather than advancing self-interest; adhering to budgets; and ensuring others' time is utilized effectively.

Illustrative Behaviors	Individual Professional	First-Level Manager	Mid-Level (Manager of Managers)	Functional Manager
1. Plans how to eliminate unnecessary activities and procedures in order to improve efficiency and make better use of resources.		X	X	X
2. Determines priorities for different activities and plans an appropriate allocation of available resources.		X	X	X
3. Deploys resources based on what is best for the organization versus advancing his or her own interests or agenda.		X	X	X
4. Monitors plans to ensure that resources are used optimally and budgets are adhered to.		X	X	X
5. Analyzes the short- and long-term financial impact of decisions.			X	X
6. In developing plans, considers how they will affect the business's financial strength and seeks to maximize this impact without adversely affecting other criteria of success.				X

Operational and Tactical Planning

Determining short-term objectives and action steps for achieving them; determining how to use personnel, equipment, facilities, and other resources efficiently to accomplish a project or initiative; and determining how to schedule and coordinate activities among individuals, teams, and work units.

Illustrative Behaviors	Individual Professional	First-Level Manager	Mid-Level (Manager of Managers)	Functional Manager
1. Creates realistic plans that clearly define goals, milestones, and results.	X	X	X	X
2. Plans in detail how to accomplish a large or complex project (e.g., identifies necessary sequence of action steps, then determines when each should be done and who should do it).	X	X	X	X
3. Understands the roles of others within the company and uses this knowledge to improve efficiency (e.g., knows whom to contact in other areas to obtain information).	X	X	X	X
4. Develops controls, checks, and balances to monitor progress against plans and ensure the accuracy of the final product.	X	X	X	X
5. Anticipates possible delays or risks to plans and determines alternative courses of action to ensure timely delivery and results.	X	X	X	X
6. Involves his or her team in planning and setting priorities.		X	X	X
7. Determines priorities for both short-term and long-term projects and plans an appropriate allocation of available resources.		X	X	X
8. Evaluates the current flow of work and information across units and identifies opportunities to improve coordination and make better use of resources to accomplish projects/initiatives.			X	X

Results Orientation

Communicating business performance measures and clarifying priorities; maintaining a focused commitment to achieving one's objectives; working on important issues first; staying with a plan of action or point of view until the desired goal has been obtained or is no longer reasonably attainable; recognizing opportunities and acting on them; looking for ways to quickly overcome barriers; persevering in the face of adversity or opposition; and translating ideas into action.

Illustrative Behaviors	Individual Professional	First-Level Manager	Mid-Level (Manager of Managers)	Functional Manager
1. Takes appropriate risks to accomplish goals.	X	X	X	X
2. Overcomes setbacks and adjusts the plan of action to realize results.	X	X	X	X
3. Focuses on high-priority actions and does not become distracted by lower-priority activities.	X	X	X	X
4. Challenges him- or herself and others to raise the bar on performance.		X	X	X
5. Focuses people on critical activities that yield a high impact.		X	X	X
6. Develops a sense of urgency in others to complete tasks.		X	X	X
7. Holds self and others accountable for delivering high-quality results on time and within budget (e.g., models high work standards and demands the same from others, criticizes mediocre or substandard performance).		X	X	X
8. Gives priority to achieving results for the company or department, even if it conflicts with one's own personal goals or agenda.		X	X	X
9. Develops a plan for execution with the team to garner commitment and buy in.			X	X

Quality Orientation

Promoting organizational effectiveness by anticipating and dealing with problems; encouraging others to suggest improvements to work processes; providing a persistent focus on quality as well as on results; determining how to improve organizational coordination, productivity, and effectiveness.

Illustrative Behaviors	*Individual Professional*	*First-Level Manager*	*Mid-Level (Manager of Managers)*	*Functional Manager*
1. Ensures the quality of the work (e.g., monitors reports, reviews complaints from customers, notices mistakes in his or her own work and in the work of others).	X	X	X	X
2. Identifies sources of mistakes and determines a course of action to prevent their recurrence.	X	X	X	X
3. Proactively raises critical issues that impact organizational coordination, productivity, or effectiveness and takes the lead in resolving them.	X	X	X	X
4. Consistently monitors the quality of products and services and the processes used to produce them.	X	X	X	X
5. Evaluates how well a major project or activity was done (e.g., monitors internal and external client satisfaction, asks people what went well and what can be done better next time).		X	X	X
6. Communicates and reinforces the importance of high work standards.		X	X	X
7. Encourages team members to take the initiative to improve work processes.		X	X	X

Mastering Complexity

Quickly integrating complex information to identify strategies and solutions; learning new concepts quickly; demonstrating keen insights into situations; assimilating large amounts of information and narrowing it down to and articulating the core idea or issue.

Illustrative Behaviors	Individual Professional	First-Level Manager	Mid-Level (Manager of Managers)	Functional Manager
1. Understands new concepts quickly.	X	X	X	X
2. Assimilates large amounts of data/ information to identify what is most important.	X	X	X	X
3. Integrates complicated ideas and approaches to develop the best possible solutions.	X	X	X	X
4. Breaks down complicated problems or concepts into clear and manageable components.	X	X	X	X
5. Focuses others on the core message or desired result of a complex plan or idea.			X	X

Business and Financial Acumen

Possessing the technical and business knowledge needed to make the best decisions for the organization; assessing the financial implications of decisions and actions; understanding how strategies and tactics work in the marketplace; and balancing data analysis with judgment and business sense.

Illustrative Behaviors	Individual Professional	First-Level Manager	Mid-Level (Manager of Managers)	Functional Manager
1. Understands how his or her role contributes to the overall success of the organization.	X	X	X	X
2. Understands the key drivers of the business, including how the business makes money.		X	X	X
3. Understands the financial impact of decisions and actions.		X	X	X
4. Analyzes data to identify trends and issues that are important to the business and interprets the results of the analyses to make recommendations for how the organization should address the issues.		X	X	X
5. Understands how internal and external business measurements are defined and influenced.			X	X
6. Continuously learns and demonstrates an in-depth understanding and knowledge of the company's core business and how the organization operates (e.g., has a thorough understanding of overall business structure, processes, policies, functions, and their interrelationships).			X	X
7. Assesses existing talent base to determine whether the right mix of skills/competencies are in place to ensure the current and future success of the work unit.			X	X
8. Has a working knowledge of profit and loss and other key financial measurements used in the business, in terms of current performance, forecasting, and longer-term business planning.				X
9. Communicates the key performance/profit levers for the business and manages to these measures.				X

Strategic Planning

Developing and driving a shared understanding of a long-term vision that incorporates people's input and describes what the organization needs to look like and how it needs to operate in the future; determining long-term objectives and the tactics to achieve them; allocating resources according to stated priorities; making sure that accountabilities and expectations for executing a strategy are clear.

Illustrative Behaviors	Individual Professional	First-Level Manager	Mid-Level (Manager of Managers)	Functional Manager
1. Translates company strategies into meaningful plans for the business; connects them to people's daily work.		X	X	X
2. Demonstrates how priorities fit into the company's overall strategies (i.e., creates a line of sight).		X	X	X
3. Pursues challenges that result in long-term business benefit (e.g., proposes challenging but realistic objectives).		X	X	X
4. Understands where the business is going and the strategic objectives of the company and knows how to support them.		X	X	X
5. Allocates resources based on strategies and related objectives.		X	X	X
6. Stays abreast of changes in the marketplace and the company's position relative to competitors.		X	X	X
7. Continuously learns and demonstrates an understanding of the competitive environment, trends in the economy, and technology that may impact the business; refers to these trends in conversations; anticipates the effect of trends on the business; and uses information about trends when evaluating alternatives and making decisions.			X	X
8. Engages in scenario planning (e.g., assesses where the organization is today against potential changes/conditions in the external environment) to determine the best path forward.			X	X
9. Communicates the company's vision, values, and strategy with conviction.			X	X
10. Communicates business priorities to all levels of the organization.			X	X
11. Does not give up the long-term vision under present-day pressure; takes a long-term perspective on problems and opportunities facing the organization.				X

Strategic Thinking

Understanding the implications of social, economic, political, and global trends; showing an understanding of market conditions and customer needs; understanding the company's position in the marketplace—both its strengths and its weaknesses; taking a long-term perspective on problems and opportunities; applying insight and creativity to the development of strategies that help the organization gain or sustain competitive advantage; proposing innovative strategies that leverage the organization's competitive position.

Illustrative Behaviors	Individual Professional	First-Level Manager	Mid-Level (Manager of Managers)	Functional Manager
1. Prioritizes actions based on what is best for the organization.		X	X	X
2. Demonstrates knowledge of customer needs and uses this information to help determine the way forward.		X	X	X
3. Understands and drives toward increasing his or her work unit's financial performance (e.g., understands the financial impact of plans and decisions).			X	X
4. Demonstrates an understanding of key business drivers and product attributes within his or her department (e.g., aligns products offered with core organizational competencies).			X	X
5. Anticipates strategic problems and opportunities and makes strategic decisions to address them.			X	X
6. Continuously identifies and evaluates viable future opportunities for the business; selects and exploits the activities that will result in the greatest return.			X	X
7. Demonstrates creative thinking to solve strategic issues (e.g., proposes innovative strategies that capitalize on the unique qualities and core competencies of the organization).			X	X

Global Perspective

Understanding the international issues facing the business; appreciating how ethnic, cultural, and political matters influence business; integrating local and global information for decisions affecting multiple sites; applying knowledge of public regulatory frameworks in multiple countries; and making deliberate decisions about how to conduct business successfully in different parts of the world.

Illustrative Behaviors	Individual Professional	First-Level Manager	Mid-Level (Manager of Managers)	Functional Manager
1. Considers wide-ranging influences, situations, and implications both inside and outside the organization when making plans or decisions, solving problems, or developing strategies.	X	X	X	X
2. Recognizes emerging patterns of business on a global basis and formulates strategies in line with these trends.			X	X
3. Demonstrates an understanding of the international issues facing the company.			X	X
4. Communicates how international and political issues may impact the business in the short and long term.			X	X
5. Implements global decisions while adjusting for local perspectives where appropriate.				X
6. Creates/validates long-term directions based on business dynamics, global trends, and the overall strategy of the company.				X

Organizational Savvy

Staying abreast of what is happening across the organization; understanding the effects of decisions and actions on other parts of the organization; recognizing the interests of others in different parts of the organization; understanding the influence dynamics of the organization and using that information to establish alliances to achieve organizational objectives; understanding the organizational culture and norms of behavior.

Illustrative Behaviors	Individual Professional	First-Level Manager	Mid-Level (Manager of Managers)	Functional Manager
1. Approaches problems with a clear understanding of organizational and political realities.		X	X	X
2. Understands how the culture of the organization impacts how the work gets done and takes this into account in planning and decision making.			X	X
3. Understands the goals/objectives of other departments/work units and uses this information to establish alliances and resolve issues.		X	X	X
4. Understands the interdependent nature of operations and the impact of various departments/work units on workflow within the organization.			X	X
5. Understands how his or her decisions may impact others across the organization and involves them appropriately.			X	X
6. Keeps up to date on what is happening across the organization.		X	X	X
7. Proactively shares information with others across the organization based on an understanding of their priorities, goals, and objectives.		X	X	X
8. Considers organizational culture and norms of behavior in making decisions.	X	X	X	X

Organizational Design

Ensuring the organization's structure and systems support its strategies; taking actions to optimize resources and work processes (e.g., reengineering, continuous process improvement); and identifying how to organize the work (e.g., grouping responsibilities, establishing appropriate linkages) to enhance efficiency and drive results.

Illustrative Behaviors	Individual Professional	First-Level Manager	Mid-Level (Manager of Managers)	Functional Manager
1. Understands the importance of aligning organizational structure and strategy.			X	X
2. Reviews organizational structure, systems, and processes to ensure they support change initiatives.			X	X
3. Identifies key skills within the work unit and determines how to best organize the work (e.g., grouping responsibilities, establishing linkages) to enhance efficiency and coordination.			X	X
4. Collects feedback from employees at all levels to understand what is working and what could be improved related to existing systems and structure.	X		X	X
5. Identifies and implements ways to optimize resources and work processes.			X	X
6. Creates clear descriptions of the work, roles, and responsibilities to help facilitate coordination and cooperation.			X	X

Human Resources Planning

Ensuring the talent base is in place to meet organizational needs; assessing current skills sets and identifying the right mix of talent to fill gaps and ensure sustained results; accurately assessing "fit" based on the requisite skills and competencies as well alignment with organizational culture.

Illustrative Behaviors	Individual Professional	First-Level Manager	Mid-Level (Manager of Managers)	Functional Manager
1. Develops clear job descriptions based on the key skills and competencies (personal, interpersonal, technical, and managerial) required for the role.			X	X
2. Clarifies the current skills and knowledge within the work unit as well as its future needs.			X	X
3. Considers the long-term implications of team performance and skills in order to ensure sustained results.			X	X
4. Makes plans to fill development or skill gaps within the work unit.			X	X
5. Accurately assesses talent and makes hiring decisions based on a clear picture of what is required for success in the role as well as cultural fit.			X	X

Monitoring the External Environment

Collecting information about opportunities and threats in the external environment that may affect work in the short or long term; analyzing trends and looking for opportunities to enhance the organization's performance.

Illustrative Behaviors	Individual Professional	First-Level Manager	Mid-Level (Manager of Managers)	Functional Manager
1. Understands industry and market trends and the impact they may have on the business in the short and longer term.		X	X	X
2. Analyzes data and creates benchmarks (based on the competition/industry) to monitor the quality of products and services and improve existing processes.			X	X
3. Identifies trends and patterns in the marketplace that may positively or negatively impact the business.				X
4. Takes action to mitigate threats in the external environment.				X

Core Functional/Technical Skills

Maintaining up-to-date knowledge within one's field of expertise; remaining abreast of developments in the industry; providing guidance or counsel on technical matters related to one's field; knowing how to use company-specific technology.

Illustrative Behaviors	Individual Professional	First-Level Manager	Mid-Level (Manager of Managers)	Functional Manager
1. Quickly masters new technical knowledge relevant to his or her position.	X	X	X	X
2. Has a comprehensive knowledge of all existing computer systems and other technologies relevant to his or her job responsibilities.	X	X	X	X
3. Offers helpful advice and guidance when others are learning technical matters related to his or her role or function.	X	X	X	X
4. Is knowledgeable about best practices relative to the technical aspects of his or her function/role and benchmarks against other organizations.		X	X	X
5. Acquires technical/functional knowledge of new areas that he or she manages to sufficient depth to be an effective manager of the overall function.			X	X

Endnotes

Chapter 1

1. Peter Senge, *The Fifth Discipline: The Art and Practice of the Learning Organization* (New York: Currency, 1994).

2. See Douglas K. Smith, *Making Success Measurable* (New York: John Wiley & Sons, 1999), p. 17.

3. See Daniel R. Tobin, *All Learning Is Self-Directed* (Alexandria, VA: ASTD, 2000) for further explanation of this model.

4. Shoshanna Zuboff, *In the Age of the Smart Machine: The Future of Work and Power* (New York: Basic Books, 1989).

5. *Return on Investment in Training and Performance Improvement Programs,* 2nd ed. (Burlington, MA: Butterworth-Heinemann, 2003).

6. For more on the misuse of ROI analysis, see Daniel R. Tobin, "The Fallacy of ROI Calculations," www.tobincls.com/fallacy.htm

Chapter 2

1. Marcus Buckingham, quoted in "The One Thing You Need to Know About Great Managing, Great Leading, and Sustained Individual Success," *Human Resource Planning, 28* (2) (August 2005), 28.

2. Stephen Drotter, Ram Charan, & James Noel, *The Leadership Pipeline: How to Build the Leadership Powered Company* (San Francisco: Jossey-Bass, 2000)

3. Justin Menkes, "Hiring for Smarts," *Harvard Business Review* (November 2005).

4. For example, the New York State Department of Labor has a good online worksheet for this purpose (www.labor.state.ny.us/careerservices/findajob/assess.shtm). Another good resource is from Northwestern University's Office of Career Services (http://www.northwestern.edu/careers/students/major/skills.htm).

5. Laura Morgan Roberts, et al., "How to Play to Your Strengths," *Harvard Business Review* (January 2005).

6. Ibid.

7. Chuck Martin, Peg Dawson, & Richard Guare, *Smarts: Are We Hardwired for Success?* (New York: AMACOM, 2007).

8. Jeffrey Pfeffer & Robert Sutton, *The Knowing-Doing Gap: How Smart Companies Turn Knowledge into Action* (Cambridge, MA: Harvard Business School Press, 2000), p. 6.

Chapter 3

1. See William Bridges, *Managing Transitions: Making the Most of Change,* 2nd ed. (New York: Perseus, 2003).

2. See Michael Hammer & James Champy, *Reengineering the Corporation: A Manifesto for Business Revolution,* revised edition (New York: Collins, 2003).

Chapter 4

1. Lynne Truss, *Eats, Shoots & Leaves* (New York: Gotham Books, 2003).

Chapter 5

1. See the Project Management Institute website for more information (www.pmi .org).
2. *Competing for the Future* (Cambridge, MA: Harvard Business School Press, 1996), p. 96.
3. Ibid., p. 83.
4. Samuel Greengard, "Moving Forward with Reverse Mentoring–Sharing the Knowledge," *Workforce* (March 2002), retrieved August 2007 from http://findarticles .com

Chapter 6

1. Thomas P. Bechet, *Strategic Staffing* (New York: AMACOM, 2002).
2. Victoria A. Hoevemeyer, *High Impact Interview Questions* (AMACOM, 2006).
3. John Brennan, "Promotion from Within Builds Strong Organizations," *M World, The Journal of the American Management Association,* 6(1) (Spring 2007).
4. Brian Libby, *How to Conduct a Job Interview on BNET.* www.bnet.com/2403-13056 _23-52947.html
5. Ram Charan, Stephen Drotter, & James Noel, *The Leadership Pipeline* (San Francisco: Jossey-Bass, 2001).

Chapter 7

1. Jay Jamrog, *The Perfect Storm: The Future of Retention and Engagement* (New York: Human Resource Planning, 2007).
2. Ibid., p. 29
3. Daniel R. Tobin, *All Learning Is Self-Directed* (Alexandria, VA: ASTD, 2000).
4. Ibid., p. 14
5. Ibid.
6. Malcolm Knowles, *Self-Directed Learning* (River Grove, IL: Follett Publishing Company, 1975).
7. Peter F. Drucker, *Managing Oneself. Leadership Fundamentals* (Cambridge, MA: Harvard Business School Press). Best of Harvard Business Review.
8. Daniel Tobin, op. cit.
9. "New Data Shows Distinct Skills Gap as Generation X Managers Replace Baby Boomers," *Chief Learning Officer Industry Newsletter,* February 9, 2007.

Chapter 8

1. Michael J. Marquardt, "Action Learning," in *By George: GW's Faculty, Staff & Community Newspaper* (February 18, 2004).

2. For a more thorough list, see David Ulrich and Dale Lake, *Organizational Capability: Competing from the Inside Out* (New York: John Wiley & Sons, 1992), especially Appendix 6-2.

3. From *The ICF Definition of Coaching,* accessed September 2007 from www.coachfederation.org

4. The roles of human resources professionals and trainers as coaches will be discussed in Chapters 11 and 12.

5. Marshall Goldsmith, "The Six-Question Process: Helping Executives Become Better Coaches," accessed September 07 from www.marshallgoldsmithlibrary.com/docs/articles/SixQuesProcess.doc

6. For example, Brown-Herron Publishing has published several study guides as e-documents sold through Amazon.com.

7. For more information, see www.getfuturethink.com

Chapter 9

1. David L. Bradford, & Allan R. Cohen, *Managing for Excellence* (New York: John Wiley and Sons, 1997).

2. David Bradford, & Allan Cohen, *Influence Without Authority.* (New York: John Wiley and Sons, 2005).

3. Marcus Buckingham, *The One Thing You Need to Know* (New York: Free Press, 2005).

4. Chuck Martin, *Smarts* (New York: AMACOM, 2007).

5. Daniel R. Tobin, *The Knowledge-Enabled Organization* (New York: AMACOM, 1998).

Chapter 10

1. Jack Stack, & Bo Burlingham, *The Great Game of Business* (New York: Currency, 1994), p. 3.

2. Larry Bossidy, Ram Charan, & Charles Burck, *Execution: The Discipline of Getting Things Done* (New York: Crown Business, 2002), p. 150.

3. B. Joseph White, *The Nature of Leadership* (New York: AMACOM, 2007), p. 4.

4. Robert Barner, *Bench Strength* (New York: AMACOM, 2006).

5. Ibid., pp. 166-167.

6. Daniel R. Tobin, *All Learning Is Self-Directed* (Alexandria, VA: ASTD, 2000). This book contains a much broader discussion of the concept and practice of a PLE.

7. Tom Schmidt, & Arnold Perl, *Simple Solutions: Harness the Power of Passion and Simplicity to Get Results* (New York: John Wiley & Sons, 2007).

Chapter 11

1. Larry Bossidy, quoted by Don Redlinger, Sr. VP of HR at Honeywell International, in Larry Bossidy & Ram Charan, *Execution: The Discipline of Getting Things Done* (New York: Crown Business, 2002), p. 167.

2. See www.i4cp.com

3. Institute for Corporate Productivity, *Highlight Report–Talent Management* (Tampa, FL: I4CP, 2007), p. 13.

4. Dave Ulrich, *What's Next for HR? Part 1–Contribution: How HR Professionals May Add Value in the Future* (Provo, UT: Results-Based Leadership Institute, 2002).

5. Ibid., p. 3.

6. Ibid., p. 4.

7. Ibid., p. 8.

8. I4CP, *Human Capital Strategies,* Issue 225, e-mail newsletter, 2007.

9. Gregory Kesler & Paul Kirincic, "Roadmaps for Developing General Managers: The Experience of a Healthcare Giant," *Human Resource Planning, 28*(3), 26.

10. Ibid.

11. Ibid., p. 29.

12. Ibid., p. 30.

13. Ibid., p. 34.

Chapter 12

1. Daniel P. Tobin, *The Knowledge-Enabled Organization* (New York: AMACOM, 1997).

Chapter 13

1. Judy London, *Graying of Society* (Tampa, FL: Institute for Corporate Productivity, June 2007).

2. Walt McFarland & Kate Morse, "From Briefcase to MySpace: Developing and Managing a Multigenerational Workforce," American Management Association, *M World* (Spring 2008).

3. Stefanie Smith, "Preserving Baby Boomer Wisdom for the Next Generation," American Management Association, *M World* (Spring 2008).

4. In reality, ROI analysis is more complicated than this because it involves a time series of benefits and costs and discounting of future benefits and costs to arrive at a net present value.

5. We are grateful to AMA's Florence Stone for conducting a number of interviews for this chapter during November 2007. The following attributions are paraphrased from these interviews.

6. Nicholas G. Carr, *The Ignorance of Crowds* (Booz Allen Hamilton, 2007).

7. Scott Cooper, *Collaborative Innovation and Swarm Creativity in the New Workforce,* a paper prepared for the American Management Association, 2007.

Index